Surviving
Debt

Surviving Debt

Counseling Families in Financial Trouble

By America's Expert on the
Rights of Consumer Borrowers

NATIONAL CONSUMER
LAW CENTER
Boston

For reprint permissions or ordering information,
contact Publications, NCLC, 11 Beacon Street,
Boston, Massachusetts 02108 (617) 523-8010.
Library of Congress Catalog No. 92-81748
ISBN 1-881793-07-9
This project was supported by the NCCE/AT&T Consumer
Credit Education Fund, the Public Welfare Foundation,
the National Consumer Law Center, the AFL-CIO,
the United Auto Workers, and others.
Printed in the United States of America
10 9 8 7 6 5 4 3 2 1

This book is intended to provide accurate and authoritative
information in regard to the subject matter covered. This book
cannot substitute for the independent judgment and skills of a
competent attorney or other professional. Non-attorneys are
cautioned against using these materials in conducting litigation
without advice or assistance from an attorney or other professional. Non-attorneys are also cautioned against engaging in
conduct which might be considered the unauthorized practice
of law.

Acknowledgments

Surviving Debt began as part of a NCLC project, funded by the Public Welfare Foundation, to stimulate private attorney representation of displaced workers. NCLC conducted a series of training sessions for pro-bono and legal services attorneys and job counselors working with the debt problems of recently displaced workers. A package of detailed written materials was developed in conjunction with the training.

The AFL-CIO, the United Auto Workers, and various church groups provided funds to expand the original materials into a legal manual. Significant interest was also expressed in developing a companion manual for non-lawyers counseling the "new poor." In response, NCLC began work on *Surviving Debt*.

In the process, we have changed the focus of the original materials in two ways. We have made this book less legalistic so that it can more easily be used by non-lawyers who counsel families in financial distress. We have also expanded the book's scope to offer assistance not just to recently displaced workers, but to any family which suddenly faces overwhelming debt.

This publication would not have been possible without the generous support of the NCCE/AT&T Consumer Credit Education Fund. Its grant not only allowed completion of this project, but an exceptionally wide distribution of the final product. NCLC has also devoted a significant amount of its own funds to the production of this resource.

The views in this book are NCLC's and should not be construed as those of the NCCE/AT&T Consumer Credit Education Fund, the Public Welfare Foundation, or any other entity contributing to the development of *Surviving Debt*.

Numerous individuals contributed to the writing and final production of this volume. NCLC and Montana Legal Services staff attorneys were largely responsible for writing this book. With an average of almost 20 years of expertise on the rights of consumer borrowers, the NCLC staff attorneys are Jonathan Sheldon, Robert Hobbs, Kathleen Keest, Robert Sable, Ernest Sarason, Gary Klein, Willard Ogburn, Yvonne Rosmarin, Roger Colton, and Nancy Brockway. The Montana Legal Services attorneys are Robert Rowe and Michael Eakin. Howard Fox, Holly Newman, and Karen Smith persisted in their faith in this project and helped keep it alive.

A number of attorneys and counselors from around the country also provided helpful materials, insights, or comments. In particular, thanks to Carolyn Carter, Director of Legal Services Inc. in Pennsylvania, Neil Fogarty of Hudson County Legal Services in Jersey City, Dan Haller of Neighborhood Legal Services in Pittsburgh, Mark Budnitz, Professor at Georgia State College of Law, Joanna George of Legal Aid Society of Northwest North Carolina, and Jesse Toca of the Christian Relief and Crisis Intervention Service and Amicus Communication Inc. in Tampa, Florida, particularly for his tips on negotiating home mortgage payment plans found in Chapter Nine.

Parts of Chapter Ten on home foreclosures are based on materials provided by Mark Kaufman. Patricia Baker and Deborah Harris of Massachusetts Law Reform and Timothy Casey of the Center on Social Welfare Policy and Law reviewed Chapter One on public benefits. Henry Sommer of Community Legal Services in Philadelphia contributed materials to Chapter Fourteen on bankruptcy. These contributors do not share responsibility for any errors or omissions in the final version.

Ann Stewart designed the book, Jean Knox edited an earlier draft, Donna Wong provided stylistic advice, and Technologies 'N Typography typeset the manuscript. Courier/Stoughton was the printer.

Contents

7 • Protecting the Family Car from the Repo Man • 102

8 • Threats to Seize Household Goods • 122

9 • General Home Defense Strategies • 130

10 • Special Home Defense Strategies • 155

11 • Utility Service • 177

12 • Dealing with Landlords • 191

13 • Government Collection of Student Loans and Taxes • 203

14 • Bankruptcy • 212

CONTENTS
xi

How to Use this Book

Millions of American families, through no fault of their own, face severe debt crises involving home foreclosures, apartment evictions, utility terminations, seizure of property, and debt collection harassment. The cause is a sudden decline in the family's income—someone loses a job, becomes disabled, or stops contributing to the family—or a dramatic rise in uncontrollable expenses, such as utility bills, medical expenses, or home repairs.

Too often these families in financial trouble have nowhere to turn for help. *Surviving Debt* makes it possible for non-lawyers to offer the required assistance, be they job counselors, clergy, social workers, veterans counselors, community workers, housing counselors, labor union personnel, vocational counselors, family services caseworkers, paralegals, JEPTA counselors, complaint handlers, or employees of charitable organizations. Although not trained to offer financial counseling, these professionals cannot be effective in their own job—be it vocational, charitable, psychological, or spiritual—when their clients are being evicted or harassed by collectors.

Since this book is designed for non-lawyers, consumers with money troubles can also use it as a self-help tool. Such consumers should talk over the strategies found in this book with someone they trust and respect. Another opinion is always helpful, particularly when an individual is under stress.

Lawyers not specializing in consumer credit should find *Surviving Debt* a useful and practical introduction to the field, with references to other treatises for in-depth information. Attorneys who do specialize in consumer credit problems should use *Surviving Debt* as a training aid for paralegals, law students or others in their office, or even as a handout to consumers whom they cannot represent.

Pinpointing What You Need to Know

Surviving Debt allows readers to quickly discover solutions to specific debt problems. Most chapters deal with one particular problem that families in financial distress may encounter, such as home foreclosure, utility termination, debt collection harassment, or collection lawsuits. To start handling a specific problem, simply read that one chapter.

Chapters One, Two, and Fourteen, however, should be read when counseling *any* family with financial problems. Chapter One lists sources of cash, medical, food, and other assistance that may be available for individuals in need. Chapter Two introduces basic consumer credit counseling concepts, particularly how to decide which debts to pay first and which to delay until the family's finances improve.

Any family with severe financial problems should at least understand its rights concerning bankruptcy, and have an idea when it is and is not appropriate to file for this relief. Chapter Fourteen explains how bankruptcy works, what it can and cannot do, when bankruptcy is the right or the wrong solution, and how to choose the right type of bankruptcy and the right time to file.

Surviving Debt packs into one, easy-to-read, accessible book the important steps that borrowers in financial trouble need to take. The book is not a treatise on the law of consumer credit. Readers who want more detailed information should refer both to the sources mentioned in each chapter and to the bibliography.

1

Government Benefits

Public Benefits Are a Key Resource

An Essential Stopgap

Benefits provided by government and non-profit agencies are a key source of assistance for individuals in financial distress. Although unemployment benefits are the most familiar of government programs, a variety of lesser known programs and benefits are also available.

The Food Stamp Program helps to meet urgent needs for food. AFDC provides cash benefits for some families, and some state and local governments provide General Assistance cash benefits to those not eligible for AFDC. Medical care is available through a variety of medical benefit programs that include Medicaid, state medical assistance, medical school teaching clinics, and public health clinics. The Supplemental Food Program for Women, Infants and Children (WIC) provides nutritional assistance for pregnant mothers and for children up to five years old. WIC also has a limited health care component.

Depending upon the duration of a family's unemployment, additional programs can assist with heating bills, or even help with emergency home repairs. Family members aged 62 or over often are eligible for Social Security retirement benefits. Even if individuals do not have enough work credits to qualify for Social Security retirement benefits, they may still qualify for Supplemental Security Income (SSI) upon turning 65 years old. Individuals should also determine if they are eligible for an earned income tax credit that could result in a $1000 income tax refund.

Those with disabilities should consider applying for Social Security Disability Benefits and Supplemental Security Income (SSI). Even family members (including children) who have never worked or have worked very little may be eligible for federal disability benefits under the SSI program if they become disabled. Where another individual's failure to pay child support is contributing to a family's financial difficulties, state agencies may assist in recovering this amount owed. Laid-off workers should take advantage of job placement, career counseling and job training services.

Not all programs are available in every state. Counselors should know of all available programs, and should be able to direct families to the appropriate agencies. Further information and resources are usually provided by local legal services offices, family service agencies, and welfare offices.

What If Someone Refuses to Receive Government Benefits?

Many individuals strongly resist applying for welfare, believing that a social stigma is attached to public assistance benefits. Others are psychologically unable to admit their difficult circumstances. While families usually are willing to apply for Unemployment Insurance Benefits, which many do not consider traditional welfare, they are often reluctant to seek cash public assistance benefits, such as AFDC or general assistance.

These barriers can be overcome through sensitive counseling. For example, emphasize that government assistance is only temporary, helping to tide families over until they secure new employment. Point out that by paying taxes and contributing to the public welfare system in the past, taxpayers have built up credit against which to draw during difficult times. Once the taxpayer has found new employment, he or she will resume paying taxes and thus repay the system.

Benefits Are Not a Free Ride

Do not raise false expectations. Public assistance benefits provide only minimal assistance and cannot replace previous income. Furthermore, the process of obtaining benefits is often slow and difficult. This is a surprise for those who believe welfare benefits are an easy handout.

New applicants for assistance are likely to face long delays and complicated paperwork. With each application, they must supply basic information and extensive documentation, and include a history of household income and expenditures. Individuals accustomed to walking into a bank and receiving the ready attention of bank representatives are surprised to find that overworked public assistance employees often do not return phone calls or mail notices when promised.

Applicants often are not prepared for the intrusiveness of agency investigations. They are shocked to learn that eligibility for many programs does not depend upon current income, but rather on an average of past and current income, which masks the severity of their current financial situation.

Take time to prepare individuals for these surprises and to explain the difficult application process. When necessary, shepherd individuals' applications through the bureaucratic maze, ensuring that application procedures are understood and that all documentation is properly assembled and delivered.

Unemployment Compensation Benefits in a Nutshell

When and Where to Apply

Unemployment Compensation is usually the first government program available to laid-off workers. Although benefits will not flow immediately after a lay-off, the worker should apply as soon as the worker is unemployed. If discharged employees do not know how or where to apply for benefits, they should call the personnel office of their former company, the state labor department, or the division of state unemployment.

The First Appointment

To expedite the award and receipt of benefits, the laid-off worker should assemble and bring all relevant documents to the first appointment, including *at least:* a Social Security card, a driver's license, a lay-off notice, and the four most recent pay-stubs. At the first appointment, the applicant should be prepared to describe accurately the nature and cause of the lay-off.

This description should be worded carefully. Characterizing the reason for leaving employment as voluntary will lead to denial of benefits. If a worker left employment in anticipation of layoff or discharge, the worker should carefully set out the reasons why the lay-off or discharge was involuntary.

Care must be taken in explaining the cause of the discharge. Unemployment Compensation applications can be denied if the state employee taking down the information misinterprets the reasons given for the discharge, and if the applicant signs the statement as true without carefully reading and correcting it. For example, an applicant's statement that a supervisor began to verbally harass him and finally told him to leave and not return might be recorded incorrectly as: "The worker was verbally abusive and fired for cause."

Steps to Take When Unemployment Compensation Benefits Are Denied

Unemployment Compensation can be denied if the employer is not covered by unemployment insurance laws, if the applicant was discharged for cause, or if the applicant quit without good cause. The worker can contest denial of unemployment benefits by requesting an administrative hearing. Applicants should request this hearing as soon as they receive a denial, because there are tight and strictly enforced deadlines to request this hearing.

After a hearing, if the claim is still denied, the worker can bring an administrative appeal to an unemployment insurance appeals board. Board decisions are publicly available for review. Decisions of the appeals boards in turn can usually be appealed to a state court, but courts are usually bound by the board's rulings about the facts.

In appealing the denial of a claim, it is risky to rely upon the inequity or unfairness of a decision. A sympathetic claimant cannot win without a legally sound argument. To be safe, a lawyer or paralegal familiar with unemployment compensation laws should be consulted whenever it appears that a worker has been unfairly denied compensation.

Counselors and workers can consult several sources if they want to research specific legal grounds why a particular claim is or is not valid. Each state has administrative regulations that explain procedure and set out the basic standard for approving claims. Appeals board and state court decisions are also important, particularly in that they may detail the reasons why benefits are granted or denied in particular situations, and may require benefits to be awarded even where a state's rules would indicate otherwise.

How to Continue Receiving Unemployment Compensation

In order to continue to receive unemployment benefits, applicants must demonstrate that they are making a diligent job search. State agencies usually require that applicants periodically submit a list of the jobs they have applied for, the addresses and dates of applications, a list of help wanted advertisements clipped from a newspaper, or proof of registration with and visits to state employment services.

Food Stamps

The Food Stamp Program is supposed to help recipients to maintain a minimally sufficient diet. Eligibility is much broader for food stamps than for most other public assistance programs. Resource and income levels are higher. All kinds of households, from individuals to two-parent families, can qualify. Because eligibility is broad, and because high quality resource materials are available, lay counselors can be particularly effective in helping households obtain food stamps.

Key Resources

The Food Research Action Center (FRAC) publishes a *Guide to the Food Stamp Program,* which is periodically updated. It is available at most legal services offices, and can be ordered directly from FRAC, 1875 Connecticut Ave., NW, Suite 540, Washington, D.C. 20009-5728; telephone (202) 986-2200. In 1992, the guide cost $12.

Another key resource is the state's Food Stamp Program Manual. Information about the Food Stamp Program and applications are also available from welfare offices. Welfare offices are sometimes called the Department of Public Assistance, the Department of Social Services, or the Department of Human Services.

How to Apply for Food Stamps

Food stamps are issued from the date the consumer signs the Food Stamps application. As a consequence, application should be made immediately, even if complete documentation has not been assembled. Application forms can be requested by mail. Once the consumer submits the form, the government processes the application within thirty days. (See the next section for receiving expedited food stamps before then.)

Food stamp offices require the following documentation:

1. Identity and social security number of household members,
2. Gross income,
3. Address (unless the applicant is homeless, a migrant farm worker, or recently relocated), and
4. Age.

In addition, food stamps are based in part on certain living expenses. It is thus helpful to provide certain additional information:

5. Utility, rent, mortgage and other shelter expenses,
6. Dependent care expenses,
7. Medical expenses, and
8. Receipt of disability benefits.

Do not delay applying because some of this information is missing. Just supply those documents after the initial application.

Some welfare offices use a combined application form for all government assistance programs. When a combined form is used, the applicant will have to bring in much more documentation, but *only* if the applicant is applying for other available benefits.

Food stamps can be denied if an applicant fails to bring in all requested documentation, supplies false or inaccurate information, or fails to meet deadlines. It is difficult for some applicants to obtain the requested documentation within the allotted time. When that is the case, ask for an extension. Another approach is to ask the state agency's caseworker for help in obtaining the documentation.

Sometimes food stamps are improperly denied either because of confusion about eligibility requirements or because of arithmetical mistakes by agency personnel. Do not take applicant rejections as definitive. (See below on contesting food stamp denials.)

How to Receive Food Stamps Before Completing the Application Process

Certain households are eligible, while their regular application is being processed, to receive expedited food stamps within five calendar days after the household turns in a simplified application. The application merely verifies the applicant's identity.

The following households are eligible for expedited food stamps:

1. Families with less than $150 monthly gross income, and liquid resources not over $100;
2. Destitute migrant farm workers with liquid resources not over $100;
3. Homeless individuals. This category includes individuals lacking a fixed nighttime residence, or making as their primary residence a shelter or other temporary accommodation, including the residence of another individual;
4. Families whose combined gross monthly income and liquid resources are less than their combined monthly housing and utility costs.

Who Qualifies for Food Stamps?

Many more individuals are eligible for regular food stamps than for expedited food stamps. Generally, to qualify for food stamps, the household must have a net monthly income (after deductions) below the poverty level, although gross monthly income (before deductions) can be at 130 percent of the poverty level. (The poverty level changes each year and varies with a family's size. The food stamp office, other state welfare offices, or a legal services office should be able to provide the precise income level for each size family.) Household income can be even higher than the poverty level if the household includes someone who is elderly or disabled.

In calculating net monthly income, it is important to consider available deductions. Deductions are allowed for certain work expenses, for nonreimbursable medical expenses, for dependent care, and for shelter or housing expenses that exceed a certain income percentage. Shelter expenses include rent or mortgage payments, heat, electricity, water, property taxes, and fire insurance.

Food stamps may be denied if a family has too many assets. The following assets do *not* affect an individual's eligibility for food stamps:

1. A house and the land it sits on;
2. Personal belongings;
3. Tools, equipment, and supplies required by an applicant's occupation;
4. A vehicle with a Blue Book equity value (that is, car's value less amount of loans that use the car as collateral) below $4,500, or used to make a living, or for transportation of a handicapped individual;
5. A catchall exemption of $2,000 in resources for families in which no one is over sixty years old, or $3,000 for families with a member over that age. The catchall can be applied so as to increase the $4500 vehicle exemption as high as $6500 or can be applied to exempt other property.

For more detail on eligibility and exemptions, carefully review program manuals and regulations, or refer difficult situations to an advocate who specializes in food stamps.

An important issue is what is a "household" for calculating household income, because sometimes an individual will be eligible for food stamps only if others are not included in the household. A household may be a single person or a group of people who purchase food and prepare meals together. More than one household can share the same residence, but still be treated as two separate households. Nevertheless, certain individuals who share a residence must always apply as one household, even if they do not shop or prepare meals together:

1. Spouses,
2. Minors and their parents,
3. Parents residing with their adult children,
4. Adult siblings (brothers and sisters).

There are certain exceptions. Parents and siblings, when either is disabled or elderly, can apply separately for food stamps, as can individuals with children under eighteen, even if they are living with their own parents or siblings.

Food Stamp Recipients Must Periodically Reapply

Qualifying households can receive food stamps for periods of from one to twelve months. If they require assistance longer, they must reapply before the end of the certification period. Some households are required to file updated reports monthly; failure to do so results in suspension of their benefits. Other households are required to file reports only when their circumstances change, and then within ten days.

Food Stamps Are Distributed in One of Three Ways

1. Food stamps are mailed directly to the household;
2. Food stamps are distributed from the welfare office or from another central location;
3. Authorization to Participate (ATP) cards are distributed, which the household returns to an issuance center in exchange for food stamps.

How to Contest Denials or Reductions of Stamps

Individuals can challenge the denial of stamps or a reduction in stamps through an administrative hearing. (The general administrative fair hearing process is described in more detail at the end of this chapter.) The first step is to review the notice that is always sent to an individual when an application for food stamps is denied. It explains the reasons for the denial and the applicant's right to appeal. File an appeal *before* the deadline listed there, or the individual forfeits his or her appeal rights.

Workers in the state agency that administers food stamps will rely on a state's food stamp program manual, which contains the state's food stamps regulations. When preparing for a hearing, counselors should note which regulations apply to their clients, and should consult with an advocate specializing in food stamps issues.

Other Food Programs

WIC Benefits Young Children and Pregnant Women

If a family includes a pregnant woman or a child under five, it should inquire about assistance from the Women, Infants and Children (WIC) program. Typically, WIC is administered by local public health departments and provides vouchers for supplemental foods important to the health of mothers and to the early development of their children. Eligibility for this program is based on family income and on whether the women, infants or children in the family are at nutritional risk. Welfare offices or health departments can provide information about WIC.

Private Food Banks and Food Pantries Are Additional Resources

Many unions, churches and community groups have community cupboards or food pantries that distribute food for home preparation. Churches and social service organizations such as the Salvation Army maintain cafeterias to which families can turn. These programs can be located by contacting local church offices, United Way offices, or other social service agencies.

Medicaid and Other Medical Care Programs

Try to Retain Medical Insurance Even After a Lay-Off

Ordinary preventive medical care, particularly dental care, tends to be postponed during times of crisis. Nevertheless, families sometimes suddenly confront large unplanned medical expenses and are caught with no medical insurance. Such nightmares can sometimes be prevented, particularly where an individual has just been laid off.

Within thirty days of being laid-off (unless the union or employment contract provides different terms), most individuals receive a notice from their former employer's health insurance company stating that their insurance has been terminated. The notice should specify a time period during which they can convert to an individual policy without any lapse in coverage.

If a family can afford to pay the premium to convert to an individual family policy, it should do so, particularly if a family member has an existing medical condition requiring care. If the laid-off worker later attempts to purchase a different health insurance policy, that policy is likely to deny or postpone coverage for such pre-existing medical conditions. Often the only way to avoid such a restriction is to maintain coverage with the existing insurer. (It is even possible that the existing insurer must continue to pay for treatments started while the consumer was covered, but continued after the policy has lapsed.)

Medicaid Is Another Important Alternative

If it is not possible for a family to maintain private health insurance coverage, consider applying for a state or federally funded medical assistance program, known in many states as Medicaid. Qualification for Medicaid varies from state to state, but hinges on available family income and resources.

Key Sources of Information about Medicaid

Medicaid is a jointly administered federal and state program. All states have chosen to participate in the basic program. At the federal level, Medicaid policy is set by the Health Care Financing Administration (HCFA), within the Department of Health and Human Services (HHS). Federal regulations governing Medicaid are especially complex. In fact, for their complexity they have been compared to the Internal Revenue Code.

Each state has its own Medicaid rules describing eligibility, services covered, and doctor reimbursement. These state rules, too, are often complicated. Most states maintain Medicaid program manuals, designed for daily use by technicians in local welfare offices. The manual is the best way to sort through complicated individual reimbursement problems, and is essential for counselors who expect to do much work in the area of Medicaid reimbursement.

The National Health Law Program (NHELP) publishes *An Advocates' Guide to the Medicaid Program* (1991), a basic resource for Medicaid advocacy. It also publishes *The Health Advocate,* a quarterly publication concerned with health law issues. Both publications are available through local legal services offices. NHELP also consults with legal services offices on a case-by-case basis. NHELP may be reached at 2639 S. La Cienega Blvd., Los Angeles, California 90034; telephone (213) 204-6010.

States Must Offer Medicaid to Some Individuals

Federal law requires that states provide medical coverage for groups described as the "mandatory categorically eligible." These individuals include recipients of AFDC, Supplemental Security Income, and pregnant low-income women. Because the AFDC Unemployed Parent program is now mandatory in all states, AFDC-based Medicaid is available to many displaced workers. AFDC families automatically meet Medicaid income and resources tests. Usually, any Medicaid-eligible service is covered in full, except for a small co-payment.

Medicaid eligibility has also been expanded in recent years. Medicaid now provides transitional benefits for up to one year to families that lose AFDC eligibility because of earned income. Children up to age six are eligible even in families with income as high as 130 percent of poverty. The scope of services required for poor children has been expanded. A few states have also expanded coverage to certain older people and disabled individuals, and otherwise relaxed eligibility standards.

Medicaid Medically Needy Program Assists Additional Families

The other major category of Medicaid eligibility is the medically needy program, now established in most states. This program assists families otherwise eligible for AFDC or SSI whose income is too high to qualify for those programs. Applicants must pass a resource test. The medically needy program, for example, benefits the families of displaced workers on severely reduced incomes who still have earnings above the AFDC level.

Medically needy participants must "spend down" their incomes to become eligible. A qualifying household must incur medical expenses (meaning expenses they owe, but not necessarily pay) equal to their spend down amount. Once they have done so, the medically needy program will pay the remaining medical expenses for the rest of the spend down period, usually one, three, or six months. During the next spend down period, the household must again incur medical expenses in order to become eligible.

Medical Expenses Covered by Medicaid

Medicaid pays the physician, the pharmacist, and any other service provider directly. Many states have co-payment systems, in which the Medicaid patient pays a small amount, usually only a few dollars, toward the service.

Under federal law, states must provide certain mandatory services, including inpatient hospital care, physician services, and skilled nursing services. States cannot deny service because of an individual's condition, although they can control service through a medical necessity review. A determination that a service is not medically necessary can be appealed.

States must also pay for transportation to necessary medical care. Optional services, which some states choose to cover, include prescription drugs, eyeglasses, dental care, psychiatric services, and private nursing. Most states provide lists of the services they cover.

How to Apply for Medicaid

As with other assistance programs, applications and information about medical assistance are available at local welfare offices. If a separate Medicaid application is required, documentation similar to that required for food stamps must be provided. Applications must be processed within forty-five days. For people applying on the basis of disability, the processing period is ninety days. Some states have shorter processing time limits.

Although states are required to inform applicants about their rights and benefits, they are not always diligent in doing so. Therefore, counselors should become familiar with several eligibility categories, optional covered services, and special programs to advise applicants about their options.

As with the food stamp program, medicaid applicants and recipients have the right to contest adverse actions. Administrative fair hearings are discussed at the end of this chapter.

Catastrophic Medical Assistance for Those Not Covered by Medicaid

For applicants not qualified for Medicaid or for state medical assistance, Catastrophic Medical Assistance is available in some states to assist with major medical expenses. When medical bills exceed a certain percentage of an applicant's household income, the balance of the bill above that percentage is reimbursed.

Hill-Burton Hospitals Provide Free Medical Assistance

The Hill-Burton Program for Hospital Renovation and Construction works directly with local hospitals. In exchange for federal money, subscribing hospitals agree to provide set amounts of free or below-cost medical care each year to qualified individuals. Needy individuals requiring hospital care should check with local hospitals to learn whether they qualify for Hill-Burton benefits, and when they can apply. Lists of Hill-Burton hospitals are available from local United States Department of Health and Human Services offices and from local legal services offices.

Hospitals Cannot Deny Emergency Care

Federal law prevents hospitals with emergency departments from turning away anyone in need of emergency care, although the hospital is not required to provide follow-up care. Further care for those unable to pay the cost of medical care is sometimes available at county and city operated public hospitals.

Other Programs Offer Free Care

A number of physicians in various parts of the county donate their services free to those who cannot afford medical care. Information about the programs can usually be obtained from local medical societies or health departments.

Local service clubs also sometimes have programs designed to meet particular needs. The best known is the Lions Club, which helps to purchase eye glasses for children.

Cutting the Cost of Medical Prescriptions

Several options are available for families unable to obtain prescription drugs through Medicaid. Any patient receiving a prescription should ask whether or not a less expensive generic drug can be substituted. In some states, doctors are required to allow patients to substitute generic drugs, while in other states doctors can make their own decisions about whether to allow generic substitutes.

Some hospitals provide free prescription drugs through their hospital pharmacy. Emergency one-time grants or small loans for drug prescriptions can sometimes be obtained from private social service agencies or church organizations.

Low-Cost Dental Care

Dental care often takes a back seat to more pressing financial obligations. However, there are several ways that families can obtain free emergency dental care or low-cost preventive care. First, some types of dental care are covered by health or dental insurance. Some dental coverage is included in Medicaid. Second, if neither insurance nor Medicaid is available, many community college dental hygiene programs and university dental schools provide preventive, diagnostic, and restorative services for free or at negligible cost as part of their teaching programs. Some hospitals have low-cost oral surgery clinics or participate in the Hill-Burton program (see page 15).

Mental Health Counseling

A financial crisis places tremendous emotional burdens on families. It is normal for such families to experience depression, anxiety, and feelings of worthlessness. These families may be served by seeking professional help. For more serious, long-standing problems, such as substance abuse, marital difficulties, or chronic depression, professional help is often essential.

Mental health assistance takes a variety of forms. Most psychologists and counselors offer both short-term intervention and long-term therapy. Group therapy is especially helpful for overcoming the feelings of isolation that often accompany job loss. Drug therapy is an alternative for serious depression; if medication seems called for, the individual should consult a physician or psychiatrist.

Most health insurance covers a portion of the cost of mental health assistance, but some plans stipulate that reimbursable care must be provided by a particular kind of professional, such as a psychologist rather than a licensed social worker. Many private counselors also provide limited free care or care at reduced cost.

Most regions of the country now have community mental health centers, where fees are generally based on income. Community mental health centers often provide both good service and referrals, and many conduct programs that address specific issues, such as chemical dependency, domestic violence, or crisis intervention. Most of these programs are free or provided on a sliding scale, though some are covered by private insurance or public medical assistance.

The AFDC Program

Key Resources

All states administer Aid to Families with Dependent Children (AFDC) programs. The federal Department of Health and Human Services has adopted general program rules, and approves state AFDC plans. States have great flexibility in setting eligibility and benefit levels. All states have passed AFDC rules or have published program manuals. Counselors who intend to work in this area should obtain a copy of their state's manual.

The Center on Social Welfare Policy and Law is a key resource on AFDC issues. The Center publishes a continuing series of bulletins, reports on litigation, and a pamphlet "Memoranda to Welfare Specialists." These items can be obtained at legal services offices. The Center also provides technical assistance, usually through local legal services offices. To contact the Center directly, write 275 Seventh Ave., 6th Floor, New York, New York 10001-6708; telephone (212) 633-6967.

How to Apply for AFDC Benefits

Application for AFDC can be made at a local welfare office, sometimes called a department of public assistance, department of social services, or department of human services. Most states require that applications be processed within forty-five days, although some states require a thirty day period or even less. Lengthy delays beyond these time limits are common. Some states pay benefits retroactive to the date of application. Other states pay benefits effective 15 or 30 days after application.

As with other programs, extensive documentation is requested. When applicants face unreasonable or multiple requests for documentation, counselors should help to simplify the process.

Who Is Eligible for AFDC Benefits?

To receive AFDC benefits a family must pass each of three tests: a family unit test, an income test, and an asset or resources test.

The Family Unit Test

AFDC benefits are available to family units in which "dependent children" live with "caretaker relatives" and are deprived of the support or care of one parent. More than one family unit can live in the same residence, and all eligible family units can receive benefits.

A key for AFDC eligibility is that the family have a "dependent child," which is defined as a child below the age of eighteen (or eighteen and attending a vocational or secondary school program that will be completed by age nineteen). Pregnant women are also eligible for the program, in that they will soon have a dependent child.

The second step is to show that the dependent child is living with a "caretaker relative," a category that includes parents, stepparents, grandparents, siblings, uncles or aunts, first cousins, and nieces or nephews. A child who is temporarily absent from the home can still be considered to be living with the caretaker relative.

The third step is to demonstrate that the dependent child has been deprived of the support or care of at least one parent in any of the following three ways:

1. *Continued absence.* The absence can be for any reason unless it is *solely* for military service. The parents need not be

divorced, so long as the child is deprived of one parent's support. Death of one parent also qualifies as a continued absence;

2. *Incapacity.* A parent is incapacitated if his or her ability to support or care for the child becomes substantially reduced by physical or mental circumstances and if this incapacity is expected to last at least thirty days. This is a much lower standard than that required for Social Security disability benefits; *or*

3. *Unemployment.* A parent had a "recent labor force attachment," but is now working fewer than one hundred hours a month. A recent labor force attachment occurs if a parent earned $50 or more in six of the thirteen calendar quarters ending within one year before the family applied for AFDC. The labor force requirement can also be met by participating in certain education, work, or training programs, or where a worker qualified for unemployment compensation within one year before applying for AFDC. At state option, four of the six quarters can be met through school attendance.

The Income Test

Like other programs, AFDC eligibility is based upon the recipient's having limited income and resources. While the exact standards vary from state to state, both gross and net monthly income is evaluated and households are allowed certain deductions. The most important deductions are for child care expenses, for a portion of earned income, and for the income of a dependent child. The first $50 of current child support, paid through a state agency, is disregarded.

The Assets or Resources Test

To be eligible for AFDC, a family can only have minimal assets, the exact amount varying from state to state. Importantly, many family assets are exempt from this calculation, so that a family with a house, car and other resources can still be eligible. Again, the specific exemptions vary from state to state, but in most states the following resources are exempt:

1. $1,000 in resources which are not otherwise exempt;
2. A house in which the family resides;
3. Basic household items;
4. Equity value in a vehicle, usually up to $1,500. The equity value above this amount might still be exempt under the general $1,000 exception. Equity value means the value of the vehicle less the amount owed on any loans which use the vehicle as collateral.

What if the Family Owns but Does Not Live in the House

While a family's home does not count toward the assets test, a house may be counted where the family does not still reside in the house, such as where a family moved to find employment, but has not been able to sell the house. In many states a house where the family is not living can still qualify as an exempt resource for up to six or nine months if the family is making an effort to sell the house. Even if a house cannot be exempted, the family may still be eligible for AFDC since the family may own the house, but have little or no equity in the house. This will require a determination of the amount of debts that are owed against the house, including mortgages, home improvement loans, back taxes, and other assessments, compared with an estimate of the house's current market value.

Pay Special Attention to the "Lump Sum" Rule

Any large amount of money (for example, a worker's compensation award) received during a month when the household receives AFDC can disqualify the household for AFDC benefits for many months into the future, even after the lump sum has been spent. If a household anticipates receiving a lump sum, it should cancel its AFDC in the month before it will receive the money. If the family subsequently spends the lump sum down below the resource level, it can then reapply for AFDC. The family should be certain not to acquire any resources that would render it ineligible.

There are several other ways to avoid lump sum problems and there are a few specific hardship exceptions to the lump sum rule. For information about these exceptions, an experienced public benefits advocate should be consulted. The best advice a counselor can give is to avoid lump sum problems.

Trust Funds Are Another Source of Problems

Try to demonstrate that a particular trust is not available to meet a family's basic needs, and thus should not be included as a family asset. For example, a trust established for a minor injured in a car accident might be restricted to cover only that child's medical care. Obtain information about the purpose of a trust from copies of court documents, letters from the attorney who drafted the trust, or letters from the judge who approved it. Sometimes it is possible to have a lawyer redraft the trust, clarifying that the trust is not available to support the family.

The JOBS Program for AFDC Recipients

The federal Job Opportunities and Basic Skills Training Program (JOBS) provides educational activities, skills training, readiness activities, job development and placement, and other job related services for AFDC recipients. In most states, caretakers of children younger than three are not required to participate in the JOBS program, although in some states only caretakers of children younger than age one are exempt.

Participants who fail to comply with JOBS requirements without good cause can be disqualified from AFDC. The first disqualification is for three months and the second disqualification is for six months. Usually, the rest of the family is not disqualified.

JOBS rules require the agency to try to resolve problems before disqualifying a person from AFDC. If conciliation is unsuccessful, a fair hearing can be requested. Disqualified individuals can shorten the disqualification period by complying with program requirements.

Counselors have an important role in helping JOBS participants with program requirements, conciliation, or sanctions. They can monitor the kinds and quality of services provided, ensuring that they are beneficial to their clients. For example, many for-profit trade school programs in recent years have been shams even though the program was accredited, qualified for federal loans, and even though the state had licensed the program. Ask prospective employers what they think of a particular school or form of training, and make sure that the participant is in a program that truly meets his or her needs.

Emergency Assistance

Many states participate in Emergency Assistance programs. Emergency Assistance is potentially available to any family with a member under age twenty-one, provided the family has not received such assistance in the previous twelve months. Unlike the AFDC program, there is no requirement that a child be without the support of a parent. There are no federally required income or resource limits, but states can set their own limits.

States have tremendous discretion in deciding what emergencies to cover. Some states require that the emergency be unforeseeable, or outside the household's control. Common emergencies include evictions and utility terminations.

Households should insist on applying for Emergency Assistance in writing. Welfare office supervisors have great discretion in granting or denying assistance; effective advocacy can influence that discretion for the benefit of a family in financial trouble. If assistance is denied, the family can request an expedited review of the decision. Request a copy of the state's Emergency Assistance rules or policy as useful background material.

Other Cash Assistance Programs

General Relief Programs

Many states also have local General Assistance or General Relief
programs. Benefits and eligibility requirements vary tremendously
among states, but the programs are usually available only to people who are ineligible for any other form of assistance, and who
have few or no resources.

Some general assistance programs cover only certain categories,
such as children or the disabled. Some programs provide benefits
for only a limited number of months each year. Most programs
require that employable people participate in a workfare or job
search program. Local legal services offices can provide more
information about these programs.

Other Emergency Programs

In addition to Emergency Assistance, some states and communities
have other emergency funds available to help with basic needs,
such as food, shelter, medical care, clothing, or transportation.
Often, these programs provide vouchers rather than direct cash.

Private Funds

Private social service groups and charitable and religious organizations sometimes have small funds available that provide limited
grants or short-term loans to families lacking other available resources. The Salvation Army is a valuable resource in many communities, as are shelters and crisis centers.

Public and private funds are often difficult to locate. Some are
listed in the social services section of the phone book. In many
communities, one agency serves as an information clearinghouse
or referral service for various sources of assistance.

Earned Income Tax Credits

Families can obtain up to a $1000 income tax refund if they are eligible for the earned income tax credit. Individuals who were laid off during the most recent tax year should be especially careful to see if they qualify.

A particularly valuable resource for counselors about earned income tax credits is a community outreach kit prepared by the Center on Budget and Policy Priorities. The kit helps counselors inform low-income families about their potential eligibility for tax refunds. The kit contains a fact sheet, eligibility guidelines, campaign posters, flyers printed in English and Spanish, and a summary of effective outreach strategies.

To receive the kit or more information about earned income tax credits, write to: the EITC Campaign, Center on Budget and Policy Priorities, 777 N. Capitol St., Suite 705, Washington D.C. 20002 or call (202) 408-1080.

Social Security and SSI Benefits

Although workers are eligible to receive Social Security benefits at age 62, many workers postpone receipt of these benefits because they will be eligible for larger monthly payments at a later date. While this strategy may make sense when the family's financial resources are adequate, it certainly does not in a time of financial distress.

Remind those age 62 or over that they may be eligible for Social Security benefits. The survivors of an insured worker may also be eligible for Social Security benefits upon the worker's death.

Social Security benefits are available only for those who have been employed a sufficient number of years in covered jobs, that is jobs contributing to the Social Security fund. Those aged 65 or over not eligible for Social Security may still be eligible for Supplemental Security Income (SSI). This is a federal program open to those whose income and assets are under established guidelines.

Disability Benefits

When Consumers Are Entitled to Disability Benefits

Many displaced workers and others are legally entitled to Social Security disability benefits. An entitled candidate might have worked for years at a good blue collar job, have limited education or skills to transfer to another job, and have suffered enough injuries or impairments over the years to qualify for disability benefits.

Disabilities take many forms—physical and mental limitations, extreme pain, depression or anxiety, and uncontrolled alcohol or drug abuse all qualify as disabilities. To qualify, the impairment or combination of impairments has to have lasted or be expected to last a year or more and has to prevent the person from engaging in substantial gainful activity in light of the person's age, education, and work experience.

Social Security is a federally administered program, separate from the other public assistance programs discussed here. Applications are made at local Social Security offices, or by calling a toll free telephone number.

Those whose past employment record does not qualify them for Social Security disability benefits can apply for SSI disability benefits. SSI is the federal Supplemental Security Income program for individuals whose income and assets fall below established guidelines.

Applicants May Have to Fight to Get Disability Benefits

Many applicants are unfairly and illegally denied disability benefits. Anyone who decides to pursue a claim under Social Security or SSI disability should contact a lawyer.

Disability benefit applicants will usually be able to hire a lawyer without paying a retainer up front. Many private attorneys specialize in disability law, and they seldom expect their clients to pay in advance. Instead, a successful claimant's lawyer can get a fee of up to one quarter of the claimant's back benefit. Moreover, many legal services programs represent disability claimants at no charge.

Disability cases proceed from an initial determination, to reconsideration, to a hearing in front of a Social Security administrative judge. If an applicant is denied benefits at any step, he or she can request an appeal to the next level. Each appeal must be filed within sixty days of the denial being received, unless the claimant has good cause for missing the sixty day deadline. It is helpful to secure early legal representation to insure that no deadlines are missed. An applicant who loses the hearing before the administrative judge can appeal the case to an appeals board and then to court. It is very important to have an attorney or other trained social security advocate once the case gets to the hearing level.

Utility Bills

Failure to keep up with electricity, gas, and other utility bills can lead to termination of service. In some cases, it can even trigger eviction. The Low Income Home Energy Assistance Program (LIHEAP) is available in some states to pay winter heating or summer cooling bills. Various weatherization and conservation programs can help reduce the size of heating bills, making them more affordable. Qualifying households can apply for a Standard Utility Allowance (SUA). Programs like LIHEAP, SUA, and strategies for dealing with utilities problems are explained in Chapter Eleven.

Child Support

Many families in financial distress are owed back child support by an ex-spouse. Even where a family cannot obtain an attorney to press their claim for child support, a state agency should be able to help in the collection attempt. Contact the local welfare office to see which state agency assists families in the collection of child support and what type of assistance they can offer.

How to Appeal the Denial of Government Benefits

Getting Started

In most states, those applying for benefits (and those already receiving benefits) can appeal adverse decisions through administrative fair hearing procedures. These procedures are usually less formal than regular court proceedings and are used for food stamps, Medicaid, AFDC, and several other programs.

After becoming familiar with the facts of a particular case, a lay counselor can help consumers assert their rights. Whenever complicated questions arise, an advocate specializing in public benefits should be consulted.

Most states have general procedural rules that explain how appeals and hearings should be conducted. These rules can usually be obtained from a legal services office, a welfare office, or a hearings office.

Guidebooks and references for various particular programs have been mentioned throughout this chapter. An excellent general reference to keep up on a wide range of government benefit issues is the *Clearinghouse Review,* published monthly by the National Clearinghouse for Legal Services, 407 South Dearborn, Suite 400, Chicago, Illinois 60605; telephone (312) 939-3830. Annual subscriptions are $75. *Clearinghouse* is widely disseminated to all local legal services offices.

Requesting a Hearing

Whenever an adverse action is taken against an applicant for or recipient of assistance, the service agency must send a written notice explaining the reasons for the denial or reduction of benefits. The notice should include citations to the regulations or policies being applied. It should also explain how the recipient can appeal the action.

The first step in challenging an adverse action is to request an administrative fair hearing. Usually, this request is made at the local office of the agency that denied the application for assistance. The request should be written, but it need not be formal or complicated. The applicant or counselor should keep a copy of the request.

Claimants who are current recipients and whose benefits are being reduced or terminated can request that current benefits continue pending a final resolution of the appeal. This request must be made promptly, usually no later than the date when the benefits are to be reduced or cut off, or within a certain number of days after the notice of the adverse action. If the claimant eventually loses the appeal, the claimant may have to arrange to repay benefits received during the appeal's pendency.

After a hearing is requested, the claimant usually (but not in unemployment compensation or social security cases) has an opportunity to meet with a supervisor at the local welfare office for an administrative review. This is an informal meeting at which both sides exchange information and learn whether they can settle the case out of court.

The administrative review is an opportunity to learn, as specifically as possible, why a particular action was taken. Counselors should request copies of any relevant items in their client's file, and of applicable state and federal policies, acquiring any additional information that might help them to resolve the matter and to settle the case favorably.

The Administrative Fair Hearing

If the case is not resolved at an administrative review, the claimant must decide whether to proceed to a fair hearing. Fair hearings are much less formal than court trials and hearing officers usually are not lawyers. Most hearings are tape recorded.

In rural areas, hearings are sometimes conducted by a telephone conference call. If it is important for the hearings officer to observe the claimant, the hearing should be in person.

Before the hearing, the hearing officer should be provided with any documents used as exhibits; copies should also be given to the agency opposing the appeal. Arrangements should be made for any necessary witnesses to attend the hearing. The counselor or claimant should make a written outline of important points; submission of a written statement of the claimant's position is optional. Claimants should insist on the right to review any documents the other side intends to use. Both sides have the right to ask questions of anyone who testifies.

Documents often include statements by people who are not present at the hearing. For example, the welfare office might rely on a report from John Smith that the claimant owns a brand new car. This kind of report is hearsay. The claimant should object to having the hearing officer consider such a statement, and should insist on the right to question John Smith in person. Whether the hearsay is kept out of the record will depend upon state law.

Many people represent themselves in fair hearings. A claimant intending to do so should first consult with a lawyer or lay counselor familiar with public benefits law. For complicated cases, it is advisable for a claimant to be represented by a lawyer or paralegal. Legal services programs often provide this kind of assistance at no charge. Even if a legal services office lacks the resources to handle a particular case, it may be able to provide enough information to enable the claimant to represent himself or herself effectively.

If the hearing decision is unfavorable, several appeals are usually possible, first within the service agency, and then in state or federal court. Most of these appeals are limited to issues and evidence already raised in the fair hearing. Therefore, it is important to thoroughly present the case at the original fair hearing. For an appeal to a state or federal court, a lawyer is essential.

2

Debt Counseling

Who Should Advise Consumers?

A family's financial difficulties will result not only in debt collection pressures, but in other forms of emotional stress. It is very important for the family to find outside support and advice. Family members will need someone to help them decide which bills to pay, what forms of assistance to seek, how to stave off creditors, and how to budget the family expenses.

Credit Counselors Need Not Be Financial Experts

The person offering this support to the family need not be a lawyer or a financial expert. Anyone who offers varying types of support services can provide this necessary credit counseling. This manual is designed to help social workers, community workers, clergy, vocational counselors, veterans counselors, JEPTA counselors, family services caseworkers, labor union personnel, paralegals, employees of charitable organizations, and others so that they can provide credit counseling.

Pros and Some Cons of Professional, Non-Profit Consumer Credit Counselors

Many cities have non-profit agencies which help financially distressed families develop feasible budgets, and also contact creditors to arrange more reasonable payment schedules. These agencies are often called "consumer credit counseling services." They provide a valuable service for many families.

There are some disadvantages to credit counseling services. The services often will not work with families whose debts are much too large for their income. The services sometimes charge a low fee. Most of their funding comes from lenders.

Many credit counseling agencies will not inform a consumer of any legal rights the consumer may have against a creditor. For example, a consumer may not have to repay a car loan if the car sale involved fraud. Few credit counseling services would bring this defense to a consumer's attention.

Avoid Profit-Making Credit Counselors

Some profit-making credit counselors have embezzled consumers' money. As a result, profit-making credit counselors are prohibited in many states. They should generally be avoided in other states. It is not always easy to distinguish non-profit and profit-making credit counselors, because profit-making entities may adopt "non-profit" type names, such as "foundation" or "service." A United Way logo on the counselor's letterhead is usually a reliable indication that a counselor is non-profit, although not all non-profit credit counselors are affiliated with the United Way.

Which Debts to Pay First

The most important function of a credit counselor is to help consumers decide which debts to pay first. Consumers with significant debt loads cannot get out of trouble simply by cutting down on expenses. (The next section does give some tips on cutting expenses.) Where the amount of debt is far beyond the family's present ability to pay, the family must make choices about which debts to pay and which debts to let remain unpaid for a period of time. (Refinancing debt often makes matters worse—the next chapter indicates when refinancing does and does not make sense.)

The first creditor to pay is not necessarily the creditor that screams at the consumer the loudest or the most often. Creditors who yell the loudest often should be paid *last* because they may have few remedies against the consumer other than yelling. Of more concern are creditors who not only threaten, but actually *can* take quick action against the consumer's residence, utility service, car, or other important assets. Consumers should direct their limited resources to what is most necessary for the family—typically food, clothing, shelter and utility service.

The fundamental principle is first to pay debts whose non-payment would result in the most harm to the family. Here are several general rules about which debts to pay first, followed by a more detailed sketch of the consequences of not paying certain types of debts.

1. Home mortgage and rent payments should always be paid first.
2. Make sure essential utility service is not disconnected. While this may not always require payment in full (such as during a winter moratorium), whatever payments that are necessary should be made.
3. Car loans should usually be paid after the really critical items (food, rent, utilities, clothing), but ahead of most other debts.
4. Generally, loans with only household goods as collateral should have lower priority and should be paid with other general debts.
5. If the consumer has not pledged any property as collateral for a loan, this makes the debt a low priority. Most credit card debts, doctor and hospital bills, open accounts with merchants, and the like are low priority debts.
6. The threat of being sued should not bump up a debt in priority ahead of mortgage, rent, utility, or car loan payments (top priority debts).

7. Generally do not pay debts where the consumer has a legal defense to repaying the loan, such as that the goods were never delivered or were defective. Instead, obtain legal representation. It is particularly dangerous to withhold mortgage or rent payments without legal representation.

8. When a creditor prevails in its lawsuit to collect on a debt, and has obtained a judgment, a consumer's home and other assets may be at risk, depending on state law and the amount of equity the consumer has in these items. If the property is at risk, make this a top priority debt, but only if the property is actually at risk.

9. Tax liabilities and student loans should generally be paid ahead of low priority debts but after top priority debts.

10. The existence of debt collection activity should have *no* impact on when a debt is paid.

11. Threats to report a consumer to a credit reporting agency, to seize household goods, or to garnish wages should have *no* impact unless the creditor has already sued the consumer in court.

The Consequences of Not Paying Different Types of Debts

To better understand the basis for these rules and how to apply them in particular cases, it is important to understand the consequences of not paying different types of debt.

Home Foreclosure

If a family owns a home and does not pay the mortgage, the bank or other creditor can foreclose on the home. This means the bank can sell the home and the family will have to move and will typically lose all their equity in the house. Often it is difficult to stop a foreclosure. Even filing for bankruptcy may not help a family permanently stave off a foreclosure. It is thus critical for families to prioritize their bills and make their mortgage payments first.

There is an important exception to this rule of always paying a mortgage first. Sometimes a fraudulent home improvement contractor, shady finance company, or other questionable company will obtain a second mortgage or lien on the home. In that case, consumers may have legal reasons why they do not have to repay the loan—e.g., the aluminum siding was never installed or the replacement windows are shoddy and overpriced.

Before making a final decision whether the consumer should repay the loan, make sure to obtain legal representation. It is dangerous for a counselor or consumer to make this decision without professional assistance because a misunderstanding of the law or legal practice can result in loss of the home. See Chapter Ten for more details on when a consumer may have defenses to repayment of a home mortgage or lien.

Creditors can only foreclose on a home if they have a mortgage, deed of trust, land contract, or lien on the home and the consumer is in default on the loan. A mortgage and deed of trust are similar and both involve the consumer putting up the home as collateral for a loan.

Sometimes consumers purchase a home through a land contract, whereby they do not obtain ownership unless they make all the required payments. If a consumer has never put up a home as collateral for a loan, a seller may still have a lien on the home under state law if the seller has improved the home, such as by fixing the roof or replacing windows.

Other creditors, such as a furniture store, a car dealer, or a hospital, cannot foreclose on a home, and it is thus less important to pay these creditors. These other creditors must sue the consumer, win the lawsuit, and then attempt to sell the home through a court procedure. Even then, state law may limit the creditor's right to sell the home and a bankruptcy filing may also save the home. See Chapters Nine and Ten for more information about home foreclosures.

Apartment Eviction

If a family does not pay its rent, it can be evicted. A family cannot be evicted for failing to pay other bills (although a utility termination may lead to eviction). While a bankruptcy may offer short term relief, the only way to stay in an apartment is to keep current on future rent payments, and, in most cases, pay any arrears in rent. See Chapter Twelve for more on consumer strategies to deal with evictions.

Utility Termination

Every household is hooked up to a series of utilities—telephone, water, gas, and/or electric service. Non-payment of the utility bill may result in disconnection of service, although in many instances this can be delayed or avoided even though the bulk of the bill is outstanding.

Failure to pay a telephone bill will have no impact on the continuation of electric service and vice versa. In fact, the only bill that can lead to utility termination is the bill for that particular utility. A bankruptcy can wipe out old utility bills, allowing service to be reconnected as long as the family stays current on new bills and provides any required deposit. Chapter Eleven discusses consumer rights concerning utility terminations.

Car Repossession

Typically, when consumers take out car loans, they put up the car as collateral on the loan. Sometimes consumers put up their car as collateral on other loans. Whenever a car is collateral on a loan, the lender can seize the car if the family gets behind on the loan. No court procedure is required; the creditor just drives away with the car, unless the consumer is there and objects to the taking. This is called "self-help repossession."

Not only will the consumer lose the car, but the creditor will usually sell the car for less than it is worth and then seek a "deficiency" from the consumer—the amount owed on the debt less the amount for which the car is sold. Chapter Seven examines consumer strategies to respond to car repossessions.

Creditors can only repossess a car through self-help if the car is collateral for a loan with that creditor. For example, the car will not be collateral for credit card debt or hospital bills; these creditors cannot repossess the car. Instead, they will have to sue on the loan, obtain a court judgment, and then ask the court to seize and sell the car. Even then the court will not seize the car if it is "exempt" under state law. (Chapter Five discusses when cars and other property are exempt.)

Seizure of Household Goods

Sometimes creditors who have taken the consumer's household goods as collateral threaten to repossess those goods, but this repossession is much more difficult and less profitable than the seizure of an automobile. Creditors cannot enter a home to seize property without the consumer's permission. Otherwise, the creditor will have to go to court to gain possession of the items.

Goods the creditor does seize rarely have any market value. From a purely financial point of view, it is generally not worth it for creditors to seize household goods collateral. Moreover, goods taken as collateral for a loan unrelated to purchasing the household goods are generally protected from seizure if the consumer files for bankruptcy. Typically, a creditor's threat to seize household goods is just that—an empty threat. Chapter Eight examines in more detail threats to seize a consumer's household goods.

Lawsuits to Collect a Debt

Consumers are often terrified by the very threat that a creditor will go to court to collect a debt. Consumers should understand that a creditor's filing a lawsuit against them does not immediately harm them. First of all, the consumer may win the lawsuit or the consumer's decision to contest the lawsuit may be enough to convince the creditor to drop the case.

If the court eventually rules in the creditor's favor, then the court will order the consumer to pay the debt. Even this court order to pay should not be viewed as especially threatening—failure to pay does not place the debtor in contempt of court. Instead, the judgment triggers the creditor's ability to take certain actions to garnish wages, seize property, and examine the consumer as to his or her assets. It is these actions, and not the filing of a lawsuit, which should concern the consumer.

This is not to say that consumers should ignore a creditor filing a lawsuit. The consumer should obtain immediate assistance from a lawyer or counselor to explain to the consumer what is happening, what should be done, and the consequences of inaction. Chapter Five examines these issues in more detail. But the threat of a lawsuit is really only a statement that the creditor *eventually*, after taking several legal steps, *may* have the right to take the additional steps described in the next two items, immediately below.

Wage Garnishment and Seizure of Bank Accounts

Creditors can only seize wages or bank accounts *after* they go to court and convince a judge that the creditor is owed the money. Before the creditor can take any action, the consumer has a right to a trial to determine whether the consumer owes the money. Only after the court orders the consumer to pay the debt can the creditor get an order to garnish, i.e., seize the consumer's wages or bank account. Depending on state procedure, this garnishment order can be from the court, a court clerk, or a sheriff. The order for garnishment is presented to the employer or bank, but even then state and federal law limit what can be taken.

Under federal law, the first $127.50 a week of take home pay is exempt from garnishment, and generally only 25% of a paycheck can be seized.[1] State law often gives consumers even greater protections. In some states, wage garnishment is not allowed at all, while in others the amount that can be garnished is less than the federal standard.

Moreover, many forms of government benefits, such as social

security payments, AFDC payments, and the like cannot be garnished. If this government benefit is placed in a checking account, particularly if no other funds are in the same account, the money may also be exempt from garnishment.

Filing bankruptcy is another method of dealing with garnishments. The bankruptcy filing generally eliminates garnishment as a threat. If all else fails, the consumer can usually negotiate a payment plan with the creditor to avoid the garnishment.

Execution and Judgment Liens

Creditors' rights to seize the consumer's property are significantly limited where the consumer has not put up property as collateral for the loan. Where property is not collateral, the lender must first obtain a court order that the consumer owes the creditor money. The consumer can contest the debt in court. Only if and when the judge decides a case in the creditor's favor can the creditor put a lien on the consumer's home or request the sheriff or a court official to seize the consumer's property.

Even then, state law protects certain family possessions from seizure, and even a home may be exempt from seizure, particularly if the family's equity in the home is not too great. Filing bankruptcy will postpone the threat of execution on personal and real property, at least for a period of time, and sometimes permanently. Moreover, creditors often are willing to work out payment schedules even shortly before a threatened seizure. See Chapters Five and Ten for further discussion of a consumer's right to protect from seizure property not pledged as collateral.

Debt Collection

Debt collectors legally cannot take *any* steps against consumers' property that are not listed above. (Most debt collectors are not even empowered by the creditor who employs them to take those steps themselves. Usually, debt collection agencies can only recommend that the creditor take those steps.) All debt collectors can do is communicate with the consumer and with others.

It is usually not difficult to stop the collector from even doing this. The federal debt collection law, for example, gives consumers the right to stop all collection contacts by simply requesting the collection agency to stop. As a result, a particular collection agency's aggressiveness in collecting a debt should have *no* bearing on whether the consumer pays that debt. Chapter Four details consumer strategies to deal with debt collectors.

Credit Record

A family in financial distress is likely to have adverse information listed on its credit record. There is no way to avoid this. Deciding to pay one creditor instead of another will usually not help a consumer's credit record. Just because one creditor says it will report the default to a credit agency does not mean it will. Moreover, other creditors who do not make such threats may in fact report defaulters to credit agencies.

Taxes, Student Loans, and Other Debts Owed to the Government

The government has special powers not available to other creditors to collect tax obligations, student loans and other debts owed to a government agency. The I.R.S., after a series of warning letters that will take a number of months, will send a final 90 day warning. At that point the I.R.S. will start putting liens on the consumer's property and then begin to seize property. While certain minimal possessions are exempt from seizure, most of a family's property can be seized. A court procedure is not required.

The consequences of nonpayment of student loans and other obligations to government agencies are not so serious. But be prepared for the government to intercept income tax refunds and earned income tax credits. The government will also utilize debt collection agencies and may seek large collection costs. Student loan defaults will definitely be reported to credit reporting agencies. Student loan defaulters also will be ineligible for future student loans and grants. See Chapter Thirteen for more on government collections.

Developing an Expense Budget

Developing a budget is a difficult but necessary step in assessing a family's financial condition and in controlling spending. Budgeting often requires support, is always unpleasant, and usually entails changing well-established behaviors. For financially distressed families, budgeting is even more unpleasant, because the family will face deficits even after severe belt-tightening.

A family's discretionary expenses must be cut to a bare minimum. Many counselors advise financially distressed families, "cut up your credit cards," and "stick to cash." However, a very disciplined consumer may find the convenience of a credit card, or the availability of a line of credit, useful in a future crisis.

Unless rapid improvement in financial circumstances is likely, belt-tightening should be viewed from both the short-term and long-term. Short-term, simple budget-reducing measures may include:

• Reducing fuel consumption;
• Reducing telephone equipment and use;
• Purchasing inexpensive foods (bulk foods are usually less expensive then packaged foods);
• Postponing clothing purchases;
• Growing or picking your own food;
• Asking a life insurance agent or carrier if the policy may be capped and payments delayed;
• Eliminating discretionary purchases.

Longer-term measures include:

• Creditors may agree to interest-only payments (leaving principal unpaid) for a realistic period, such as four to six months;
• Some creditors may allow entire payments to be deferred for months, but deferral charges should be checked; creditors who

have not taken collateral, and to whom the balance owed is a few hundred dollars or less, are most likely to allow deferrals;

• In colder states, ask the utility company to accept a twelve-month repayment plan, spreading high winter fuel costs into the summer. Most northern states also forbid winter utility shut-offs, and some offer guaranteed service at reduced levels of payment for low-income families;

• In some areas, wood for heating can be obtained free from federal or state forests, although investment in wood cutting tools and a wood stove might make this uneconomical;

• Child support payments may be reduced by a court or child support agency in light of reduced income;

• The family home may be leased to another family, and less costly rental housing obtained;

• Sell an extra car or trade in an expensive primary car for a "junker." While the more expensive trade-in car may be worth less than the amount of the debt on that car, at least the family will stop having to make installment payments on the more expensive car;

• Selling unnecessary personal possessions;

• Applying for assistance such as Food Stamps, Medicaid, SSI or Social Security energy assistance, weatherization, or cash benefits. (See Chapter One.)

For a substantial number of financially distressed families, poverty is only temporary. For others, it may be long-term. A different strategy will be called for in each case.

3

Refinancing Do's and Don'ts

Refinancing an unaffordable debt load is one of the most tempting but potentially disastrous steps a debtor in distress can take. Refinancing's attraction is that it seems to resolve the consumer's problems even though the consumer's income has not gone up and the consumer's expenses have not gone down. The stroke of a pen pays off creditors who have been threatening all sorts of things. The consumer now only has to make monthly payments to a new creditor who is not (yet) threatening anything.

There are times when refinancing is a good idea, but there are also times when it is a very bad idea, and there are times when the offered refinancing is just a scam to steal the debtor's house or other property. This chapter warns about cons to avoid and gives tips to determine when refinancing is a bad idea and when it is a good one.

Refinancing Scams

Many unscrupulous companies prey on those most in distress, believing that these individuals' financial plight makes them vulnerable to rip offs. Here are ten tips to help consumers steer clear of frauds:

• Be wary of anyone who solicits the consumer about refinancing or loan consolidation, particularly if the solicitation does not come from an established financial institution in the community. In addition, be skeptical of any solicitation from a finance company even if the company has "helped out" the consumer before. Well known finance companies have engaged in egregious frauds.

- Particularly avoid anyone who comes to the consumer's home. It is very expensive to market anything door to door, and odds are someone coming to the house to help bail homeowners out of trouble is really coming to get them in deeper.
- Never sign documents without knowing what is in them. Homeowners should be especially wary, because odds are any deal to "help" them will involve giving up rights to their home.
- Avoid any company that suggests that the homeowner sell it the home, with an option for the homeowner to buy the home back.
- Be careful of advertised schemes to save homes from foreclosure or personal solicitations to help the homeowner avoid foreclosure.
- If the local banker, credit union, or other person a family has been dealing with for years cannot help the family, odds are someone who advertises cannot either.
- Do not use a middleman to sell or lease a car. Always get the permission of the car creditor or lessor before turning a car over to someone else.
- Beware of anyone who wants to consolidate all of a consumer's debts into one loan. This *never* makes sense. The solicitation shows that the person suggesting the loan consolidation is not out to help consumers but to fleece them.
- Do not send an "application" or "processing" fee to an out-of-state lender who advertises "Bad Credit, No Problem" and then asks consumers to call an 800 or 900 number. This may just be a scam to make off with the fee.
- If it is too good to be true, it is not true.

How to Help Scam Victims

It is much easier to avoid a refinancing scam than to get a scam victim's money back. Do not expect the con artist to negotiate in good faith or to be responsive to complaints. A consumer's only hope is that the con artist does not want to alert law enforcement officials and is willing to "buy off" one victim with the hope of snaring more. So threats to go to a state attorney general office or district attorney or the local press may help.

The better course is usually to get legal help. But most lawyers will not want to handle such a case, and, if they do, many will not do so aggressively. So carefully pick a lawyer who will really go to bat for the fraud victim. There may be grounds to cancel any mortgage the con artist has placed on the home and to undo the whole agreement.

The consumer filing bankruptcy is one way to stop in its tracks a scam operation's attempt to foreclose a consumer's home. A bankruptcy filing temporarily stops all actions against the debtor's property. To be effective in the long run, though, the consumer's bankruptcy attorney must aggressively challenge the scam operator in the bankruptcy proceeding, something not all bankruptcy attorneys are prepared to do.

Competent legal representation may save the consumer's home, and even cancel the remainder of the consumer's obligation to the scam operator. It will be more difficult to recover money from a fly-by-night con artist.

Alerting Others to the Fraud

Probably the best course for a victim of a financial swindle is to first threaten to go to law enforcement officials. See if this obtains a quick settlement. Even if the threat does succeed in getting a settlement with the creditor, the consumer should still let law enforcement officials, the press, and others know about the scam. That way neighbors will not also be duped. The consumer should keep all paperwork and make records of all conversations with the scam operator.

Deciding When to Refinance

Often there is a fine line between a scam operator and an aggressive finance company that urges a consumer to consolidate or refinance debt. Do not assume that a finance company or other creditor will structure a loan so it is best for the consumer—in fact, one might even assume the opposite. The consumer must make an independent judgment as to which debts to refinance and which to leave alone. The rule of thumb is that when in doubt, do *not* refinance—this will only make matters worse.

To see why refinancing usually does not make sense, it is imperative to understand the characteristics of different types of debt.

Unsecured Debts

Most debts are called "unsecured." This means that a home, car, or other property is *not* collateral for the loan. Good examples are hospital and doctor bills and most credit card debt. Generally speaking, unsecured debt is "good" debt. The creditor will have to go to court before it can do anything to the consumer to collect on the debt, and even then may have difficulty taking any effective action against the consumer or the consumer's property. (For more about this, see Chapter Five.) It is almost always a bad idea to refinance unsecured debt into secured debt, particularly since the new loan will probably take a family's home as collateral.

Secured Debts

When a family puts up its home, car or other property as collateral on a loan, this is a secured loan. The creditor is said to have a "security interest" in the consumer's property. Common examples are home mortgages (both first and second mortgages) and auto loans. Be sure to look at the fine print in any loan to see what property the family is putting up as collateral. Every credit agreement has a statement disclosing in a readable format the important loan terms. That statement should clearly describe whether the consumer is giving the creditor a "security interest" in any of the consumer's property.

Secured debt is "bad" debt because the creditor has expedited rights to seize the consumer's property if the consumer gets behind on the loan. When refinancing, do not convert an unsecured debt into a secured debt, particularly if the family is putting its principal residence up as collateral for the new loan. Also never "trade up" on security. For example, do not refinance a car loan into a second mortgage, or turn a loan secured by household items (which creditors rarely if ever seize) into a home mortgage loan.

Utility Bills

Utility debts should not be refinanced. Obviously, the consumer does not want to lose heat or electricity. But there are many preferable ways to stave off a utility termination or to get service turned back on. (See Chapter Eleven.)

Refinancing a utility debt begins a downward spiral. If the consumer was having trouble paying the utility bills, refinancing these low or no interest debts will not improve matters. Instead, the consumer will have to pay both the *past* bills now refinanced at anywhere from a 10% to 36% interest rate and the current monthly utility bills. Particularly unwise is folding a utility debt into a home mortgage debt. Not only is the consumer paying more in interest, but the risk of default is that much more serious.

Low Cost vs. High Cost Credit

Believe it or not, many times when consumers consolidate or refinance loans, they turn low cost loans into high cost loans. Many existing bills charge *no* interest or charge only minimal late charges. Existing mortgage loans usually have a relatively low interest rate.

Refinanced loans, on the other hand, will generally be high cost loans. Not only will the stated interest rate be high, but the creditor will assess points, closing costs, insurance charges, maybe even a broker's fees or hidden charges.

One way of determining the real cost of the new loan is to request a "disclosure statement" explaining all the terms for the new loan. The federal Truth-in-Lending law requires that creditors provide this statement before the consumer signs the loan papers.

Unfortunately, creditors typically will only show consumers this form as the consumer signs the loan papers. Consumers should not wait to the last minute to get the loan, so that if the loan terms as disclosed are not advantageous, he or she can walk away and shop around for another loan. If the consumer has to put up his or her principal residence as collateral for a refinancing, federal law allows the consumer to cancel the loan *for any reason* up to three days after signing the loan.

Here are some items to look at in the loan's disclosure statement. What is the Annual Percentage Rate or "APR" (that is, the interest rate)? What is "the finance charge" (the total interest payments over the life of the loan)?

The "amount financed" is supposed to be the money the creditor is "giving" the consumer. However, often much of the amount financed never goes to the consumer or to pay off the consumer's obligations, but instead goes to purchase insurance or to pay various fees and charges. As far as the consumer is concerned, the amounts going to insurance, fees, etc. are really part of the finance charge, making the true interest rate higher than the stated rate. Request an itemization of the amount financed which will explain where the consumer's money in fact is going and why.

Bank Loans vs. Finance Company Loans

In general, do *not* refinance a bank loan with a finance company loan. (In fact, try to avoid finance companies entirely.) Finance company loans tend to be at higher interest rates and have more "padding" of insurance, fees, and hidden charges. Many consumers think only finance companies will deal with them, that banks do not make loans to credit risks. Do not make assumptions—ask a few banks. Also beware of finance company "flipping." Many finance companies encourage frequent refinancings, each time making the loan *less* advantageous for the consumer, and each time assessing prepayment penalties on the old loans.

Long-Term vs. Short-Term Credit

Always look at the length of a loan and whether there is a balloon payment (that is, a very large payment that is due as the last payment). Consumers will not want to refinance a loan they are paying out over 15 years with a loan they have to pay off in four years.

Particularly watch out if the monthly payments for the shorter loan are the same or lower than the longer term loan. This almost invariably means the shorter term loan has a large balloon at the end. Families in financial distress will not be able to pay the balloon payment when it comes due. Forced to refinance the balloon, the consumer at that point will have no leverage and may be stuck with whatever loan terms the creditor wants to offer.

Points, Broker's Fees and Other Up-Front Charges

New loans may assess points, broker's fees, or other up-front charges. Since any such charges on the old loan have already been paid, these charges assessed on a new loan must be viewed as an extra cost of the refinancing. These charges may make the new loan more costly even if the new loan's stated interest rate is lower.

Make sure the "APR" (Annual Percentage Rate) on the new loan is lower than the *interest* rate stated on the old, existing loan note. This is because the "interest rate" on the old loan will not reflect points, broker's fees, closing cost, and other up-front fees that are reflected in the note's APR. The stated interest rate reflects the continuing cost of the old loan *after* up-front costs have been paid. The APR is a measure of the total cost of a loan with all of these up-front costs factored in.

Insurance and Other Extras

Consumer debt frequently is loaded up with a lot of extras. Just as auto dealers make their real profits selling rustproofing and other extras, so, too, lenders sell overpriced extras or tack on fees and charges. Unless a consumer has a special reason for wanting these extras—they are usually fantastically overpriced and a really bad deal—the consumer should not purchase them. That sounds easy, but consumers often do not know what extras they are buying and lenders have sophisticated techniques to sell these extras.

One of the worst offenders is credit life and credit accident and health insurance. Consumers will be asked to initial that they want this. They should not do so. Only a small percentage of these insurance premiums are ever paid out as losses to policyholders.

For other extras there will be no choice. Consumers must purchase them if they want the loan. Examples are credit property insurance on the collateral and title examination fees. Some creditors take household goods as collateral for a loan for the sole purpose of requiring the consumer to purchase wildly overpriced insurance on this household goods collateral.

Do not assume that all creditors will load up a loan with these mandatory extras. Shop around because some creditors are a lot more guilty of loan padding than others. When comparing the cost of the old loan with the new loan, do not forget to factor in the cost of all the extras.

Prepayment Penalties

When a consumer pays off an old loan through refinancing, there are almost always significant prepayment penalties. These should be treated like extra charges on the new loan. Add them to the finance charge on the new loan and consider that they increase the interest rate on the new loan accordingly.

Most consumers will find it difficult to measure the size of these penalties, but they almost always exist. Even if the creditor does not have an explicit prepayment penalty, most states allow creditors to compute payoff figures using a fudge factor significantly to the creditor's advantage. Moreover, if the consumer purchased insurance on the old loan, that insurance will be canceled and the consumer will receive less than a pro rata rebate. (The creditor will then try to sell a new insurance policy with the new loan.)

Consumer Defenses

Consumers often have legal grounds not to pay a debt, for example, that the goods were never delivered or that repair work was shoddy. If this is the case, never refinance the loan with a different creditor because the consumer may lose the ability to raise these defenses against the new creditor. The more removed a creditor is from the original seller, the harder it is to raise defenses.

Twelve Simple Refinancing Rules

This discussion can be simplified down to the following twelve rules:

1. When in doubt do not refinance or consolidate debts.
2. Do not refinance because of pressures from debt collectors. Only refinance if, after careful consideration of all the numbers, the consumer is better off in the short term and in the long term under the new loan. A classic example of a good refinancing decision is if a local bank converts an 11% mortgage to a 9% mortgage with a minimal prepayment penalty and no points or hidden charges and only minimal closing costs.
3. Never or almost never refinance unsecured debt into secured debt. Do not trade "good" debt for "bad." Creditors want to do this because they cannot do much about an unsecured debt, but can really squeeze a family with a secured debt. Some people believe it is better to turn an unsecured loan with a 30% interest rate into a secured loan with a 12% interest

rate, but even then a better course may be just not to pay the 30% loan and work something out with that creditor. This is better than a new loan which puts a home further at risk.

4. Do not refinance utility debts. Work something out with the utility company instead.

5. Do not refinance credit card debt with secured debt.

6. Do not refinance doctor, hospital, lawyer or other professional bills.

7. If the debt is with a finance company or high-rate second mortgage company, do not refinance a debt with the same company. Consumers can ask the company to agree to lower payments on the existing loan, but should not allow the creditor to write out a new loan, which invariably will involve a prepayment penalty and new extra charges. Definitely do not allow the company to add new security—such as a home.

8. Consumers should not turn a car loan into a second mortgage unless they would rather lose their home than their car.

9. Do not refinance a loan with household goods collateral into a second mortgage loan.

10. Do not refinance low interest loans with high interest loans. Even if the new loan has a lower stated interest rate, make sure it is low enough to offset prepayment penalties, extra fees, and other charges involved in the new loan. Make sure that the "APR" (Annual Percentage Rate) of the new loan is lower than the *stated interest rate* of the old loan, that is the rate stated in the note. (This adjusts for certain up-front fees in the old loan which the consumer has already paid.) Also factor in the cost of insurance, closing costs, and other up-front fees.

11. Keep long term first mortgages. Lenders may try to "wrap around" or pay off a first mortgage. That is, instead of extending a second mortgage on top of the existing first mortgage, they may try to pay off the first mortgage and extend the homeowner a new first mortgage equal in size to the old mortgage plus the new loan. Do *not* let the lender do this unless the new loan is for the equivalent length of time and the interest rate is significantly *lower* than the old first mortgage—to offset prepayment penalties and fees and charges.

12. Do not refinance loans when a consumer has a valid legal reason for not paying that particular debt.

Backing Out of a Refinancing

If the consumer rethinks the advisability of a refinancing, federal law allows the consumer to cancel the loan within three days of signing the loan *if* the consumer's home is collateral on the loan. The consumer simply fills in and mails the form that the creditor is required to provide the consumer at the time of signing the contract. Federal law also provides other grounds for canceling refinancings where the consumer's home is put up as security. See Chapter Ten for more details.

Alternatives to Loan Refinancing

The consumer should only refinance if it makes sense for the consumer in the short run and long run. If refinancing is not appropriate, the consumer in financial distress still has lots of other options.

The consumer can try to get the lender to forbear payments or even rewrite the loan, arguing that the lender will do better that way than if the consumer files for bankruptcy. This will particularly be the case if the collateral is worth less than the loan, because the bank will definitely lose money in a foreclosure. Tell them they do workouts for commercial developers, so they should do the same for consumers.

In fact a growing number of mortgage lenders are being very flexible in changing loan terms. The lenders view this as superior than a forced foreclosure sale, with a low resale price and high expenses. See Chapters Nine and Ten for more details on possible work out arrangements.

For many types of unsecured debt, the consumer's best alternative may be to simply default on the loan and tell the creditor he or she cannot pay. For home mortgages, car loans, or for secured debt, the best debtor strategy may depend on the precise nature of the collateral. Other, different tactics may be appropriate for utility bills, rent payments, student loans, debt collection harassment, or collection lawsuits.

Because the appropriate strategy varies so much by the type of debt and the type of creditor collection action, this manual is broken down into chapters separately covering each situation. One thing is for sure though. Refinancing is almost never the right strategy.

4

Dealing With Debt Collectors

Do Not Let Collectors Pressure Consumers

Individuals in financial distress should not let debt collectors push them around. The last two chapters showed which bills a consumer should pay first and when to refinance. It is the job of some bill collectors to persuade consumers to pay the wrong bills first and to refinance bills that should not be refinanced.

Do not let debt collection harassment force families into making wrong decisions that will hurt them later. If a certain bill is less important, consumers should explain to a creditor why they are not paying and when they propose to pay: "I have to pay my rent and utility bills first. I just got laid off, but when I get a new job I will do may best to meet my credit card debt. I understand that you will want to cancel my card, and I will pay you when I can." If the creditor or a bill collector still calls at all hours and writes threatening letters, treat the collector as the enemy and use these tips to stop debt collection harassment.

Collectors Cannot Legally Do Much to Harm Debtors

Debt collectors are experts at making threats as to the dire consequences of nonpayment. It is important to know what a debt collector can and cannot legally do when a consumer does not pay a particular debt. Most debts, such as virtually all credit card obligations, doctor bills, small amounts owed merchants, and many small loans are "unsecured." This means the consumer has not put up any collateral, such as the family home or car, to secure the loan's repayment. An *unsecured* creditor can legally do only the following three things:

Stop Doing Business With the Consumer

Such action is most relevant with utility bills which are discussed in detail in Chapter Eleven.

Report the Default to a Credit Reporting Agency

Obviously, if a family cannot pay all its debts, at some point someone will report a default to a credit reporting agency, and the family will have to live with a bad credit rating for a while. For families in real financial distress, bad credit reports are unavoidable and should not be the reason to pay any particular bill. Moreover, those threatening to report a default may be the last to do so, since a collection agency has no financial incentive to actually report the family to a credit reporting agency.

Sue the Consumer

This is the threat that consumers worry about. Nevertheless, there are four reasons why the threat of a lawsuit is far less serious than many imagine. First, it is hard to predict whether a particular creditor will actually sue on a past due debt. It is expensive to take consumers to court. Many creditors will not do so for small debts, say under $200, although some creditors do take even small debts to court. Still other creditors do not take even large debts to court. How aggressively a collection agency threatens suit is no indication whether the creditor will actually sue, even if the threat appears to come from an attorney.

Second, if the creditor sues the consumer, the consumer has a right to respond to explain why the money is not owed. Do not let the creditor win by default. The consumer does not have to hire an attorney to respond to the lawsuit. Often when a creditor sees that a consumer will contest the action, it will stop pursuing the lawsuit. How to respond to a lawsuit is detailed in Chapter Five.

Third, even if the creditor does pursue the lawsuit and eventually wins, the worst that can happen is that a court judgment will be entered against the consumer. A consumer will *not* be in contempt of court for failure to pay the judgment. The judgment only gives the creditor the legal right to *try* to seize the consumer's property or wages.

Fourth, "judgment proof" consumers have nothing to fear from even these special collection techniques. A consumer is "judgment proof" if all the consumer's assets and income are protected by law from a creditor trying to enforce a court judgment.

It is thus very useful to know whether a consumer is judgment proof or whether the creditor can legally seize either the consumer's income or property after prevailing in its lawsuit. State exemption laws usually protect a certain amount of a family's property from seizure pursuant to a court judgment. A local attorney can provide a list of exempt property and advise whether a state's laws allows a home or any other valuable property to be taken and sold by a creditor with a judgment against the consumer.

To be judgment-proof, a consumer's wages or other income must also be exempt from seizure. Federal law sharply limits the amount of wages that a creditor can seize. In all states the first $127.50 a week of take home pay is protected, and only a portion of the amount over $127.50 can be seized. Moreover, in certain states no wages can be garnished at all; in other states more than the first $127.50 is protected. Social security and other government benefits cannot be seized at all.

As can be seen, the threat of a court action is not nearly as real or dangerous as the threat of a landlord's eviction action, a bank's foreclosure on a mortgage, a car's repossession, or a utility's termination of gas or electricity service. These latter four actions usually happen quickly with a minimum of legal process and expense to the creditor. Moreover, state laws will provide consumers only minimal protection from these latter four creditor actions.

Debt Collectors Cannot Legally Take Other Actions to Collect on Unsecured Debts

A creditor, if it chooses to, can stop doing business with a consumer, report a default to a credit bureau, or sue on the past due debt. A collector's veiled threats to do anything else on an unsecured debt are deceptive and violate federal law. The collector cannot seize wages or property before the creditor has obtained a court judgment, nor can it send the consumer to jail or send the consumer's children to foster care. Remember the cardinal rule about debt collectors—unless they work for the debtor's landlord, utility, or a secured creditor, they often have no bite behind their bark. Creditors who growl the loudest should not drive debtors into the teeth of a creditor with real bite.

Dealing With Debtors' Guilt Feelings

Consumers in financial distress are not deadbeats. Circumstances outside their control prevent them from paying their debts. Consumers with excess debt burdens must repay their most important debts first, and must postpone payment of other debts.

Believe it or not, the collector knows this even better than the consumer. Creditors know from long experience that most people pay their bills and, when they do not, it is because of job loss, illness, divorce, or other unforseen events. Creditors take this risk of default into account when the creditor sets the interest rate—creditors make enough money off debtors in good times so that when consumers default, the creditor is covered.

Do not be fooled by collector statements to the contrary. Debt collectors are *instructed* to ignore the reasons that consumers fall behind on their debts, to show no sympathy, and not to listen to reason.

A consumer has no moral obligation to pay one debt at the cost of not paying another debt, particularly where the debt not paid is more central to the family's survival. Creditors know this. They should not be rewarded for trying to pressure consumers to pay them off at the expense of another creditor.

Six Different Ways to Stop Debt Collection Harassment

Because bill collectors have no bite behind their bark, they will bark very loudly, hoping to intimidate. Do not let them. This section lists six different approaches to stop debt harassment. Filing for personal bankruptcy is *not* one of these six, even though it is very effective at stopping debt harassment. A bankruptcy filing should be saved for more serious financial problems because debt collection harassment is usually easily stopped without having to resort to a bankruptcy remedy. In fact, be wary of any attorney offering to file bankruptcy for a consumer where the only problem is debt harassment.

Keep in mind that the effectiveness of any of these six approaches may depend on whether the creditor is doing its own collection (for example, the doctor's office is calling the consumer up) or whether the creditor has hired a debt collection agency or attorney. Consumers have more rights if they are dealing with a debt collection agency or an attorney. The key federal law regulating debt collection, the Fair Debt Collection Practices Act (FDCPA),[1] applies only to debt collection agencies and attorneys, and generally does *not* apply to creditors collecting their own debts. Nevertheless, state laws regulate creditors collecting their own debts, and the six approaches listed here generally will work with creditors collecting their own debt, and not just with collection agencies.

1. Head Off Harassment Before It Happens

When families have more bills than they can pay, they by definition cannot pay all their bills. A natural, but usually counterproductive response is for a consumer to ignore certain bills, maybe just tossing a series of warning letters in the trash. But creditors will not forget about a bill just because the consumer fails to respond. Instead, a likely result is that the creditor will hire a collection agency or turn the matter over to an in-house collection bureau. The job of these collectors is to get the consumer to notice the bill, and sometimes they are not very nice in the methods they choose to attract the consumer's attention.

To avoid this result, before the creditor refers a loan out to a collection agency, and before the debt gets into the machinery of the collection process, the consumer should call up the creditor and explain the family situation. Promptly contacting the creditor is most important with hospitals, doctors, dentists and similar creditors who would otherwise quickly turn a debt over to a collection agency. Although retailers, banks and finance companies are more likely to have an in-house collection arm, it still pays to try to avoid the transfer of the debt to that office.

Consumers should say that they have to pay the landlord or mortgage, utilities and certain other bills first. The consumer has not forgotten the creditor and will pay when he or she can. Make it clear that the consumer cannot afford to pay the bill, and will not pay a collection agency either. The consumer should not over-promise, but should be polite and honest.

Make sure the creditor understands the consumer will pay the creditor when he or she can and there is no need or advantage to go to the expense of hiring a collection agency. The consumer will not pay a collection agency any sooner than the creditor.

The creditor then has a financial interest *not* to turn the matter over to a collector. Collection agencies usually charge the creditor a fee of approximately one third of what they collect, or sometimes charge the creditor a flat fee per debtor. The creditor can avoid this fee by sitting tight.

The consumer also has a financial interest in heading off referral of a debt to a collection agency. Creditors are generally more flexible than debt collection agencies, and are more willing to work out payment plans. Consumers may waste a lot of time trying to negotiate with debt collectors, where they would have been more successful dealing directly with the creditor.

The only danger of calling the creditor is that the creditor might

convince the consumer to start making reduced pay~~ment~~
consumer cannot afford to make. For this reason, a
friend might help the consumer in talking to the crea

2. The Cease Letter

Assuming the consumer fails in explaining the situation to the
creditor, and the consumer is being harassed for the debt, the
simplest and best strategy to stop collection harassment is to write
the collector a cease letter. Federal law requires collection agencies
to stop their dunning after they receive a written request to stop.
The federal law does not apply to creditors collecting their own
debts, but even these creditors will often honor such requests.

The letter need not give any special explanation why the collector should cease contacts. Nevertheless, it is generally a good idea
to explain why the consumer cannot pay and the consumer's
hopes for the future. The letter might also describe the abusive
tactics of the collector's employees and the family's resulting distress, and request termination of any future unbusinesslike collection contacts. It is very important to keep a copy of the written
request.

Here is an example of such a letter (delete references to billing
errors, debt harassment, or any other statements that do not apply
to the consumer. A simple request to stop collection contacts is
sufficient):

Sam Consumer
10 Cherry Lane
Flint, MI 10886

January 1, 1993

NBC Collection Agency
1 Main Street
Flint, MI 10887

Dear Sir:
I am writing to request that you stop communications to me
about my account number 000723 with Amy's Department Store

as required by the Fair Debt Collection Practices Act, 15 USCA § 1692c(c).[2]

I was laid off from work two months ago and cannot pay this bill at this time. I am enrolled in a training program which I will complete in March and hope to find work that will allow me to resume payments soon after that.

Please note that your letters mistakenly list the balance on the account as $245. My records indicate that the balance is less than that.

You should be aware that your employees have engaged in illegal collection practices. For example, I received a phone call at 6:30 a.m. from one of them last week. Later that day I was called by the same person at my training program which does not permit personal phone calls except for emergencies. My family and I were very upset by these tactics.

I will take care of this matter when I can. Your cooperation will be appreciated.

Very truly yours,

Sam Consumer

cc: Better Business Bureau
    10 Main Street
    Flint, MI 10887

3. The Lawyer's Letter

A consumer does not need a lawyer to send a cease letter. Believing that they need to file for bankruptcy, people too often go to lawyers, when all they actually need is relief from a few abusive bill collectors. When such relief is all that is needed, the debtor or a counselor can send a simple cease letter without the cost of legal assistance. If these letters do not stop the abuse, a letter from a lawyer usually will.

Collection agencies must stop contacting a consumer known to be represented by a lawyer, as long as the lawyer responds to the collection agency's inquiries. Even though the federal Fair Debt Collection Practices Act requirement does not apply to creditors collecting their own debts, these creditors also will generally honor requests from a lawyer. A collector's lawyer also is generally bound by legal ethics not to contact debtors represented by a lawyer.

4. The Work-Out Agreement

Probably the most common consumer strategy, though not the best, to deal with debt harassment is to work out a deal with the collector. Collectors will generally stop collection efforts after the consumer works out a payment plan with the collector.

Many collection agencies and creditors claim initially that they must receive payment of the balance in full. They will urge the consumer to borrow from a loan company or from relatives to pay off the debt. As described in Chapter Three, this is almost always a bad idea.

If a consumer resists this suggestion, eventually most collectors will agree to an installment plan. Again collectors initially will ask for payments beyond the consumer's financial capability. If the consumer sticks to his or her guns, the collector will agree to a realistic plan, one that often greatly reduces the amount of the debt.

While a consumer may feel flushed with victory in negotiating a large debt down to small monthly payments, even this may be offering too much to the collector. As described in Chapter Two, consumers must prioritize their debts. Even a small payment to an unsecured creditor is unwise if this prevents payment of the consumer's mortgage or rent. There are other, better ways to stop debt harassment.

5. Complaints About Billing Errors

Collection letters are sometimes in error, mistaking the amount due or the account number, or billing the consumer instead of his or her insurance company. When a collection letter contains a mistake, the consumer should write to request a correction. Collection agencies, by law, must inform consumers of their right to dispute the debt. If the consumer disputes a debt in writing within

30 days of receiving this notice, the collection agency must stop collection efforts while it investigates.

If the dispute involves an open end account, a credit card, or an electronic transfer of money, the consumer has the additional legal right under the federal Fair Credit Billing Act to require the creditor to reexamine the bill. The consumer must write a letter pointing out the mistake within 60 days of receipt of the disputed bill. The consumer's rights to correct billing errors are periodically included with credit card statements. Although other creditors are not required by this law to investigate errors, they usually do so as well. Even after deadlines have passed, most collectors will stop their collection efforts and investigate.

6. Complaining to a Government Agency

Another strategy is to write to government agencies responsible for enforcing laws that prohibit debt collection abuse. A government agency is not likely to investigate immediately unless it has other complaints against the same collector, a fact that probably cannot be known beforehand. Nevertheless, sending a copy of the complaining letter to the collector often produces good results.

The complaining letter should be sent to the Federal Trade Commission, Bureau of Consumer Protection, Washington, D.C. 20580. Copies of the letter should be sent to the consumer protection division within the state attorney general's office, usually in the state capitol, and also to any local office of consumer protection listed in the local telephone book. Addresses can be obtained from a local better business bureau or office of consumer affairs.

If the collection tactics include abusive telephone calls, a copy of the same letter should be sent to the local telephone company and to the public utility commission in the state capitol. If the collector's abusive behavior appears part of its routine practice, either because of form letters or because of lack of provocation, this should be pointed out to the agency. An example of such a letter follows:

Sam Consumer
10 Cherry Lane
Flint, MI 10886

January 25, 1993

Federal Trade Commission
Bureau of Consumer Protection
Washington, DC 20580

Dear Sir:

I am writing to complain of abusive debt collection tactics used by ABC Collection Agency, 1 Main Street, Flint, MI 10887 which I request that you investigate.

I was laid off by U.S. Steel two months ago and have not been able to maintain all payments on all my bills. ABC began contacting me in December about my account with Amy's Department Store in Flint. ABC's abusive collection tactics have included:

1. Telephoning my sister asking her to lend me the balance when she does not have anything to do with this account.

2. Calling me at 6:30 a.m. at home and using offensive language, calling me a "God damned deadbeat."

3. Writing that they would sue me if they did not receive payment in ten days (this was a month and a half ago) whereas all they have done since then is to call and to write. (A copy of that letter is enclosed).

4. Continuing to contact me after I sent them a letter asking them to stop. (Enclosed is my letter to them and a later letter from them).

5. Billing me for $245 when no more than $185 is owed on the account.

My family and I are doing our best to get back on our feet, and this abuse is very distressful. Your assistance will be appreciated.

Very truly yours,

Sam Consumer

cc: Attorney General's Office
Bureau of Consumer Protection
Lansing, MI 10826

Flint Office of Consumer Affairs
14 Main Street
Flint, MI 10887

ABC Collection Agency
1 Main Street
Flint, MI 10887

Upper Michigan Telephone Co.
36 Main Street
Flint, MI 10885

Public Utility Commission
Lansing, MI 10826

Getting Money For Families Subjected to Serious Debt Harassment

Families in financial distress are subjected to more debt collection harassment than most families. Such harassment is illegal and the families should be compensated for any injury suffered. These families are already experiencing difficult emotional issues, and they do not need further harassment by debt collectors. Obviously, any money collected—or any amounts written off existing debts in settlement of a harassment charge—will be particularly welcome. At the same time, any money collected will deter future misconduct by debt collectors.

The consumer should consider suing the collector for a large amount of actual and punitive damages where the collector's conduct is egregious. Examples of such conduct are threats to throw the consumer in jail, to deport the consumer, or to have children put in foster care. A lawsuit may also be appropriate where emotional and psychological injury is severe, such as lost sleep, nausea, headaches, or where harassment results in the consumer seeking medical treatment. A collector's willful or wanton conduct may result in a court awarding not only the consumer's actual damages, but, in most states, "punitive damages," meaning an amount to punish and deter the collector from future misconduct.

Where a large recovery is possible, the family may be able to find a competent attorney to take the case on a contingency fee basis. While a few cities have lawyers who regularly handle debt collection harassment cases, in most places the family should seek a personal injury lawyer willing to pursue the case on a contingent fee basis. A lawyer new to this type of claim may save substantial time by using the National Consumer Law Center's *Fair Debt Collection* (2d ed. 1991 and Supplement), a legal practice manual covering all aspects of consumer remedies for debt collection harassment. Even if a local collection agency has inadequate assets to pay a large judgment, point out to the attorney that collection agencies usually are bonded or have insurance coverage.

Once an attorney is found, the family or counselor's job is just to document the extent of collector misconduct and the impact on the family. Although a debtor may not want to discuss his or her feeling about the harassment, it is key to determining what kind of legal case the debtor has. All symptoms of emotional distress should be discussed: anxiety, embarrassment, headaches, nausea, indignation, irritability, loss of sleep, and interference with family or work relationships. Did the consumer consult a doctor? Are there symptoms of psychosomatic illness brought on by the harassment? One survey of 1300 consumer judgment debtors revealed that just less than half suffered psychosomatic illness as a result of their financial distress and about a quarter of them consulted a doctor.

Out-of-pocket losses should also be listed, ranging from loss of employment to loss of wages because of time taken off from work to try to resolve the dispute. In addition, telephone charges, transportation, medical bills, and counseling services could all be part of the consumer's actual damages.

Consumers should keep a record of all expenses related to the collection effort. They should prepare a statement, with or without the help of a counselor, describing their physical and emotional response to the collection efforts, and listing all costs incurred as a consequence of that response. If a doctor or counselor had to be consulted, that expense should be included. Supporting statements should be obtained from family members, relatives, friends or co-workers.

A verbatim telephone log of collection contacts would also be helpful. Pen and paper should be kept near the telephone to record all telephone contacts.

Recovering Up to $1,000 for Less Serious Harassment

Other times a family is subject to illegal debt harassment, but the conduct is not so egregious that a court will award large damages. As a result, the economics of hiring an attorney appear doubtful. Nevertheless, the United States Congress has determined that families need a viable remedy to prevent less serious debt harassment. Congress has enacted a law that makes consumer recovery for less serious debt harassment both practical and meaningful.

Consumers Can Recover Up to $1000 Even Where Injury Is Minimal

The federal Fair Debt Collection Practices Act (FDCPA) allows consumers to recover up to $1000 plus their attorney fees even when their injury is only minimal. FDCPA violations are easy to prove because the FDCPA specifies with some particularity types of prohibited collector conduct. Any violation in turn entitles the consumer to an automatic recovery of up to $1000.

This means that even if the consumer cannot prove actual damages, the court has discretion to award the consumer as much as $1000 for any violation, but can also award the consumer a smaller amount. Courts occasionally award more than $1000 for multiple violations of the Act.

Actual damages can be awarded on top of the $1,000 statutory award for any actual injury caused by the illegal collection activity. A survey of FDCPA cases indicates that the average award for *actual* damages is over $2,000, and that actual damages have been awarded for such emotional injuries as loss of happiness, loss of energy, loss of sleep, tension headaches, crying spells, and marital problems. Consumers have been awarded as much as $6,000 for emotional distress when the stress aggravated pre-existing medical problems.

When a consumer wins an FDCPA case, the collector must pay the consumer's attorney fees, which may encourage a private attorney to take the case on a contingent fee basis, particularly where the claim appears strong. In fact, the collector may end up paying more in attorney fees than in damages.

Even though many debt collectors are small operations, consumers can usually recover their judgments against the collectors. Many collectors carry professional liability insurance to protect themselves against consumer claims. The existence of such insurance can usually be discovered during the pretrial stage of a lawsuit and is often important in settling claims.

A consumer thus has a lot of leverage in dealing with a collector that violates the FDCPA. It pays to be familiar with the specific requirements of the federal Act so that violations can be pointed out to the collector or to an attorney who might represent the consumer.

Finding an Attorney to Pursue FDCPA Claims

It is not always possible to find an attorney to handle a FDCPA claim. Families with low incomes and limited assets may be eligible to obtain free legal services from a neighborhood legal services office, and those offices may pursue such claims. Other consumers can contact bar association pro bono attorneys who might handle the case. The key to convincing a pro bono or other private attorney to take the case will be the availability of an attorney fee award paid by the collector if the consumer prevails.

Another key is that private attorneys unfamiliar with the FDCPA can find everything they need in the National Consumer Law Center's *Fair Debt Collection* (2d ed. 1991 and Supplement). This is the most thorough resource for bringing cases under the federal Fair Debt Collection Act as well as under other debt collection laws. The 683-page manual analyzes the statute, agency interpretations, court decisions, and reprints the statute, legislative history, agency interpretations, sample court documents, interview checklists, damage awards, and other important practice aids. With the use of this manual lawyers should be able to pursue a debt collection harassment case with a minimal expenditure of time. The manual will also be helpful to counselors who wish to determine with more specificity whether particular forms of debt collection violate the FDCPA.

The Federal FDCPA Applies Only to Collection Agencies and Attorneys, Not To Creditors

The FDCPA applies to collection agencies and lawyers; it does not generally cover creditors or their employees collecting their own debts.[3] That is, when a creditor hires an independent company to collect its debts, the actions of the independent collection company are subject to the FDCPA. Similarly, when a creditor hires an attorney to collect its debts, the attorney is covered by the FDCPA. On the other hand, the FDCPA does *not* apply to collection attempts by a creditor's employees or officers collecting for the creditor and in the creditor's name.

Other than this serious restriction, the Act applies broadly to most attempts to collect consumer debts. The debt need not arise from the sale of goods on credit. For example, the FDCPA applies to collection agencies and lawyers' attempt to collect medical bills, rent, utility bills, loans, and dishonored checks.

The Act does not apply to sheriffs, marshals, and other state and federal officials when collecting a debt in the performance of their official duties. However, private collection agencies who are collecting debts owed to a state or federal agency *are* subject to the Act.

What if the FDCPA Does Not Apply?

If the FDCPA does not apply to collection efforts, the consumer still has legal remedies for debt collection harassment. These remedies will mostly involve state law, not federal law. While there will be variations from state to state, in every state there will always be at least some remedy for debt collection harassment. For more detail on these other state remedies, see the National Consumer Law Center's *Fair Debt Collection* (2d ed. 1991).

Conduct Violating the FDCPA

Any conduct violating the Act is sufficient for a consumer to recover up to $1000 in statutory damages. The Act requires collection agencies to take certain affirmative actions:

- The collection agency must stop contacting consumers if the consumer so requests in writing or disputes the debt in writing.
- The collection agency, in its initial communication or within five days of that communication, must send the consumer a written notice. That notice identifies the debt and the creditor, and tells consumers of their right to dispute the debt or to request the name and address of the original creditor, if different from the current one. If the consumer asserts either of these rights, the collector must suspend collection efforts on the disputed portion of the debt until the collector responds to the request. (Note that a consumer's failure to dispute a debt is not an admission of liability. The collector would still have the burden of proof in any court action to collect the debt.)
- Any lawsuit by a collector must usually be brought in the same county or other judicial district where the consumer resides or signed the contract.

The following conduct violates the FDCPA:

- Communicating with third parties, such as the consumer's relatives, employers, friends, or neighbors, about a debt unless the consumer or a court has given the collector permission to do so. Several narrow exceptions to this prohibition apply. Collectors may contact creditors, attorneys, credit reporting agencies, cosigners, the debtor's spouse, and the debtor's parent if the debtor is a minor. Third-party contacts are also permitted if the contacts are solely for the purpose of locating a debtor and do not reveal in any way the contact's underlying purpose.

- Communicating with the consumer at unusual or inconvenient times or places. The times 8:00 a.m. to 9:00 p.m. are generally considered convenient, but daytime contacts with a consumer known to work a night shift may be inconvenient.
- Contacting the consumer at work if the collector should know that the employer prohibits personal calls, or contacting the consumer at other inconvenient places, such as a friend's house or the hospital.
- Contacting a consumer represented by a lawyer, unless the lawyer gives permission for the communication or fails to respond to the collector's communications.
- Contacting the consumer when the consumer writes a letter asking the collector to cease communications. The collector is allowed to acknowledge the letter and to notify the consumer about actions the creditor or collector may take.
- Using obscene, derogatory or insulting remarks.
- Publishing debtors' names.
- Telephoning repeatedly and frequently.
- Telephoning without disclosing the collector's identity.
- Making communications that intimidate, harass or abuse the consumer, such as a threat to conduct a neighborhood investigation of the consumer, or telling debtors that they should not have children if they cannot afford them.
- Making false, misleading or deceptive representations in collecting debts, such as pretending that letters carry legal authority.
- Falsely representing the character, amount or legal status of a debt, or of services rendered or compensation owed.
- Falsely stating or implying a lawyer's involvement, such as where form letters written on an attorney's letterhead and bearing an attorney's signature in fact came from a collection agency and were not reviewed by a lawyer.
- Threatening arrest or loss of child custody or welfare benefits.
- Stating that nonpayment will result in arrest, garnishment or seizure of property or wages, unless such actions are lawful, and unless the creditor or the collector fully intends to take such action.
- Threatening to take actions that are illegal or that are not intended. To verify a collector's intention to file suit, counselors could check the plaintiff's index at their local courthouse to see

whether the company making the threat has a history of filing similar suits. Suit is less likely the smaller the debt (e.g., less than $500), the more distant the collector, and the stronger the consumer's dispute of the debt. Other common threats that may be false are that the collector will refer the action to a lawyer, harm the consumer's credit rating, or repossess household goods.

- Using any false representation or other deception to collect or to attempt to collect any debt or to obtain information about a debtor.
- Failing to disclose in communications that the collector is attempting to collect a debt.
- Using unfair or unconscionable means to collect debts.
- Collection of fees or charges unless expressly authorized by the agreement creating the debt and permitted by law.
- Depositing post-dated checks before their date. The collector also must give at least three days but not more than ten days notice before depositing the postdated check, or using the check for the purpose of threatening or filing criminal charges.
- Causing expense to another party while concealing the purpose of the communication, for example, by making collect telephone calls and sending collect telegrams.
- Threatening self-help repossession without the legal right to do so, or if the collector has no present intent to do so.
- Using any communication, language, or symbols on envelopes or postcards that indicate that the sender is in the debt collection business.

5

Lawsuits to Collect on a Debt

Will a Creditor Sue on a Debt?

Creditors frequently threaten to sue to collect on overdue debts, and families in debt obviously worry about being sued for the money. So the first question many people ask is—"Will I be sued?" Usually it is clear that the family *can* be sued, but the question is *will* they be sued. Creditors do not always make rational decisions. However, the following are good predictors whether a creditor will sue.

Creditors typically will not resort to a lawsuit if they have a more effective remedy available. The lawsuit process is slow, somewhat expensive, and, as will be detailed later in this chapter, may not get the creditor much anyway. So if the creditor can do something else more effective, it will. A business will not go to court initially if, instead, it can repossess a car, foreclose on a house, evict a tenant or terminate utility service.

Creditors also are unlikely to file a collection suit: (1) when the amount of the debt is small, (2) when the consumer disputes the debt and is likely to raise a strong defense, or (3) when the creditor has no history of filing suit. One might check with the local court clerk or legal services office to see if certain common creditors in the area—for example large retailers or finance companies—have a reputation for filing suit or not. When a creditor is out-of-state, it is even more unlikely that it will file suit over a small amount, particularly if the consumer will raise a defense.

Certain creditor threats to take legal action can also be discounted. For example, a collection agency's threat to garnish the consumer's wages is deceptive because the collection agency cannot garnish wages until it obtains a court judgment. When the same collection agency in its next letter threatens a lawsuit, that statement should be viewed with skepticism. Evaluate who is threatening action and the intent behind that threat.

How to Respond to a Collector's Lawsuit

Get Professional Advice

It is important that families not ignore a lawsuit. Often they can take steps that will significantly improve the outcome; doing nothing usually is the worst tactic. If a lawyer or counselor cannot give the needed advice, determine if a self-help manual has been written for your state on how to defend a lawsuit. Often someone will have published a pamphlet about how consumers can represent themselves in small claims court. Make sure you get a manual for *your* state.

Another option is to contact the clerk of the court. Families should feel that the court offices are not just for lawyers—that they have as much right to ask questions as someone with a law degree. One problem with court clerks though is that in busy courts they may not be that helpful. Another is that the advice they give may not be accurate. Sometimes the clerks in the individual courtrooms are more accurate than a clerk in the clerk's office. It certainly cannot hurt to ask several clerks the same question and compare their answers. Whenever relying on information from a court clerk, write down the clerk's name.

Carefully Read All Court Documents the Family Receives

To start a lawsuit, the creditor files a document with the court called either a petition or a complaint. This document asks the court to enter an order or judgment that the consumer owes the creditor a certain amount of money.

Along with the complaint filed with the court, the creditor usually must prepare another document, to be delivered to the consumer. This document stating that a suit has been filed is often called a summons or original notice. It usually tells the consumer what kind of suit is being instituted, what the creditor wants, and the actions the consumer must take to respond to the lawsuit.

The summons must be delivered to the consumer according to state procedure. Sometimes a constable must personally deliver the summons. Sometimes mail is sufficient. Dropping the summons on the consumer's doorstep is not sufficient.

Each court has its own procedures for responding to a summons. The summons should tell the consumer what steps are proper to respond to a lawsuit *for that particular court.* Do not assume that a response appropriate for one type of court will be correct for another court or another type of case. Instead, read the instructions on the summons.

Summonses are sometimes written in legal jargon that is difficult to understand. Carefully read all the documents, noting any deadlines. If something is unclear, make sure that a lawyer or someone familiar with legal documents explains what the document means. As described above, a court clerk may or may not be helpful in explaining the documents. In using a publication to understand the notice, make sure the publication is current, deals with your state, and with the particular court at issue.

Check Which Court Is Hearing the Case

The consumer obviously will want to read which court issued the summons, so that the consumer can direct all questions and documents to the correct court. Which court the case is filed in will also be critical in determining if consumers can plead their own case and how much legal help they need.

The most common court used by creditors to sue consumers is "small claims court," a court designed to hear claims for relatively small amounts of money. For example, in some states the small claims court can only handle cases seeking $2000 or less. If the creditor is seeking more money than the small claims court limit, the suit must be filed in the state's general, all-purpose court, often called a district court, circuit court, or common pleas court.

Because small claims courts are designed to handle claims for small amounts of money, the procedure is usually simple and quick. In many small claims courts a lawyer is not required; in fact, in some states, lawyers are not permitted. If a creditor can sue in small claims court, it will often do so without hiring a lawyer. The consumer should also feel confident appearing in that court without a lawyer.

A state's other trial courts follow more formal procedures. Creditors are represented by lawyers, and formal rules of pleading and evidence apply. Although consumers can represent themselves in this type of court (this is called appearing "*pro se*"), their wisest course most often is to use a lawyer.

How to Answer the Summons

To avoid the creditor winning the lawsuit by default, the consumer *must* follow the instructions on the summons (sometimes called the original notice). If those instructions are unclear, a lawyer (not the creditor's lawyer) or other professional should be consulted. Another alternative is to contact the clerk of the court where the suit was filed. The summons will tell the consumer to appear at a hearing, to file a written response, or to file an appearance at the clerk's office.

If the summons requests the consumer appear at the hearing, the summons usually specifies a time, a date, and a place at which the hearing will be held. In more formal courts, it is unusual for a hearing to be scheduled immediately, without allowing time for the consumer to file an answer. In some states hearings are scheduled right away for small claims courts cases. Whatever the court, eviction cases and demands for the immediate possession of property are also usually handled promptly.

A summons often will tell the consumer to file a written answer to the summons, also called an appearance, within a certain number of days, usually less than thirty. Although the summons may read "appear and defend," this may not mean that the consumer must physically appear on the date mentioned, but only that a written document must be filed with the court by that date.

Most small claims courts that require written answers provide prepared answer forms, which only need to be signed and returned to the court clerk. The answer form states that the defendant (i.e. the consumer) denies the justice of the plaintiff's (i.e. the creditor's) full claim. Other small claims courts require no written answer.

In more formal courts, there are usually no prepared answer forms. For these courts, the answer should be written by a lawyer, and should include reasons why the consumer denies being required to pay all of the creditor's claim.

Although answers not written by lawyers are accepted by many courts, they are likely to be found insufficient on technical grounds. If a consumer needs more time to find a lawyer and prepare an answer, a time extension is usually allowed, either by written agreement with the creditor's attorney or by a court order.

Most courts require that the consumer send a copy of the answer and any other document he or she files with the court to the creditor or the creditor's lawyer. The consumer should indicate on the original court document filed with the court clerk that a copy was mailed to the creditor. Of course, the consumer should also keep a copy, stamped and dated by the clerk.

Respond to the Court Summons in a Timely Manner

It is important that the consumer scrupulously meets all time deadlines set out in the summons, whether the deadline is to appear at a hearing, to file an answer or to file an appearance. (In many states there is no distinction between filing an answer and an appearance.)

If the deadline is missed, a default judgment can be taken against the consumer. This means that the court will order the consumer to pay the money, plus court costs and any attorney's fees, even though there was no hearing on the lawsuit. The consumer will have no opportunity to raise any defenses or explain why he or she should not have to pay. Instead, the creditor will be granted whatever it requested.

Fewer than ten percent of consumers who are sued file answers, even though 50 percent or more have good reasons why an entire claim should not be granted. It is thus important that the consumer respond.

Filing an answer will also slow down the court process and may result in the creditor either ceasing to pursue the lawsuit or agreeing to a reasonable settlement. The creditor may be counting on the case being among the over 90% that result in a quick default judgment in the creditor's favor. Merely by answering, the consumer changes the creditor's evaluation of the case. The cost of actually trying the case and the possibility of losing may persuade the creditor to drop the case. Certainly if the consumer wants to settle the case, the consumer will obtain a much better deal just by answering the summons and contesting the case than if the consumer lets the creditor win by default.

Even if the consumer informally reaches an agreement with the creditor, it is still important to file an appearance and answer. Creditors have been known to proceed with a case and take a default judgment despite having previously reached an agreement with the consumer. Any agreed upon payment plan should be in writing and there should be a clear written statement that the creditor will drop its lawsuit. An oral agreement with the creditor is *not* a substitute for filing an answer to the summons and cannot alone prevent a default judgment. In fact, the safest course is to file a copy of the written agreement with the court clerk to be entered into the court record.

Submit Defenses and Counterclaims to the Court

A consumer can tell the court why the creditor should not collect on a debt by presenting a defense, a counterclaim, or both. A defense is a reason why the consumer need not pay the creditor on the debt that forms the basis of the suit. A counterclaim is a claim by the consumer that the creditor owes money to the consumer, regardless of whether the consumer owes the creditor on the debt. Sometimes the difference between the two is only technical. For example, where a dealer finances the sale of a car that turns out to be a lemon, the consumer might use the car's defects both as a defense on the loan and as an affirmative claim against the dealer.

It is extremely effective for consumers to raise defenses and counterclaims in debt collection lawsuits, particularly if the amount at stake is small. Frequently, creditors do not want to be bothered with a case and will let it drop just because the consumer raises a defense.

Creditors often find lawsuits cost-effective only if large numbers of cases can be disposed of quickly, usually where the debtor never shows up and the creditor wins by default. Creditors may just not want to bother with a case that eats up any time—do not forget the creditor's attorney may be billing out his or her time at $100 dollars an hour or more. Just waiting for a trial to be called may eat up attorney costs greater than the size of the debt.

Many attorneys take debt collection cases on a contingent fee basis, meaning they keep about a third of the debts they collect. When the attorney takes the case on this basis, often it will be the attorney who will not want to pursue a lawsuit if the consumer can raise valid defenses. Since the attorney's recovery is capped at one-third of the debt, it will not pay to put several hours into a small case.

Each state and each type of court will have its own procedures as to how a consumer presents a defense or counterclaim. Some courts require a written statement filed at the beginning of the case specifying the consumer's defenses and counterclaims. Some small claims courts require only that the consumer raise the defenses and counterclaims in his or her statements at the trial.

A wide variety of defenses are possible in consumer cases: for example, failure to deliver the item purchased, defects in the item, misrepresentation or duress in the creation of the debt, or violations of applicable laws. Other defenses are available if the consumer has not defaulted on the loan or if the loan happened too long ago to be heard in court.

An important type of defense involves challenging the creditor's calculation of the amount due. The creditor may be seeking attorney fees or collection costs that are either excessive or not allowed by law. The creditor may also have improperly computed the loan's payoff figure.

The consumer can raise not only defenses, but also counterclaims that the creditor owes the consumer money. In consumer cases, counterclaims frequently arise when creditors or debt collectors violate consumer protection laws. Claims can also be based on a seller or creditor engaging in unfair or deceptive conduct to induce a sale or loan. Also ascertain if there are subsequent problems with the goods or services purchased.

Chapter Six details available consumer claims and defenses. Remember to look at all stages of the transaction, from the original sales solicitation all the way through to the creditor's debt collection procedures.

Attend All Court Proceedings

In small claims court, the consumer generally only has to go before the judge once to resolve the case (unless the hearing is rescheduled). In more formal courts, a case could be more complicated. The creditor could, but rarely does, take the consumer's deposition. This means that the creditor's attorney asks the consumer questions before the actual trial date and without a judge present. Either side before the trial can also ask for a judgment without a trial because there are no important facts in dispute.

When any type of a hearing or deposition is scheduled, the consumer should make every effort to attend. A default judgment probably will be taken in the consumer's absence, even if the consumer filed an answer or appearance earlier. If the consumer cannot attend, the consumer should send someone else to ask for a continuance, explaining the compelling reasons why the consumer could not attend the hearing that day.

The hearing or trial is the opportunity for both parties to tell their story to a judge or magistrate. In many small claims courts, the hearing is informal. Usually, the creditor first explains the consumer's legal obligation. In most consumer cases, the creditor simply gives the judge a copy of the purchase contract and the accounting card that shows the lapsed payments.

Next, the consumer presents a defense or counterclaim. Unfortunately, many consumer defenses and counterclaims are somewhat technical. To be most effective, the consumer should at least consult a lawyer about the presentation of the case. The consumer should not hesitate to ask for a delay in the court date if needed to find an attorney.

Some good tips to help a consumer prepare for the hearing include:

- Collect all relevant documents. Courts generally give a lot of credence to written documents. It may be helpful to have extra copies available. Particularly in more formal courts, the consumer may need to bring someone to identify the documents and prove they are authentic.
- Bring witnesses if available. The consumer has the right to present witnesses, and their impact may be all the greater because the creditor will rarely present witnesses.
- Do not rely on written statements of your witnesses, because the court usually will not allow them into evidence. Have the witnesses attend the trial.
- Go to court beforehand just to acclimate yourself as to where the courtroom is, how the court works, how people dress, when to stand, how to tell when your case is called, where you sit during the hearing, whether a microphone is used and how to use it, the judge's personality, whether an interpreter is available, etc.
- Take a companion to the actual hearing to offer emotional support, to provide objective feedback, and to offer a second opinion if you must respond on the spot to a settlement offer.
- Prepare in advance a written chronological report of events, a checklist of points to make, and a checklist of documents to be given to the court, and take the checklist with you.
- Assume that the judge has not read any of the documents already presented to the court and knows none of the facts of the case. Start at the beginning and tell your story in a clear and organized fashion in the order it happened.
- Do not be afraid to be forceful, but do not make personal attacks on individuals.

Setting Aside a Default Judgment

As explained earlier, by not filing a written answer or appearance within the specified time, or by failing to attend the hearing, a consumer loses the opportunity to raise defenses. It is important that the consumer not lose by default unless a lawyer has evaluated the case and determined that the consumer will lose nothing by allowing a default to be entered.

If a default has been entered, opportunities still exist to set aside the ruling and obtain another chance to be heard. Specific court rules govern these opportunities. Usually, a default judgment can be set aside only for specific reasons and within a short, specified period of days after the judgment has been entered into the court records. Reasons for setting aside a default commonly include unavoidable circumstances that rendered the consumer unable to answer within the required time.

The Judgment and Appeal Rights

The judgment is what the court decides after hearing the case. If the creditor wins, the judgment gives the creditor the right to use governmental power to force payment. Consumers cannot be forced to pay debts until a judgment is entered. Once the judgment is entered, if the consumer does not pay, the creditor has special rights to seize the debtor's property or income, unless this property or income is protected by federal or state law.

A party that loses a lawsuit at the first court level can appeal to a higher level. For cases heard in small claims court, that usually means appealing to one of the state's general purpose trial courts. This may be the only appeal that is allowed from a small claims court decision. Further appeal can be granted only if a higher court specifically says that it wishes to hear the case. If a case starts in a more formal trial court, the losing party can appeal to the state court of appeals or to the state supreme court.

Deadlines for filing an appeal are generally short and strictly enforced. Procedures for what papers to file in an appeal may be quite technical and may also be strictly enforced.

The costs of an appeal vary widely, but can be significant. Typical costs include a filing fee, typing a transcript of the trial, and posting a bond to cover the judgment being appealed. In some circumstances, a party unable to pay these fees can request that some of them be waived.

Creditors' Attempt to Collect Court Judgments

Even if the consumer loses the lawsuit, this does *not* mean the consumer must repay the debt. If a family is in financial distress and cannot afford to repay its debts, a court order to pay may not really change anything. The family did not have the money to pay and the court saying that the family has to pay will not make it any more possible for the family to pay.

What the court order does do is allow creditors to use several extraordinary tools to try to squeeze money from the family. How effective these tools are will depend not only on how much income and property a consumer has, but on the *types* of income and property involved. In some cases these tools are effective in recovering money and may even result in the family losing its home. In other cases, these extraordinary tools will have *no* impact on the family.

Where losing a lawsuit has no adverse effects for a consumer, that consumer is called "judgment proof." The consumer's assets and income are small enough and are of a type that federal and state law fully protects them from seizure by creditors. In that case, the consumer does not really have to worry about the judgment until his or her financial situation improves. The family should ignore the judgment and save their minimal income to pay bills whose payment is critical to the family's survival, such as a mortgage, rent, or utility payments.

Consumers faced with collection lawsuits thus need to know whether they are judgment proof, that is whether the creditor can use the judgment to the consumer's detriment. Creditors can utilize four different special remedies to coerce payment after they obtain a court judgment against a consumer. If any of these remedies produce partial payment, the creditor can continue to resort to the same or different remedy to try to recover the full amount. The remainder of this chapter discusses these special remedies.

Garnishment

A creditor with a court judgment against a consumer has the right to "garnish" money belonging or owed to the consumer that is in the hands of a third party. In this context, to "garnish" means to take. Most often, garnishment takes money from a consumer's wages or bank account.

Garnishment can only take place *after* the creditor obtains a judgment against the consumer. After obtaining a judgment, the creditor can file a request for garnishment with the court or sheriff. A notice is then issued to the "garnishee" (a bank, an employer, or another third party holding the debtor's property), directing that party to turn over the property at a specified time.

The consumer must be given notice of the garnishment. The consumer can then request a hearing to prove that state or federal law protects the funds at issue from garnishment. Federal and state law protect consumers from garnishment in two ways:

1. A portion of wages is protected from seizure. Current federal law[1] provides that the first $127.50 from weekly take-home pay, after taxes and Social Security are deducted, cannot be garnished at all. If the weekly take-home pay is more than $127.50, an employer, in response to a garnishment order, must pay the *smaller* of the following amounts to a sheriff:

The weekly take-home pay (after withholding) minus $127.50
or
Twenty-five percent of that take-home pay.

The standard described above is based on federal law and sets out minimum protections for consumers in all fifty states. In addition, in many states, consumers have even greater protections against wage garnishment. Some states prohibit all wage garnishment or allow a smaller amount of wages to be garnished than the federal standard. Moreover, federal law and some state laws forbid employers from firing employees solely because their wages are being garnished.

2. Certain types of income, primarily government benefits, are completely exempt from garnishment. Even if a consumer's income is large enough so that a portion may be garnished, some sources of income are *completely* protected under federal or state law. Federal law completely exempts from garnishment certain federal benefits, including Social Security payments, Supplemental Security Income, and veterans' benefits. States with AFDC and unemployment insurance programs usually exempt those benefits from garnishment as well. If the government benefit is placed in a bank account, particularly if no other funds are in the same account, the money is also exempt from seizure.

As can be seen, federal and state law do a better job protecting wages than bank accounts. Consumers threatened by a court judgment must weigh the benefits of a bank account against the risk of having the money seized. Creditors will have more difficulty finding and seizing a bank account in another state or jointly held in the consumer's and in another individual's name.

If a significant amount of income or cash in a bank account is still subject to garnishment, the consumer may wish to work out a deal with the creditor rather than allow an imminent garnishment. The creditor may be just as happy to accept a certain amount a month instead of going through the garnishment procedures. A settlement makes particular sense in states where part of the amount garnished goes to pay court costs and the employer's administrative costs, and does not go to the creditor.

Attachment and Execution

A creditor with a court judgment can also arrange for the sheriff to seize a debtor's property. Because the creditor is armed with a court judgment and is asking the sheriff to do the seizure, the creditor need not have taken that property as collateral for the loan. After seizure the sheriff sells the property at public auction, and applies the proceeds to the judgment.

These auctions are usually poorly attended and bring low bids. For this reason, creditors rarely seize used household goods, which will have minimal resale value. If property is sold at auction, the consumer can encourage friends to attend the auction and purchase back the possessions (in the friend's own name) at a bargain price.

The right to execute, like the right to garnish, is not unlimited. State law specifically protects from attachment and execution certain types of property and/or certain amounts of property. State execution statutes allow debtors to prevent the seizure of exempt property by filing notice of exempt property, or by taking similar steps. This right to protect property from seizure is detailed below under "Exemptions Prevent Creditor From Seizing Property."

Judgment Liens

Any outstanding judgment generally becomes a lien on real estate owned by the consumer in that state. Unless the real estate is legally exempt from execution, creditors can force its sale in much the same manner as they can force the sale of other property. The next subsection discusses when real estate is exempt from execution.

Even if the real estate is exempt from execution, state law will usually allow the lien to remain in effect. The lien will "cloud the title" because, if a consumer wants to sell the real estate, the judgment will have to be paid first. One way of getting rid of judgment liens is to file for bankruptcy. To the extent the property is exempt, the lien can be removed.

Exemptions Prevent Creditors from Seizing Property

State exemption laws protect debtors and permit them to keep the basic necessities of life. Exemption statutes provide little or no protection from a creditor seizing *collateral.* For example, if the consumer puts up a home or car as collateral on a loan, exemption laws do not prevent the creditor from seizing the home or car if the consumer gets behind in the loan payments.

Exemption statutes do provide significant protections against property being seized by *other* creditors. Exemption statutes give very important rights when the consumer has not put up any collateral when taking out a loan, but where, *after a court judgment,* the creditor seeks an order to seize the consumer's property.

Some exemption statutes specify dollar amounts of property that are exempt from seizure. For example, $4,000 worth of personal property might be exempt. Under such statutes, debtors can choose which property they want to keep within the category of personal property up to the protected amount. Homestead exemptions protect a consumer's residence, and can be as high as $100,000, but can also be significantly less in other states. Under some exemption statutes, if husband and wife own property, they may be entitled under the exemption law to double the amount of protection.

It is important to understand that an exemption for only a few thousands of dollars may in fact be sufficient to protect a home or car worth significantly more. The key is that the family have a mortgage or lien on the property, so that the consumer's equity is less than the value of the property. The amount that may be exempted refers not to the dollar value of the *property,* but to the value of the family's *equity* in the property. Equity is how much the property is worth in excess of mortgages, tax and water liens, liens from home improvement work, or other secured debts.

For example, consider a state homestead exemption of $30,000 in equity and a home worth $150,000. If the consumer has a $100,000 first mortgage and a $20,000 home equity loan, the homeowner has $30,000 in equity. Since the homestead exemption is $30,000, the home is exempt from execution by a judgment creditor.

Other states specify certain property items that are totally exempt, sometimes placing an upper limit on the value of specific items. The list of totally exempt property typically includes such items as tools and supplies required for the debtor's occupation, clothing, a car (usually with a value under a specified amount), and household goods. Some states also totally exempt a principal residence on a certain size plot of land.

If a homestead or other exemption allows the consumer to exempt only a certain portion of the consumer's equity in the property, the creditor can force a sale. The consumer would retain the amount of the exemption from the sale proceeds. In the prior example, if the home's value increases to $160,000, a creditor with a court judgment could force a sale. The first $100,000 would go to the mortgage holder, the next $20,000 to pay off the home equity loan. The next $30,000 of sale proceeds would be kept by the consumer. Only the last $10,000 of sale proceeds would go to the creditor initiating the whole sale.

If a consumer files for bankruptcy, in some states the property that can be exempted from seizure is increased because the consumer can choose the federal bankruptcy exemptions that may or may not be better than a state's exemptions. But some states have opted out of the federal exemptions, meaning that even in a bankruptcy, the consumer must rely on state exemptions.

Some creditors attempt to force consumers to turn over exempt property, pointing to a small print contract clause in which the consumer agreed to waive rights under state exemption laws. These blanket waivers are now illegal under federal law.

Even if exemption laws fully protect a family's property at one point in time, the family may be at risk when their equity in their property increases. Court judgments remain on the books for many years. If the consumer's equity in a home or other property increases beyond the exemption limit or if a household acquires nonexempt income or property, creditors may be able to reach it. At that point, if the judgment is still unpaid, the consumer will have to work out a payment plan with the creditor or reconsider a bankruptcy filing.

Debtor's Examination

After obtaining a judgment, a creditor can ask the court to order the consumer to appear to answer questions about his or her income and assets. The purpose is to find income or property that is not protected by law and which the creditor can seize.

In some states this procedure is called a debtor's examination, but the procedure goes by other names in other states. Some creditors routinely request a debtor's examination. Others never do. Three important things to remember about a debtor's examination are:

- It is a court-ordered appearance. Failure to show up can result in arrest, citation for contempt, and a jail sentence. A notice to appear for a debtor's examination should *never* be ignored. The consumer should appear or make a written request to the court for a postponement. The court will usually grant a postponement if the creditor agrees to the request.
- The consumer's answers are made under oath, and often are recorded by a court reporter. Lying under oath is perjury, a crime punishable by jail.
- If the creditor does find assets or income not protected by law, the creditor can obtain a court order requiring the consumer to turn over those assets to the judgment creditor. Failure to comply with the order could be considered contempt, and could result in jail.

Because of all the various ways a debtor's examination can get a consumer into trouble, it is imperative that the consumer promptly obtain legal representation. If this is impossible, the counselor should work closely with the consumer to try to avoid the worst outcomes.

The first step in responding to notice of a debtor's examination is to review the consumer's assets *well before the examination.* Determine if all the property is protected by law and if all the income is exempt from garnishment. If so, immediately apprise the creditor. This may be sufficient to get the creditor to drop the request for an examination since it will just be a waste of everyone's time. Be sure to get this in writing; do not rely on the creditor's oral assurance that it will drop the examination.

If there is property that legally can be seized, the consumer may consider "exemption planning" just like wealthier families engage in tax planning or estate planning. Exemption planning involves the consumer in maximizing the protection of existing laws by converting property that could be seized (for example, cash) into property that cannot be seized (for example, household goods or equity in the home).

Consider a homeowner with $10,000 in cash and $10,000 equity in the home. Assume the homestead exemption is $20,000 and the personal property exemption is $3,000. At least $7,000 in cash can be seized. But if the cash is used to prepay the mortgage in part, the increased equity in the home is fully protected by the homestead exemption. The mortgage holder may even excuse a year's worth of payments because of the cash prepayment.

Generally this is a better approach than giving non-exempt property to relatives or friends. This latter type of transfer is more likely to be undone by a court.

If there is still property important to the consumer that a creditor can seize, the consumer can approach the creditor about a work out agreement. The consumer can offer to pay all or a portion of the amount due over a period of months or even years. The amount the consumer offers to pay should be directly related to what the creditor could seize after the debtor's examination. Do not offer to pay $3000 over 12 months when the only items the creditor could seize have a market value of $500.

There are two important points about work out agreements. First, get the agreement in writing. The writing should excuse the consumer from attending the debtor's examination, and contain the creditor's promise to forego wage garnishment or execution on the consumer's property as long as the consumer continues to make payments.

Second, finalize the agreement before the debtor's examination. Consumers have a habit of not showing up at the examination, and this could lead to a contempt of court citation and make any subsequent settlement with the creditor that much more difficult.

A final option is a bankruptcy filing. The bankruptcy will immediately stop any seizure and may allow the consumer to keep the property permanently. See Chapter Fourteen for a discussion on consumer bankruptcy filings.

6

Fighting Back

This book provides advice on defending against the creditor's collection efforts. Consumers also have complaints concerning the conduct of lenders and sellers. In fact, seller or creditor misconduct is often a contributing cause to the family's financial problems.

Essential to responding to any debt collection effort is raising any and all claims the consumer has against the seller, creditor, or collector. Consumers must fight back whenever they have a chance, because the best defense is a good offense.

Why Fight Back?

Consumers should take the offensive and raise all their legitimate claims for three reasons.

There May Never Be Another Chance

If consumers do not raise all their claims in response to a debt collection lawsuit or other collection action, they may never have another chance to do so. After a debt is resolved, consumers generally no longer possess the drive, initiative, or motivation to mount an affirmative action against a seller or creditor, an action that could drag on for years.

Moreover, by the time a consumer initiates an affirmative case, the court may say that the action was brought too late and is time-barred under court rules. A court may also throw out a consumer's lawsuit, saying that the consumer should have raised the issue at the same time the collector brought its case—that it is a waste of the court's time to hear essentially the same case twice.

Raising claims immediately in response to a debt action will avoid all of these problems. The consumer is still highly motivated—no one likes to pay a debt where one was treated unfairly. It is cheaper and easier to respond to a lawsuit than to initiate your own suit. The delays caused by the court process are now in the consumer's favor, because the collector cannot recover the amount it wants until the consumer's claims are resolved. Moreover, courts will allow consumers to raise even very old claims if they are raised as a defense to a collection action, as opposed to as an affirmative lawsuit.

Consumers Should Receive Compensation for Legitimate Complaints

If a consumer has a good claim, the consumer is entitled to recover for any injury suffered. Many consumer laws also authorize a consumer to recover much more than the injury actually suffered if the seller or creditor's conduct is egregious. Where the consumer's injury is very small, some consumer statutes still award the consumer $100 or even as much as $1000 as a way of encouraging consumers to complain. Particularly where the consumer cannot afford to pay a debt, it is always welcome to cut that debt down to size.

Raising Claims Provides Consumers with Excellent Settlement Leverage

Creditors collecting on relatively small consumer debts depend on consumers not contesting the debt. This allows them to collect their money quickly and inexpensively. When a consumer raises claims in response to a collection action, the economics of collection change dramatically. Not only does the collector have to factor in the value of the consumer's claim, but also the time and expense it will take to finally resolve the case.

Often collectors will drop cases where consumers present strong claims. Other times they will agree to settlements very advantageous to the consumer. Of course, not every creditor will cave in at the merest mention of a consumer claim. Some creditors are more litigious than others. Obviously, a creditor will also give more credence to a claim it considers legitimate or to a consumer represented by a competent attorney than it will to a consumer's frivolous complaint.

Identifying Claims to Raise

Consumers often do not realize all the different claims they can raise relating to a debt. Sitting down with the consumer and discussing all aspects of a transaction is likely to uncover a surprising number of legitimate claims. It is also important to try to assemble and examine all documents relating to a transaction. Where a consumer's explanation of what happened is fuzzy, the documents provide a good road map as to the nature of a transaction.

Nevertheless, do not rely just on the documents. Find out what type of promises and other oral claims the seller or creditor made. In talking over a debt, it is imperative to explore *all* of the following six stages to any transaction.

1. The Original Sale of Goods or Services

Most debts arise from the purchase of goods or services. Even if a consumer goes to a creditor just for a loan, the money often is earmarked for the purchase of particular goods or services.

Explore what oral representations were made to the consumer to lure the consumer to the seller or to clinch the deal. Were the seller's statements false? Did the written documents jibe with the seller's oral statements? Were high pressure tactics used. Did the seller hide key information?

Too often consumers feel that they will lose a swearing match between the seller and consumer, that a court will always believe an established businessman over an individual trying not to pay a debt. Quite the contrary, many used car dealers, aluminum siding sellers, and the like will have very low credibility for juries and even for judges.

Without getting into legal technicalities, any relevant oral or written misrepresentation, non-disclosure, or high pressure tactic is likely to lead to a legitimate consumer claim. Anything that you find to be outrageous, unfair, unjust, or fraudulent is likely to form the basis of a viable consumer claim.

Give special scrutiny to any door-to-door sale. Look for high pressure tactics and oral misrepresentations. In addition, such sellers have to give the consumer a right to cancel the sale for any reason within the first three days. Was the consumer given such a notice?

The National Consumer Law Center's *Unfair and Deceptive Acts and Practices* (3d ed. 1991 and Supplement) provides the best description of the innumerable types of claims and legal theories available to consumers relating to sales abuses. The book lists thousands of practices, categorized by type of sale, that have been found to be deceptive or unfair.

2. Subsequent Warranty Performance

Often goods or services do not turn out as expected. The goods are later discovered to be defective, work is not completed, or the work is found to be substandard. These problems provide a legitimate basis for a consumer's claims.

A common mistake consumers make is to assume that, where a product is sold "as is" or "without warranties," that the consumer cannot complain about problems with the product. In fact, "as is" disclaimers often do not prevent consumers from winning court awards from sellers.

Of course, consumers should always raise claims where goods or services are not delivered, the wrong services are performed, or the work is not completed. Similarly, where goods or services come with a warranty, the seller's failure to comply with the warranty should be actionable. For more detail on consumer claims based on the actual performance of the goods or services, see two National Consumer Law Center publications, *Sales of*

Goods and Services (2d ed. 1989 and Supplement) and *Unfair and Deceptive Acts and Practices* (3d ed. 1991 and Supplement).

3. The Credit Terms

Most debts begin with a credit contract. Anything that you find to be outrageous, unfair, unjust, or deceptive about the solicitation or terms of the credit agreement is likely to form the basis of a valid claim. Oral misrepresentations should be actionable. So should a lender's attempt to confuse the consumer and hide important terms. High pressure tactics should also be challenged.

The consumer may also have a claim where a creditor signs a consumer up for a loan where the creditor knows the consumer cannot afford the payments or where the creditor knows that a refinanced loan will be worse for the consumer than sticking with the original debt. Bogus charges, double-charging, sale of useless insurance and the like may also be actionable.

In addition, the federal Truth in Lending Act, state installment sales laws, and other state credit legislation set up various requirements as to what the creditor must tell the consumer about a loan. Violations often lead to $1000 statutory damages in addition to any actual damages the consumer suffers.

These statutes are technical and claims should not be pressed without the assistance of a lawyer. The National Consumer Law Center's *Truth in Lending* (2d ed. 1989 and Supplement) is the best volume available about a consumer's rights under the federal Truth in Lending statute.

Many states have usury laws that set maximum interest rates and limits on certain types of credit charges. Creditors violating these "usury" statutes will have to pay significant damages, but again a lawyer is usually necessary to press such claims. Usury laws are examined in detail in the National Consumer Law Center's, *Usury and Consumer Credit Regulation* (1987 and Supplement).

4. Creditor's Subsequent Performance

Consumers can also raise claims and defenses based on a creditor's conduct servicing a loan. Consumers should check whether payments have been properly applied, whether escrow amounts are handled correctly, and whether late charges are appropriate.

Creditors often purchase property insurance for consumers if the consumer's coverage lapses. Make sure this substitute coverage was not purchased for periods when the consumer had coverage in place, did not contain unnecessary coverages, or was sold at an inflated price.

Determine if the creditor's employees made false promises that the creditor would not repossess the collateral or call in a loan if certain payments were made. If the creditor assigns the loan to a second creditor, was the consumer clearly notified of a new address to send payments?

5. Debt Collection Tactics

Chapter Four analyzes what types of debt collection practices are illegal. Even though a consumer's primary concern is a repossession, a debt collection lawsuit, or a foreclosure, do not forget to ask the consumer about *earlier* debt collection contacts. If these earlier contacts were illegal, they will form the basis for legitimate consumer claims against the creditor or collector. Consumers may be able to obtain up to $1000 in damages for collection agency misconduct even if the consumer's actual injury from the harassment is hard to quantify.

As a result, refer to Chapter Four if a consumer is presently subject to debt harassment or if at *any* time in the past has been subject to such harassment concerning the same debt. This may result in a monetary claim against the collector and/or the creditor.

6. Attempts to Enforce a Court Order or Security Interest

Often a consumer has problems with the way a creditor attempts to collect on a judgment, repossess a car, seize household property, foreclose on a home, evict a tenant, or terminate utility service. Consumer rights in these areas are spelled out in Chapter 5 and Chapters 7 through 12. Creditors often are sloppy in the way they sue consumers, garnish wages, or repossess or seize property. Their failure to follow proper procedures may lead to consumer claims against the creditor.

A Concrete Example

Consider a consumer who is sued in the next county concerning the balance owed on a car loan after the car has been repossessed. In defending that lawsuit, the consumer should raise all of the available claims.

These might include the seller's misrepresentations about the car and the credit terms, and problems with the car's performance or the seller's repair of defects. The creditor may also have misapplied several car payments, engaged in illegal debt collection harassment, and then have illegally repossessed the car over the consumer's objections. The repossession sale of the car may been improper, the creditor may have miscalculated the amount still owed after the sale price is credited, and then engaged in further debt collection harassment in trying to collect the deficiency. Finally, the lawsuit itself may violate federal law by not being initiated where the consumer resides.

All of these claims may more than offset the amount the consumer owes the creditor for the deficiency. In fact, it is not uncommon for an aggressive attorney to be able to settle a case so that the consumer owes the creditor nothing, the creditor pays the consumer several thousand dollars, and the creditor pays for the consumer's attorney fees.

How to Raise a Consumer's Claims

When to Raise a Consumer's Claims

Usually a consumer will want to raise all available complaints as early and as often as possible. Waiting too long may diminish a consumer's credibility. Warning a collector at an early stage that the consumer has significant claims to offset a debt may be sufficient to get the creditor to drop collection activity. If the consumer waits to raise the claims during a creditor's collection lawsuit, the creditor may be less likely to drop the case because the creditor already has invested resources in the action.

Consequently, every time a creditor contacts a consumer about payment, mention the consumer's claims. If the creditor still pursues a lawsuit on the debt, raise the claims at that point also. Chapter Five explains how to raise counterclaims and defenses to the creditor's lawsuit.

A consumer's claims should also be raised in any foreclosure proceeding on the consumer's home. Where the creditor intends to seize the home or car without a court procedure (that is a "non-judicial foreclosure" or "self-help repossession"), the consumer may want to obtain an attorney to bring a court action to try to stop or undo the seizure based on the consumer's claims.

After a seizure, a creditor may seek the remainder due on a debt, after crediting the consumer with the sale price of the property. This is called an action to collect the deficiency. Raise all the consumer's claims in response to such a deficiency claim.

Complaints About the Sale Should Be Directed to the Creditor

Often the creditor collecting a debt is not the seller who sold the goods or services to the consumer. Debt collectors usually do not want to hear about problems the consumer had with the seller or with a prior creditor involved with the debt. The collector may tell the consumer to go talk to the seller or that prior creditor.

Although the collector might not want to hear about the consumer's complaints, the consumer should tell the collector anyway. The very fact that the collector does not want to hear about these problems is a good indication how important it is to press these claims with the creditor.

There are several reasons why it is critical that the consumer press available claims against the collector, instead of tracking down the original seller or creditor. By the time the consumer gets a court order against the original seller, the seller may be bankrupt or may have skipped town. Moreover, a court order against a seller may take years to obtain, and involve costly filing fees and legal bills.

On the other hand, when a consumer raises defenses against the creditor collecting on the debt, it is the collection action that may take years to resolve. Raising a consumer's claims as a defense to a collection suit is also free because there are no court fees to defend an action. All the consumer need do is tell the court and creditor that the consumer has defenses to the collection of the debt. Any subsequent delay in the case is now to the consumer's advantage.

If the consumer obtains legal representation, the consumer's attorney may decide to add to the case not only the creditor bringing the action, but also the seller, the original creditor, or even the debt collection agency. But the key thing to remember is that it is always better to defend the creditor's attempt to collect a debt than to give the creditor the money and try to get it back from someone else. When the creditor tells the consumer to go talk to the seller, firmly answer "no thank you, I am raising my claims against you."

Why the Creditor Is Responsible for the Seller's Misconduct

Creditors collecting on a debt are almost always responsible for the actions of the seller, original creditor, and any debt collector or repossessor. In most cases the loan documents will say right in the documents themselves that any holder of the loan is subject to all claims and defenses that the consumer has against the seller. In other words the very loan the creditor is trying to enforce will say that the consumer can raise the seller's misconduct as a defense.

Another black letter legal principal is that the consumer can raise against a subsequent assignee any defense the consumer could raise against the assignor. What this means is that if one creditor transfers the loan to another creditor, all the consumer's defenses against the first creditor are also available against the second creditor. It is easy to see who the first creditor is on a loan by just looking at the loan and seeing who is identified as the lender.

Where the seller is the original creditor, which is often the case where goods or services are purchased on credit, the consumer is in a good position to raise the seller's misconduct as a defense to the loan. For example, where a car dealer or home improvement contractor is the original creditor, the consumer can raise as defenses on the loan anything the consumer could raise with the car dealer or home improvement contractor, no matter who is trying to collect the loan.

The principle is the same where the original loan is with a finance company and then sold to a bank. If the finance company misrepresents the terms of a loan or makes a mistake in servicing a loan, the consumer can raise that as a defense against the bank's subsequent collection action.

Sometimes creditors try to claim they are "holders in due course." This special status would free them of any responsibility for the conduct of an earlier creditor. Fortunately for consumers, the law in recent decades frowns on the holder in due course status in consumer matters. Creditors almost never are able to avoid such responsibility.

Creditors frequently make a related, but different claim. They say they did not purchase the loan papers from the seller, but originated the loan themselves. In response, first, look in the loan documents to see if the documents themselves state that the lender is liable for what the seller did. This is usually the case because the Federal Trade Commission has a regulation requiring this notice in all consumer loans where the seller and creditor have a business arrangement.

If the notice is not in the loan documents, the consumer should still pursue such claims if the seller referred the consumer to the lender. About half the states have laws that say that the lender is responsible for what a closely related seller did. In the other half of the states, there are various arguments that a lawyer can make on behalf of the consumer that the creditor is liable for what the seller did.

7

Protecting the Family Car from the Repo Man

When to Worry About the Repo Man

When consumers buy a car on credit, they put up their car as collateral on the loan. Some consumers also put up their car as collateral on a loan unrelated to the purchase of the car. By leasing a car or putting up their car as collateral on a loan, and then getting behind on their payments, consumers risk the immediate loss of their car. The car may simply disappear some night as a repossessor breaks into the car and drives it away.

The car is always subject to seizure if the consumer is delinquent on car *lease* payments. A car that is *purchased* is at risk only if the consumer gets behind in loan payments where the car is security for that loan. The car cannot be immediately seized if the consumer is behind on other debts.

For example, if a family does not pay its credit card bill, the credit card company cannot repossess the car. All the credit card company can do is sue the consumer, obtain a court judgment, and ask the sheriff to seize the car, if the car is not otherwise exempt under state law. This rarely happens in practice, and if it does, it might occur a year of more after default. The situation is very different for car loans and car leases. Miss one or two payments and the car may be gone.

For anyone recently laid-off from work, car repossession is disastrous because the loss of transportation makes it much harder to look for and get a new job. But that is only the beginning of the consumer's problems after a car repossession. The creditor will sell the car for much less than it is worth, and the consumer's equity in the car will be wiped out. On top of all that, consumers may find themselves being sued for thousands of dollars that the creditor claims is the difference between the amount owed on the loan and the sale price of the car.

This chapter provides advise to consumers on how to avoid repossession and what to do if a car is repossessed—how to get the car back or avoid the worst consequences after repossession. While repossession law varies somewhat from state to state, this advice is generally applicable nationwide.

Key Resources

To learn more about how consumers can protect themselves from repossession and the worst problems of its aftermath, the best practice manual is the National Consumer Law Center's *Repossessions* (2d ed. 1988 and Supplement), which is the source of much of the information in this chapter. The manual covers all the federal and state laws governing consumer repossessions. *Repossessions* includes step-by-step checklists for different types of repossession situations, and samples of different documents a lawyer will have to prepare in a repossession case.

Many repossessions today involve car leases—even if the consumer thinks he or she actually bought the car. Key resources for auto leases are two other National Consumer Law Center manuals, *Truth in Lending* ch. 9 (2d ed. 1989 and Supplement) and *Unfair and Deceptive Acts and Practices* § 5.4 (3d ed. 1991 and Supplement).

How to Tell if a Car Can Be Repossessed

A car can be repossessed only if the consumer has put up the car as collateral on a loan or if the consumer has leased the car. Usually this is easy to ascertain. Identify and examine the loan the consumer used to purchase the car. Look on the front page of the loan or on a separate one page disclosure statement and see if the car is listed under "security." Sometimes this loan will in fact state that it is a lease, in which case the car is also subject to repossession.

Next, examine the car's certificate of title. Creditors that have rights to the car will usually indicate this right on the title. If the title is not in the consumer's name, but in the name of a company, the consumer probably is leasing the car.

It is possible, but not likely, that a creditor will take a car as collateral and not indicate this on the certificate of title. The only way to discover this is to look at all loans the consumer has taken out and examine the "security" provisions to see if the car is listed.

How Self-Help Repossession Works

Self-help repossession is a very real and dangerous threat whenever a consumer is behind on even one car payment. Creditors in most states have the right to seize the car even when the consumer is only a few weeks late in making payments or even if the creditor just thinks the consumer will not make payments when due.

The creditor need not obtain court permission to repossess the car. The creditor on its own initiative has one of its own employees or a hired "repo man" seize the car. In most states, the creditor does not even have to notify the consumer that a repossession is about to take place. As long as the seizure does not "breach the peace," it is perfectly legal.

There are important exceptions to a creditor's right to seize a car on its own (these exceptions prevent a creditor from seizing a car, but may not prevent a lessor from retaking its own car):

• The creditor must have taken the car as collateral.
• In thirteen states, the creditor must first give the consumer notice of the right to catch up on delinquent payments. See "Right to Cure," below.
• Self-help repossession is generally illegal in Louisiana and Wis-

consin and on certain Indian reservations. Self-help repossession is allowed in Maryland only if the credit agreement so stipulates.

- A creditor cannot repossess a car owned by military personnel or their dependents if the debt was incurred *before* the individual entered the military.

Strategies to Prevent a Car from Being Repossessed

Keep Current on Car Payments

The consumer should not pay credit card debts, doctor bills or other low priority debts ahead of car payments. Skipping payments on low priority debts for several months will have little or no bad consequences. Skip one or two car payments, and the consumer risks losing the car.

Cure a Default

In Colorado, District of Columbia, Iowa, Kansas, Maine, Massachusetts, Mississippi, Missouri, Nebraska, New Hampshire, South Carolina, West Virginia, and Wisconsin, creditors (but not lessors) must give consumers a second chance to make up late payments before repossession. This is called a right to cure. The creditor sends the consumer notice of how many months are past due; the consumer can prevent repossession by paying just these back payments and some late charges.

In other states making all back payments may *not* prevent a repossession. Creditors generally insert into their agreements the right to call the whole loan due if the consumer misses a payment. This is called "accelerating" a loan—the entire amount borrowed must be repaid immediately. When the creditor accelerates a loan, then the consumer is only secure from repossession if the whole loan if paid—which may be thousands of dollars. Paying just the delinquent payments at that point will not necessarily stop a re-possession.

This is why the right to cure is so valuable for consumers in the fourteen states listed above. The creditor cannot call the whole loan due until the creditor gives the consumer a second chance to pay only the back due monthly payments.

If the creditor has called the whole note in, do not pay just the overdue payments without first obtaining a *written* agreement from the lender. That agreement should specify that the lender will not repossess the car unless the consumer fails to make future payments. Otherwise, the creditor can usually pocket the back due payments and still repossess the car.

Negotiate a Work-Out

Many creditors are willing to negotiate a work-out arrangement, where the consumer's monthly payments are lowered, and where the lender agrees not to seize the car. Particularly where the loan amount is higher than the car's worth, a work-out may ultimately be less expensive for the lender. The work-out can be a good deal for the consumer as well if the consumer wants to keep the car.

Any work-out proposal should be carefully evaluated before taking it to a creditor. The importance of keeping the collateral should be balanced against the cost of doing so. Consideration should be given to how much has already been paid, to the risk of a deficiency if the car is repossessed (see below), and to the importance to the consumer of possessing the car. For example, a well-running car worth $1,500, with only $300 still owed on the car loan, is worth trying to save. The same may not be true of a $10,000 car with $8,000 still owed and where car and insurance payments are beyond what the consumer can hope to afford.

Work-out arrangements should also take into consideration whether the consumer has any claims or defenses relating to the car loan or to the car purchase. Was the car a lemon? Were promised repairs made? Did the seller misrepresent the car? Were illegal debt collection contacts pursued? See Chapter Six for more on raising the consumer's complaints about the car as a defense to repayment on the loan.

Attorneys representing consumers will be able to raise these claims and defenses with more credibility than if the consumers do so themselves, and thus should be able to negotiate a more favorable work out agreement. Nevertheless, a consumer's clear and factual documentation of illegal conduct by the dealer, creditor, or collector should assist a consumer's work out negotiations, even if not represented by an attorney.

Sell the Car

Sometimes consumers simply cannot afford car and insurance payments and maintenance costs necessary to keep a car. One option is to sell the car rather than wait for the lender to repossess the car and sell it at a repossession sale at a fraction of its real worth. When consumers sell their car themselves, they can get a *much* higher price. Just as important, the consumer avoids selling, repossession, storage and other expenses which the creditor would eventually charge back to the consumer. Consumers can also get a rebate on car insurance when they cancel the coverage early.

There are several important caveats about selling a car. First, identify whether the consumer leased the car or owns it. If a lease, the consumer cannot sell the car or even sublease the car without the lessor's permission. A sublease will usually mean that the consumer is liable for all monthly payments if the sublessee fails to send those in to the lessor.

Second, any sale of the car must be coordinated with the creditor. The creditor is unlikely to allow a new purchaser to assume the car loan. As a result, the consumer will have to pay off the car loan in full to give the new purchaser clear title. The consumer will have to get a pay-off figure from the creditor and work out with the creditor the mechanics of canceling the lien when the debt is paid.

If the consumer cannot sell the car for as much as is owed on the loan, the lender is unlikely to cancel the lien. It will hold out for payment in full. The consumer should point out to the creditor that this is not in its own self-interest, that it will not net as much if the lender repossesses the car and sells the car itself. The creditor's self-interest is to release its lien on the car in return for the purchase price the consumer has arranged.

If a creditor proves obstinate, make sure the consumer has

written record of the offer for the car. If the creditor eventually seizes the car, the creditor may have difficulty justifying a sale price significantly lower than the bid received by the consumer.

Third, consumers must avoid anyone who offers to broker a sale or lease of the consumer's car. In many states car brokerage is illegal. A widespread scam is for con artists to take money from both the consumer and the new "purchaser," but not effect a real transfer in ownership. Instead, the consumer will still owe the creditor or lessor the full amount. These brokers do not get the lessor's permission or release a creditor's lien on the car. The broker may not even forward monthly payments to the lessor or creditor.

Turn the Car Into the Creditor, But Make Sure the Consumer Gets a Deal

This strategy is similar to selling the car, only the consumer lets the lender do it. Although generally not a good idea (because the lender will do such a bad job selling the car), the strategy is acceptable if the consumer gets a *written agreement* from the lender that the consumer does not owe anything else on the loan.

Make sure the agreement is in writing because one department of a lender may agree orally to certain terms while another department may disregard the terms entirely. The consumer can also try to negotiate a concession that the lender will not report the default to a credit reporting agency.

The consumer turning the car in voluntarily is attractive to the lender who then need not go to the expense of seizing the car or fear a legal battle to justify the repossession. Giving up the right to a deficiency may not be viewed as too great a cost where the consumer is largely judgment proof.

Too often consumers surrender the collateral voluntarily without trying to negotiate any terms. Passive, voluntary surrender of collateral requires less effort for the consumer, sometimes creates good will with the creditor, and generates fewer expenses (for towing, attorney's fees, and the like) than self-help repossession. However, voluntary surrender has serious disadvantages.

Voluntary surrender will not prevent the creditor from seeking a deficiency claim (the amount of the debt less the re-sale price of the car). The creditor will sell the car for a low price and then come after the consumer for the difference. In addition, a surrender can unwittingly waive some of a consumer's claims or defenses, such as a claim that the creditor did not have a valid security interest, the consumer was not in default, or that the creditor had no right to accelerate the debt.

The situation is similar when consumers turn in a leased car. Consumers mistakenly believe that they will have no further obligation, just because they have no obligation at *scheduled* termination. They later discover that their liability at *early* termination will be thousands of dollars, as high as $10,000 in some cases. Before turning in a leased car, negotiate with the lessor the consumer's liability for the early termination of the lease.

Resist the Repossession

Consumers can try to frustrate the creditor's efforts to seize the car, although this approach is fraught with risk and may be only a temporary solution. The major leverage the consumer has is that the repossessor in seizing the car cannot "breach the peace." Consumers in turn can make it difficult for repossessors to seize a car without breaching the peace.

Breach of the peace is a technical term, and the law sets out strict rules as to when repossessor conduct breaches the peace:

- The repossessor cannot use bodily force or threats. Physical contact is prohibited.
- The repossessor can seize the car from the street of even a driveway, but cannot break open a locked garage door to get at a car.
- The repossessor cannot take property over the debtor's oral objections.
- The repossessor cannot be accompanied by a government official, such as the police, unless the official has a court order.
- Courts are divided over whether a repossessor can use trickery to seize the car, such as agreeing to make free repairs as a pretext for seizing the car.

In practice, this means that the repossessor cannot take a car if the owner or the owner's family is present at the repossession and objects to the seizure just *before* the seizure takes place. The consumer's objection should *not* involve force. The consumer does not even have to scream. Just politely and firmly tell the repossessor not to take the car. Obviously, the consumer should decline to turn over the keys when requested to do so. The consumer should not be swayed by any legal advise offered by the repossessor. The consumer has an absolute right to object to the repossession, and does not have to assent to the seizure.

The consumer should *never* resort to force. Never meet force with force. Never use force to object. Never use force to impede a government official. If the repossessor uses force or threats, or otherwise breaches the peace, the consumer should call the police. Consumers should not take matters into their own hands. After the fact, the consumer can consult an attorney. There are significant legal remedies available to challenge such conduct.

To avoid consumers objecting to the seizure, repossessors tend to take cars away in the middle of the night. This is perfectly legal, even if the car is parked in the consumer's driveway or in a company parking lot. On the other hand, repossessors cannot break open a lock and force themselves into a garage.

Consumers should never resist government officials in the performance of their duties. But it is appropriate to verify the identity of any alleged government official appearing at a repossession and the basis for the official's presence. Government officials should only operate pursuant to written court orders and should not assist self-help repossessions.

Remember that people in uniforms are not necessarily government officials. If the "official" does not provide proper identity, politely object to the seizure—but do so orally, not physically.

Obviously, repossessors cannot seize a car they cannot find. They will have the consumer's address and place of employment, but will not know the address of every friend and relative. Consumers should know that some state statutes makes it a criminal offense to conceal collateral or to move it out-of-state.

Consumers who do not want their car repossessed should never turn the car over to the dealer or anyone else the creditor would know for repairs. Do not drive the car to the creditor's to discuss a work-out agreement. The consumer may have to walk home after failing to come to a satisfactory arrangement.

Minimize the Loss of Personal Property Inside the Car

If a repossession is imminent, the consumer should leave as little personal property as possible in the car. Property left in a car has a way of disappearing after the car is seized. For example, tools, tapes and tape deck, clothes, and sporting equipment should be removed. Some items like child seats or even spare tires can be removed when the car is not being used and returned when the car is being used.

Before the repossession, friends should be asked to verify the items left in the car and their condition. The consumer should also make a written inventory. A consumer can try to require the creditor to pay for items not returned.

File for Bankruptcy Protection

Another possible course of action when repossession is threatened is to file for bankruptcy. If the consumer's only problem is the threatened repossession, a bankruptcy filing may not be justified. But where a threatened loss of a car is just one of many financial problems, consumers should know how bankruptcy can deal with the threatened repossession.

Just filing with a bankruptcy court several simple forms (with the rest of the not-so-simple forms to be filed later) initiates the bankruptcy case and automatically triggers what is known as "the automatic stay." Under the automatic stay, no one, including car repossessors, can take any action against a debtor's property. Although a lender can later ask the bankruptcy court for permission to take the car, any attempt to repossess before such court permission would be illegal.

The repossessor could be held in contempt of court and may have to pay the consumer both actual and punitive damages as well as the consumer's attorney fees. In practice, creditors are careful not to seize property after the consumer files bankruptcy, particularly after the consumer lets them know about the bankruptcy filing.

Once the automatic stay freezes everything, the consumer can take several steps to try to permanently keep the car from being taken (discussed below). Because bankruptcy protection often allows consumers to keep their car and other valuable assets, it is an effective approach. Bankruptcy should not be used solely to obtain temporary relief from repossession through the automatic stay. See Chapter Fourteen for a more detailed discussion of a consumer's bankruptcy rights.

What to Do *After* the Car Is Repossessed

Get Back Personal Property Left in the Car

Creditors cannot keep property left in the car when it is repossessed. The lender can only keep the car itself. As soon as possible, a consumer should demand any property left in the car—tapes, clothes, car seats, sporting goods, etc.

A lender's failure to return the property promptly is just like theft. (A grey area is whether certain improvements to a car have become so much a part of the car that the consumer does not have a right to their return, such as a tape deck or radio semi-permanently installed.)

Put the request in writing and specify anything that should be in the car and do so *quickly*. The longer the property is left in the car, the more likely it will be "missing." Moreover, some credit contracts require (probably illegally) that the consumer's request for return of property be made within a certain number of days.

The Consumer Can Reinstate the Contract in California, the District of Columbia, Illinois,[1] Maryland, Mississippi, New York, Ohio, and Wisconsin

Reinstating the contact allows the consumer to recover the repossessed car and pay only the back due payments, not the full amount of the note. (Reinstatement applies to loans and not to car leases.) The consumer must act quickly. In most of these eight states, the consumer only has a few weeks to reinstate after repossession.

The Consumer Can Redeem the Car

In every state, after a repossession, the consumer can redeem the car (assuming the consumer bought the car and did not lease it). The creditor must send the consumer written notice of the date of the car's sale or a date after which the car will be sold. The consumer can redeem the car up until the very moment before the car is sold.

To redeem the car, the consumer must pay off the whole note in one lump sum, plus reasonable repossession and storage charges. Be sure to get a breakdown from the lender of how much the consumer owes. The breakdown should include a refund for unearned interest and insurance that has not accrued because the note has been paid off early.

Redeeming the car will rarely be a practical solution because the consumer could not afford a monthly payment, never mind paying off the whole note in one lump sum. But where a car is worth more than the loan, the consumer should consider whether a friend wants to purchase the car or whether the consumer can borrow from friends or relatives.

Try to Negotiate With the Creditor

If a repossession has just occurred, it is often possible to negotiate for the return of collateral and for a reinstatement of the original payment schedule or even for a new schedule. The same considerations apply as when negotiating a work-out arrangement prior to repossession.

The consumer is in a particularly strong position if the consumer has significant claims or defenses relating to the car, its credit terms, or its repossession. If a car has minimal resale value, the creditor should also prefer a work-out agreement to a worthless asset.

If the consumer does not want the car back, it is still worthwhile trying to get a creditor to permit the consumer to sell the car privately. In the alternative, the consumer should learn whether the creditor intends to sell the car at wholesale or retail, and should encourage a retail sale, which can produce a price at least 40 percent higher than wholesale.

Get the Car Back by Filing Bankruptcy

Even after a car is "lost" through repossession, a consumer can get it back by filing bankruptcy. If the loss of the car is the consumer's only problem, a bankruptcy filing may not be justified. But if the family has other financial problems, a bankruptcy may be justified and the consumer should know how bankruptcy can help to get the family car back.

The consumer would have to file for bankruptcy before the lender resells the car. Then the consumer may be able to obtain a court order directing the creditor to "turn over" or return repossessed property. The car is not returned to the consumer, but is, in effect, given to the bankruptcy court to decide who should keep the car, the consumer or creditor.

There are several reasons why the court could decide to give the car back to the consumer instead of the creditor. If the consumer files a straight bankruptcy (known at a chapter 7 bankruptcy), the consumer can keep the car by "redeeming" it.

Redeeming a car in bankruptcy is different than redeeming a car outside of bankruptcy. Outside of bankruptcy, the consumer would have to pay the full balance of the loan plus all the lender's costs. In bankruptcy, the consumer merely pays the car's value. Although this value often is less than the amount of the loan, most consumers will not be able to come up with the cash.

Some creditors let the consumer redeem in installments. Moreover, since other debts are wiped out by the bankruptcy filing, the consumer can take any cash the consumer gets to keep and apply that to redeem the car. Of course, the consumer may have more pressing needs for his or her cash, such as to pay rent or utilities.

The better way to keep a car is to file a chapter 13 bankruptcy, sometimes known as a "reorganization." In a chapter 13, the consumer has several ways of keeping the car. Probably the best one is to set up a plan to pay off the car loan in monthly installments over a period as long as 5 years.

The interest rate charged in this plan usually can be far lower than what the consumer is paying on the car loan. The consumer may even reduce the amount owed to only the value of the car. The bottom line is the consumer gets to keep the car and significantly lower the car payments. See Chapter Fourteen for a more detailed discussion of a consumer's bankruptcy rights.

Where the Repossession Was Wrongful

Sometimes cars are seized even though the creditor has no right to seize the car or no right to take the car at that time. Other times, the repossession company will not follow proper procedure in seizing the car.

In each of these situations, the consumer has a right to get the car back and be paid money damages. As a practical matter, this will usually require a lawyer or someone who understands repossession law. The next major section provides an overview of this law in items one through four. (Items five and six deal with situations where the creditor or lessor has already sold the car.)

Increasing the Car's Selling Price

Creditors must notify consumers of the time and place of any sale of the car. Consumers can then take steps to increase the sale price, thereby reducing the amount the consumer owes the creditor. (The consumer will still owe the amount of the debt plus expenses less the car's sale price.) Consumers can:

- Encourage other buyers to bid at public auction or to buy the collateral at a private sale, announcing the sale in a classified ad that lists the property, the creditor, and the location;
- Discourage creditor use of the collateral prior to the sale;
- Encourage the creditor to recondition the collateral (at reasonable expense) prior to its sale.

Creditors' Collection Efforts *After* the Repossession Sale

Creditors seize cars to pay off car loans. Often creditors will sell the car for so little money that the sale price only pays off some of the amount owed. Creditors then usually come after the consumer for the balance due on the debt. This is called a deficiency action. (When a lessor repossesses a leased vehicle, the result is the same. The car is sold and the lessor seeks a further amount under the lease. Technically, this is called an early termination charge.)

The most common time for a consumer to come for help on a loan is when the creditor seeks this deficiency. The consumer may not object to losing the car or being sued for the debt, but will feel unfairly treated if the creditor does both.

Two factors make a deficiency claim less serious than many consumers realize. First, the obligation is no longer backed up by any collateral. The creditor can take no immediate steps if the consumer does not pay. The deficiency debt is just like a hospital bill or a credit card debt. (For more on these types of "unsecured debts," see Chapter Five.)

Second, fortunately for consumers, many defenses are available where a creditor seeks a deficiency. Because the repossession and subsequent sale of the car occurred without court supervision, the creditor was required to comply with many technical requirements.

If the creditor trips up on even one technical requirement, the deficiency action may be thrown out or the creditor may even end up owing money to the consumer! Because creditors frequently trip up on these requirements, it is always a good idea for the consumer to get legal advise before agreeing to pay any deficiency.

Usually, deciding to defend the deficiency claim entails a careful review of all the documents and the procedures the creditor uses to sell the repossessed car. A counselor may be able to help the consumer make a preliminary determination whether an attorney is needed. But be aware that the creditor is threatening legal action and that proper presentation of many of the consumer's defenses will require legal expertise.

This section provides an overview of six types of defenses a consumer has when the creditor seeks a deficiency. The first four defenses also apply where the creditor has not yet sold the repossessed car and the consumer wants to get the car back. The sixth defense deals with deficiency claims for leased cars only.

1. Claims Concerning the Car or the Credit Terms

In many cases the consumer can fight a deficiency claim by showing the car was a lemon, the dealer misrepresented the quality of a used car, the credit terms were illegal or not disclosed accurately, or the creditor engaged in debt collection harassment. These type of defenses are summarized in Chapter Six.

The mere threat that the consumer will raise these claims is helpful in negotiating a work-out agreement. Depending upon the value of the consumer's claim, a work-out can even lead to a "wash," so called because both parties agree to call the debt even, or a "wash," and release each other from liability for further payments.

2. Is the Car Collateral on the Loan?

Sometimes the creditor trips up on a technical requirement to make the car collateral for a loan. If the creditor has not taken the car as collateral, it cannot repossess the car, even if the consumer defaults on a loan used to purchase the car.

The consumer's agreement to put up the car as collateral must be in writing and signed by the consumer. The agreement must also correctly identify the consumer's car and the car must be in the consumer's own name. Otherwise, the lender has no right to seize the car.

For example, if the wife alone signs a loan, but the car is in the husband's name, the creditor may not have a valid security interest in the car. A repossession may also be illegal if the lender only took the car as collateral on an earlier loan, but not on the loan at issue. For more analysis as to whether a creditor has properly taken a car as collateral, see NCLC's *Repossessions* ch. 3 (2d ed. 1988 and Supplement).

3. Was the Consumer in "Default" When the Car Was Seized?

Creditors can repossess cars only if the consumer is in default on the car loan. Being late on payments does not necessarily place the consumer "in default".

For example, if a creditor routinely accepts late payments from the consumer, the creditor cannot surprise the consumer and seize the car just because a payment is late. A consumer sometimes can also avoid a default by giving the lender notice that the consumer is withholding payments because the car is a lemon.

Moreover, if state law gives the consumer the right to cure the default, the creditor cannot repossess the car before the right to cure has expired. More detail on when a consumer is actually in default can be found in NCLC's *Repossessions* ch. 4 (2d ed. 1988 and Supplement).

4. Did the Car's Repossession Breach the Peace?

See "Strategies to Prevent a Car From Being Repossessed, Resisting the Repossession," above, for a discussion when a seizure breaches the peace. See also "How Self-Help Repossession Works," above, for situations where self-help repossession is not permitted at all. When a seizure is wrongful, the creditor generally should not keep the car or collect a deficiency. The creditor may owe the consumer money instead.

5. Improper Repossession Sale or Calculation of the Deficiency

Creditors must either keep the cars they repossess or sell them. If they keep the car, which is rare, the creditor cannot seek any more money from the consumer. To keep the car in full satisfaction of the debt, the creditor must meet two conditions. The consumer has had to have paid less than 60% of the debt, and the creditor must give the consumer notice that it intends to keep the car. The consumer can then object and ask that the car be sold.

Creditors usually sell cars after repossessing them. The law is very strict on the exact procedure the creditor must utilize. Consumers can defeat the creditor's attempt at a deficiency simply by showing that the creditor did not take the correct steps in selling the car. Tripping up on one technical requirement is usually enough to stop a deficiency. While these technical requirements are very briefly summarized below, see NCLC's *Repossessions* ch. 10 (2d ed. 1988 and Supplement) for more details.

- Consumers, even if they turned the car in voluntarily, must be sent advance notice of the creditor's intention to sell the repossessed car. The notice must include the time and place of a public auction or the date after which the car will be sold off a lot. The creditor must make reasonable efforts so that the consumer receives a fair warning of the sale date. This notice is very important and many a consumer has won their case by showing errors in the notice of sale.

- The sale cannot be too rushed. There must be time for the consumer to receive the notice of sale and for others to read advertising about the sale. On the other hand, the creditor cannot wait too long to sell the car, or the car's value will depreciate.
- *Every* aspect of the sale, including the manner, the time, the place, and the terms must make business sense, must be "commercially reasonable." Particularly if the sale price was unreasonably low, look at every aspect of the sale, including the decision to sell at retail or wholesale, and to use an auction or to sell the car off a lot. Advertising for the sale must be sufficient, an auction must use competitive bidding, and the car should be available for advance inspection. At a private sale, neither the creditor nor original dealer can usually purchase the car.
- Check to see if the creditor correctly calculated the size of its claimed deficiency. Was the consumer given proper credit for all payments? Were the late charges correctly calculated and unearned finance charges and insurance premiums properly rebated? Was the consumer credited with the car's actual sale price and not the car's "estimated" cash value? Were the creditor's expenses (repossession, reconditioning, sale, attorney's fees) reasonable and accurate?

6. Auto Leases

Special laws and rules apply where the consumer is leasing a car instead of buying a car on credit. The lease will specify the formula used to calculate how much the consumer owes upon default or early termination of the lease. These formulas are quite complex and difficult to understand.

The bottom line is that many formulas that lessors utilize are unreasonable, and lessors often incorrectly utilize their own formulas. Federal and state law provides powerful consumer remedies when lessors apply unreasonable formulas or do not clearly disclose the formulas they use.

Aggressive attorneys can usually force lessors to settle for a "wash." That is, although it is not uncommon for a lessor to demand $5,000 to $10,000 at a car's early termination, proper legal advocacy can often get lessors to drop the whole claim. For more detail on challenging auto lease early termination penalties, see NCLC's *Truth in Lending* ch. 9 (2d ed. 1989 and Supplement).

Consumer Rights When the Creditor Trips Up

If the creditor trips up in its efforts to repossess and sell the car, the penalties are severe. In many states, any mistake will lead to the creditor being barred from seeking any deficiency. In other states, the creditor will have a difficult time proving how much the creditor is owed because the sale price of the car is thrown out. The creditor will have to show how much a car is worth that it no longer possesses.

Moreover, if the creditor trips up on one of the requirements, it may have to pay the consumer as a penalty 10% of the car's original purchase price plus the whole finance charge on the car loan. This penalty can run into many thousands of dollars.

If repossessor conduct is egregious, the consumer may also be able to recover punitive damages running into many thousands of dollars. Sometimes, the creditor will even have to pay the consumer's own attorney fees. Usually to recover any of these penalties, legal representation is essential.

8

Threats to Seize Household Goods

Understanding Creditor Threats to Seize Household Goods

One of the worst creditor practices is the threat to seize household goods, such as the family photo album, wedding rings, bedroom furniture and the like. These threats can be very effective because of the special personal significance these items have for many consumers, even if the items have little or no monetary value.

There are two reasons why consumers ordinarily have little to fear from such threats. First, the goods' limited economic value means that it is rarely economical for a creditor to follow through with its threats. Second, federal and state laws limit which household goods a creditor can seize. This chapter examines exactly how serious are various threats to seize household goods, and lists strategies for preventing such seizures.

Keep in mind four different types of seizure of household goods:

1. When a consumer takes out a loan specifically to purchase certain household goods, and puts those goods up as collateral for the loan, the creditor has a "purchase money security interest" in those household goods. If the consumer defaults on that loan, the creditor can seize those goods if it wants to go to the expense of a court procedure or if the consumer makes the mistake of letting repossessors into the consumer's home.

2. When a loan is *not* used to purchase household goods, but the creditor insists that household goods be put up as collateral for the loan, this is known as a "non-purchase money security interest." Federal law gives consumers special protections from the seizure of such goods.

3. When household goods are not put up as collateral for a loan, creditors can seize these goods only *after* obtaining a court judgment on the debt. The creditor uses that judgment to try to "execute" on the household goods. State law generally protects most household goods from such executions.

4. When a consumer rents the goods with the option to purchase them after all payments are made, this is called a "rent-to-own" or RTO transaction. Because this type of transaction is relatively new, states are still in the process of defining when creditors can seize these goods.

These are the *only* four situations where creditors have *any* legal right to follow through on their threat to seize household goods. Outside these four situations, the creditor has *no* right to seize the goods.

One can usually determine if one of these four situations apply simply by looking at the loan documents. The credit agreement should clearly disclose if household goods are taken as collateral, and should indicate if the loan was used to purchase those goods. Agreements will also indicate if they are rent-to-own transactions. If a transaction is not a rent-to-own transaction and household goods are not taken as collateral, determine if the creditor has sued the consumer and received a final court judgment.

Consumer Strategies to Protect Household Goods

This section lists nine strategies for consumers to keep their household goods despite creditor threats to seize them. For more details, see the National Consumer Law Center's *Repossessions* (2d ed. 1988 and Supplement).

1. Do Not Panic. Get Professional Advice Instead

The first thing to realize is that the creditor often is bluffing. The value of most household goods sold at auction, after deducting repossession, storage, and selling expenses, is negligible. The creditor has no economic interest in the goods.

The creditor is using the threat as leverage to force the consumer to pay off that creditor's debt first, even though it is in the consumer's overall best interest to pay off other debts instead. Sometimes creditors also make these threats to build up their reputation as being tough on defaulters.

As outlined below, the consumer has a series of strategies to protect the goods or make it very expensive for the creditor to seize them. The consumer should feel he or she has the upper hand, and should not be terrorized into doing something stupid.

These factors make it particularly important for the consumer to get competent advice whenever household goods are threatened. Many legal aid offices will treat the threat as enough of an emergency to give the consumer prompt legal attention. The risk is not only the loss of items of great personal significance to the consumer, but that an unrepresented consumer will be coerced into giving up important rights to stave off the seizure.

Where legal representation is not feasible, a review of the remainder of this chapter will at least provide an overview of the consumer's rights to stave off seizure of household goods. Supplement this chapter with specific information from your state, in particular determine which household goods are exempt from execution after a court judgment. Local attorneys should be able to provide this information.

2. Determine If the Threat Is False

A threat to seize household goods is false if the debt does not fall within any of the four categories listed at the beginning of this chapter. Even if one of these four situations apply, the threat is still usually false. This is particularly the case where the creditor is threatening to execute on household goods under a court judgment. Most state laws protect household goods from such execution. Check with a local attorney.

Beyond that, evaluating a threat will often depend on the value of the collateral, the difficulty of seizing it, and the nature and reputation of the creditor. For example, a consumer electronics store is more likely to seize $2000 worth of its own stereo and video equipment it sold to the consumer a few months ago than a loan company is to seize the family photo album or the fifteen-year-old kitchen refrigerator.

If the threat is false, obviously the family should not worry about it. Moreover, the threat is probably illegal and can be remedied under the federal Fair Debt Collection Practices Act or some other legal theory. See Chapter Four.

3. Do Not Consent to the Creditor Coming Into the House

If someone comes to seize household goods, the consumer must determine if the repossessor is a government official or an agent of the creditor. A consumer can easily thwart an attempt to seize household goods where the seizure is not performed by a government official.

Simply refuse to allow the repossessor to come into the house. The consumer should politely but firmly refuse to consent to the creditor entering the consumer's dwelling. Consumers should repeat the objections each time a repossession threat or effort is made, and instruct landlords, spouses, children, and/or roommates *not* to consent to repossessors entering the consumer's residence. (Permission to enter granted by a six year old is not effective.)

The consumer should not physically resist the entry, just politely and firmly object to the entry. Repossessors can only legally enter a consumer's house if they are invited inside. Walking uninvited through an open door makes the repossession illegal. If a repossessor still forces himself in, the first concern should be for the safety of individuals in the house. After the repossession, contact the police and an attorney because the repossessor's action was a blatantly illegal breach of the peace. Witnesses of course are helpful.

4. *Do* Cooperate with the Sheriff

In rare cases, it will not be the creditor who is seizing the goods, but a sheriff or constable. This situation is unusual because the creditor first would have had to obtain a court order to arrange for the sheriff to come. Obtaining a court order is likely to cost more than the goods are worth. If it is the sheriff (and not the creditor claiming to be the sheriff), ask for identification and then comply with any order the sheriff makes.

5. Claim that the Household Goods Are Exempt

When a sheriff is seizing the goods, it is important to determine the creditor who instituted the seizure. In particular, a consumer is vulnerable if the consumer has already put up the goods being seized as collateral with that creditor. Furniture and appliance stores are the most likely creditors to obtain a court order sending a sheriff to seize collateral.

If the creditor had *not* previously taken the goods as collateral, but is merely attempting to seize them after obtaining a court judgment, the consumer has important rights under state law. States almost uniformly protect certain household goods from seizure to satisfy a court judgment.

The state laws offering this protection are usually called exemption statutes. They may provide blanket protection for all household goods, for household goods under a certain dollar figure, or for certain types of household goods. It is important to know the exemption law for your state. If you are unsure about your state's exemptions, ask a legal services office or other attorney.

If property is exempt, this should be pointed out to the sheriff, or even better to the court before the sheriff comes. If the sheriff still takes the goods, *quickly* go to court after the sheriff takes the goods to explain that the household goods are exempt under state law. The court clerk's office or sheriff's office may have a form to fill out to claim goods as exempt.

6. Can the Creditor Take the Household Goods as Collateral?

The Federal Trade Commission's Credit Practices Rule declares it illegal for creditors to take "non-purchase money security interests" in most household goods. This rule is particularly important in dealing with finance companies, but usually not helpful in dealing with furniture or appliance dealers.

A creditor *can* take household goods as collateral when the consumer uses the loan to purchase those particular goods. A creditor *cannot* take most household goods as collateral for a loan unrelated to purchasing the goods.

Household goods that cannot be taken as collateral for a loan unrelated to the purchase of the goods include: clothing, furniture, appliances, one radio, one television, linens, china, crockery, kitchenware, and other personal effects such as wedding rings and photographs. Creditors can take as collateral (even if unrelated to the loan) art, lawn equipment, tools, audio systems, a second television or radio, cameras, boats, sporting goods, typewriters, firearms, bicycles, musical instruments or jewelry (other than wedding rings). Obviously, a creditor cannot take a security interest in "all" a consumer's household goods.

Some states also provide stronger protections in dealing with household goods collateral. In addition, every state prohibits creditors from taking as collateral goods which the consumer does not yet own at the time of the loan, but will own in the future. As a consequence, a creditor, for example, cannot take a security interest in all tools or audio systems, only in identified items the consumer owns at the time of the loan.

7. Challenge the Replevin Procedure

Sometimes a sheriff is seizing goods pursuant to a state proceeding called (depending on what state you are in) "replevin," "sequestration," "detinue," "claim and delivery," or "bail." This is a technical way of saying that the creditor has gone to court claiming that it owns the goods and should get them back.

In the consumer credit context, typically the creditor is saying that the consumer had put up the goods as collateral and the consumer has now defaulted on the loan. As a result, the creditor claims the collateral now belongs to it.

Creditors will rarely go to court to recover household goods collateral. Usually they will do nothing or try self-help repossession. But the creditor does have the option of going to court to get an order that the collateral be turned over.

Just as in other types of lawsuits, the consumer has a right to notice of the lawsuit and a hearing to contest the matter. Also, as in other types of lawsuits, the creditor is not expecting the consumer to contest the matter or to be represented by an attorney. A consumer raising a serious defense may be enough for the creditor to drop the suit.

If the court gives the creditor the right to seize the property *before* a hearing, the creditor cannot dispose of the goods until the judge has finally ruled in the creditor's favor. The creditor will not get permanent possession until the court makes a decision *after* a hearing.

8. RTO Repossessions

Consumer rights to challenge rent-to-own repossessions are less clear than with seizure of household goods collateral. Many RTO agreements authorize the company to come into the consumer's house and take the RTO appliance. Nevertheless, this right is highly suspect and is unlikely to be upheld by a court. RTO companies may be able to utilize certain states' lease larceny statutes to threaten criminal action if the consumer does not return rented goods.

Unless a consumer has made a lot of payments on a rent-to-own contract, it is usually a good idea just to return the goods and stop paying. Typically the rent is fantastically overpriced.

Consumers may also have legal rights if they want to keep RTO goods. More and more states are enacting special statutes covering rent-to-own situations, and some of these statutes allow the consumers to reinstate delinquent payments and keep the rented goods. Another option, if a consumer believes he or she does not owe any more on the contract, is to refuse to return the goods, but get legal advice quickly. The best approach in most rent-to-own situations is to ask an attorney in your own state about the current state of the law as to rent-to-own seizures.

9. File for Bankruptcy

Obviously, a consumer will have to carefully weigh the cost and other complications of filing bankruptcy against the benefits of protecting household goods. While consumers may not wish to file bankruptcy just to protect household goods, often there will be other benefits to a bankruptcy filing in adjusting other debts. It is thus important to know how bankruptcy can protect a consumer's household goods.

Filing for bankruptcy provides immediate relief by automatically stopping *any* threatened seizure of the household goods. This applies to seizures of collateral and even to rented items.

Bankruptcy also can usually protect a consumer's household goods in the long run as well. If the household goods are exempt under applicable law, then bankruptcy permanently prevents their seizure to satisfy a court judgment.

Moreover, non-purchase money security interests in household goods can also be canceled in bankruptcy. If the creditor had a purchase money security interest, that interest may be voided in certain situations if the creditor has since refinanced the original loan used to purchase the goods. Even if a creditor retains the original purchase money security interest in certain household goods, a consumer may be able to keep the property after a bankruptcy filing by paying the creditor only what the property is worth.

In a RTO transaction, a consumer wanting to keep the goods can pay the delinquent payments over time and just keep current on future rent payments. In some states consumers can categorize the RTO transaction as a credit sale, and this will give the consumer additional strategies in bankruptcy for dealing with RTO transactions. For more on bankruptcy, see Chapter Fourteen.

9

General Home Defense Strategies

How to Use the Next Two Chapters

A home is more than an important asset. It is linked with socio-economic status and access to the work place, to schools, and to friends. Foreclosure—the sale of a home to pay debts—threatens everything.

It means the loss of a major investment, since, even in a strong housing market, the price of a home sold at foreclosure sale will be significantly less than the home's retail value. This will mean a substantial loss in the homeowner's equity. In fact, usually the home will be sold only for the amount of the indebtedness, totally wiping out the consumer's equity in the property. An eviction will usually force the former homeowners to a find a rental unit in a different neighborhood, where the new rental unit may be less desirable but more expensive than the cost of owning the original home.

This chapter and the next discuss strategies that can save homes from foreclosure or that at least allow the owners to recover their equity, or minimize the amount still owed creditors after the foreclosure. Chapter Nine analyzes strategies that apply to most home foreclosures. But consumers generally have their strongest defenses when a foreclosure involves one of seven specialized situations, and Chapter Ten discusses special consumer rights in these seven situations:

1. FHA and HUD mortgages;
2. VA mortgages;
3. Farmers Home (FmHA) mortgages;
4. Mortgages (both first and second) not used to purchase the home (for which Truth in Lending rescission is available);
5. Liens and mortgages resulting from a home improvement contract (where the seller's misconduct can be raised as a defense on the loan);
6. Shady lenders, that is where credit terms are unfair or oppressive;
7. Where the loan was not secured by a mortgage, but where the creditor is foreclosing based on a court judgment.

If a home foreclosure involves one or more of those seven situations, it is important to read both this chapter and the relevant sections of Chapter Ten. Otherwise, it is sufficient to review just this chapter.

How Foreclosures Work

Foreclosure procedures vary from state to state. The procedures are established by state statutes, by case law, and by local practice. In some states, foreclosures are court proceedings. First the creditor files a suit in a court located near the property. Unless the homeowner files an answer successfully contesting the foreclosure, a judgment is entered for the creditor. The home is then sold under court supervision.

Other states have "non-judicial foreclosures." Creditors foreclose by simply advertising the home for sale, using a legal notice in a newspaper. If homeowners want to contest this type of foreclosure, they must file a lawsuit and ask the court to stop the sale. Sometimes if the homeowner wants the court to stop the foreclosure, the homeowner must file a bond to protect the creditor. Unless the homeowner initiates a court proceeding, there is no judicial involvement in such a foreclosure.

Some states allow both types of foreclosure, judicial and non-judicial. Practicality and local custom usually dictate a creditor's choice of one type over the other.

Certain states allow homeowners a second chance. Defaulting homeowners can avoid foreclosure by "curing" the default. This gives them an opportunity to undo whatever led to the default in the first place. For example, they can pay foreclosure costs and make up missed mortgage payments.

Most states also allow homeowners to "redeem" the home up to the time of a foreclosure sale. To redeem, the consumer must pay off the full amount of the note in one payment plus the creditor's costs to date. That is, instead of just paying off the delinquent payments, the consumer would also have to pay the whole remainder of the mortgage. The right to redeem allows homeowners to pay off foreclosing creditors and stop the foreclosure by taking out a new loan or privately selling the redemption right to another family that wants to buy the house. In some states the right of redemption continues for a certain time *after* the foreclosure sale.

Generally a foreclosure sale is a poorly advertised auction. Often no one attends except the foreclosing creditor, who bids no more than the balance of the debt, and maybe significantly less. If the foreclosure is a judicial proceeding, the auctioneer might be a sheriff or other court official.

If the sale does not bring in enough to pay off the creditor, in many states the creditor can seek a deficiency, that is the remainder due on the note plus certain costs, less the sale proceeds. Some state laws prevent creditors from seeking this deficiency.

Using Conferences to Educate the Public on Foreclosure Rights

Frequently, families in financial distress are reluctant to ask for legal and financial support services. With no job possibilities in sight, they may either deny the seriousness of their situation, or simply not know where to turn for help. When a community suffers widespread foreclosures, after a large plant closing for example, homeowners can benefit by participating in a public education conference on available support services. By meeting together, they can find strength and motivation in numbers and obtain valuable information.

Such a conference was held a number of years ago in a local Pittsburgh civic center auditorium. The full day conference featured a variety of speakers and was advertised by public service announcements in the local media. To ensure accommodation of all participants, reservations were requested.

The conference focused on how to avoid mortgage foreclosure. Speakers included representatives of unemployed workers, lawyers, judges, and government officials. They explained the basics of mortgages and foreclosure, government mortgage forbearance and assistance programs, bankruptcy relief, unemployment compensation, and welfare programs. A psychiatrist talked about the emotional problems created by unemployment and financial distress.

Many families in financial distress who had been reluctant to seek legal and employment counsel were encouraged by the conference to take those steps. They understood for the first time the consequences of not responding to foreclosure notices. The conference helped many families to begin thinking constructively about the future.

An unexpected benefit of the conference was that it focused the attention of public and governmental officials more sharply on the workers' plight. It encouraged judges and public officials to reexamine their roles and resulted in greater forbearance in the foreclosure process. Ultimately, because enough people had become aware of the foreclosure crisis in Pennsylvania, the legislature passed a law establishing an effective homeowners' emergency assistance program.

Consumer Strategies When Foreclosure Is Threatened

This section lists strategies when a homeowner first becomes worried about meeting mortgage payments. The next section provides advice when a lender has actually started the foreclosure process.

Often strategies in this section will also work even after the foreclosure process has actually started, but the homeowner will be
under more time pressure. Moreover, the strategies are usually
most effective if instituted as early as possible.

Get Legal Advice

Because foreclosure is a harsh legal process, homeowners threatened with foreclosure should immediately obtain legal help. Possible sources of legal help are the neighborhood legal services
office and a bar association panel of pro bono attorneys.

Too often, homeowners either postpone consulting a lawyer
until after the time to assert their legal rights has passed, or walk
away from their homes in frustration, leaving themselves without
any equity and vulnerable to deficiency claims. For each foreclosure situation, a counselor or lawyer must carefully evaluate the
homeowners' objectives and interests.

Homeowners however should avoid "quick fix" attorneys who
may advertise or solicit through the mail from published foreclosure lists. Many times these practitioners will push the homeowner
to file a bankruptcy prematurely. A bankruptcy may be necessary
at some point. But, as with many things, proper timing may be
critical.

Keep Current on Home Payments

The consumer should not pay credit card debts, doctor bills or
other low priority debts ahead of home mortgage payments. Skipping payments on low priority debts for several months will have
little or no bad consequences. Skip one or two home mortgage
payments, and the consumer risks losing the home. If the consumer is several months behind, the consumer usually can cure the
default simply by paying the amount in arrears. Again, the consumer should stop paying other bills and try to catch up on the
home mortgage.

Negotiate a Temporary Delay in Payments

One of the most important strategies today for homeowners in financial trouble is to work out with the lender a temporary delay in payments or a period of reduced payments. More and more creditors are realizing that foreclosure is a losing proposition for the lender, and that the lender is better off keeping the consumer in the home making whatever payments the household can afford. Here are some forms of forbearance that lenders are increasingly likely to accept:

- Skipping one payment, that is letting the consumer remain "30 days down";
- Extending the grace period for making late payments;
- Skipping two to six payments for a year or two; or
- Accepting reduced payments for anywhere from one to eighteen months.

There are several keys to effective negotiation of such forms of temporary forbearance. First, contact the lender as soon as the family begins experiencing financial difficulties. The longer one waits to talk to the lender, the farther behind the family gets, and the less likely the lender is to be helpful.

Just calling up the lender on the telephone is a fine way to start communication. Immediately follow up all phone calls with a letter to the lender confirming what has been discussed. The homeowner should keep a copy of the letter.

Second, the homeowner must resolve any negotiation quickly. Too often homeowners take no action, waiting for the lender to respond to their offer. The next letter from the lender (often months later) may announce that the foreclosure process has already started.

In any communication with the lender, give the lender only a short period of time to respond, and indicate that the lender's silence will be viewed as a refusal to negotiate. Alternatively, get a *written* promise from the lender that there will be no action taken toward a foreclosure for a pre-determined number of weeks while discussions proceed.

It is also important to convince the lender that the family is trying as hard as it can to keep up the mortgage payments and that the family's present financial difficulty is only temporary. Lenders do not like to offer forbearance to a family with no potential for ever getting back on track with mortgage payments. Lenders are similarly skeptical of homeowners whom the lender perceives as not intending to hold up their end of the bargain.

Having an independent counselor help with lender discussions is another good idea. It is important to clearly present the consumer's case—that the family is presently experiencing difficulties, that these difficulties can be resolved with time, and that the lender is better off helping the consumer than allowing a foreclosure to take place. Also review the next item "Negotiate a Permanent Loan Restructuring" for further negotiating tips.

Negotiate a Permanent Loan Restructuring

Although a temporary forbearance is easier to negotiate, for some families the financial problem is more long term. To keep the house, they will have to lower mortgage payments not just for a period of months, but perhaps as long as the mortgage has to run.

Fortunately, many lenders are realizing that the lender permanently receiving less interest may be a better solution for the lender than foreclosing on the home. Where a home's likely sale price at foreclosure is less than the mortgage, the lender is usually better off keeping the consumer in the home and receiving lower mortgage payments. Moreover, more and more consumers are utilizing their rights in bankruptcy, and lenders are discovering that they are worse off if the consumer files bankruptcy than if the lender negotiates a new repayment plan.

Consequently, homeowners report success in achieving the following types of negotiated mortgage restructuring:

- Capitalizing delinquent payments on top of the present principal balance, allowing the consumer to repay these delinquent payments slowly over the whole term of the loan;
- Giving the homeowner up to four years to repay, in installments, delinquent amounts, with no interest accruing on these back due amounts;

- Lowering the interest rate for a certain number of years or even for the remaining term of the loan, thus reducing monthly payments without lengthening the term of the mortgage;
- Lengthening the term of the loan, thus reducing monthly payments (but increasing the total interest payments over the term of the loan);
- Substituting some other more valuable property or asset for the home as collateral for the mortgage, thus putting this substitute property at risk of foreclosure, but protecting the family home; or
- Some combination of the above forms of loan restructuring, such as allowing back due payments to be paid gradually, lengthening the term of a loan, and lowering interest payments.

Resolve quickly any negotiation to restructure a loan. Too often homeowners take no action, waiting for the lender to respond to their offer, when the next letter from the lender (often months later) announces that the foreclosure process has already started. The homeowner would be better served to have initiated alternative strategies in the interim.

In any communication with the lender, give the lender only a short period of time to respond, and indicate that the lender's silence will be viewed as a refusal to negotiate. Alternatively, get a *written* promise from the lender that there will be no action taken toward a foreclosure for a pre-determined number of weeks while discussions proceed.

One of the most important points in negotiating a permanent loan restructuring is to know what type of lender is involved. Many conventional home mortgages originate from a local bank, but then the bank sells the mortgage to another entity, such as Fannie Mae, and then continues to service the mortgage for that entity.

It is important to know who actually owns a loan. Any negotiation, even though conducted with a local bank, will be based on the guidelines established by the lender actually owning the mortgage, such as Fannie Mae. Moreover, the final approval of the loan restructuring may have to come from Fannie Mae or some other entity actually owning the mortgage.

Fannie Mae (the familiar name for the Federal National Mortgage Association) is the leading institutional investor in home loans, purchasing mortgages from banks and mortgage companies and then contracting out with lenders to service the loans. Fannie Mae has detailed written guidelines that these servicers must follow. The servicing guidelines spell out procedures servicing banks should take to avoid foreclosure and to restructure loan terms.

The Fannie Mae "Servicing Guide" costs three hundred dollars and can be obtained from a Fannie Mae regional office. Call (202) 752-7000 for the address of the regional office for your area. For example, for the Northeast, the Servicing Guide can be obtained from Fannie Mae, 510 Walnut St., 16th Floor, Philadelphia, PA 19106. Upkeep is free after the initial investment.

If a Fannie Mae servicer is not following Fannie Mae guidelines, contact Fannie Mae to complain, and let the servicer know you are doing so. If initial contacts with Fannie Mae are not successful, try to speak to a staffer higher up in the organization. Because Fannie Mae is a federally chartered organization, some counselors report success in having a homeowner's Congressman write a letter to Fannie Mae asking Fannie Mae to follow its own guidelines.

Freddie Mac (the familiar name for the Federal Home Mortgage Corporation) is the second largest investor in home mortgages. It operates in a manner very similar to Fannie Mae and all of the discussion above concerning Fannie Mae applies to Freddie Mac as well. The Freddie Mac servicing guidelines are available for two hundred and seventy five dollars. Ask for the Sellers' and Servicers' Guide, available from Freddie Mac, Attn: Subscription Services, 8200 Jones Branch Drive, McLean VA 22102. The guide comes with one year free upkeep.

Most lenders also require that homeowners whose down payments are less than twenty percent purchase mortgage insurance. This insurance covers any loss the lender incurs as part of the mortgage loan. The private mortgage insurance (PMI) companies thus have a direct financial interest in any foreclosure. If the lender loses money, the PMI company has to absorb the loss.

Several major PMI companies, such as GECC Mortgage Insurance, MGIC, and Commonwealth Mortgage Assurance, are pressuring lenders to restructure loans as an alternative to costly foreclosures and consumer bankruptcies. Sometimes a PMI company will even make up a few missed payments for the homeowner to avoid the consumer filing bankruptcy or the lender foreclosing. If negotiations are not going well with a lender, consider contacting the PMI company to ask their help. PMI companies may be more interested in restructuring a mortgage than the lender.

Lenders who do not sell their mortgages to Fannie Mae, Freddie Mac, or a similar entity are called portfolio lenders. In negotiating a loan restructuring with portfolio lenders, consumers are dependent on these lenders' own internal policies. A local savings and loan or other bank may be amenable to negotiation. A lender whose real motivation in making the loan was to steal the consumer's home may not be open to any type of negotiation.

If you believe a lender is treating a homeowner unfairly, contact the government agency that regulates that lender. Many finance companies, mortgage companies and banks are regulated by a state banking department. Lenders offering federal insurance are regulated by the Federal Reserve Board, federally chartered banks by the federal Comptroller of the Currency, and certain savings and loans by the federal Office of Thrift Supervision. The National Credit Union Administration regulates certain credit unions.

In negotiating a new payment schedule, remember that a lender's first offer is not necessarily its last. Explain to the lender or PMI company how much it has to lose if the consumer files bankruptcy or if the lender forecloses. Compare the amount outstanding on the mortgage with the home's present value if it had to be sold in a hurry. Then discount that value significantly because foreclosure sales traditionally bring in low values. Then subtract the lender's foreclosure expenses, including attorney fees. If that amount is less than the mortgage, this is how much the lender has to lose if it does not reach a new payment plan.

Also review this chapter's discussion of consumer rights in a bankruptcy filing and the more detailed analysis in Chapter Fourteen. This will give you and the lender an indication as to how the lender might fare if the homeowner files for bankruptcy.

Refinance the Home Debt

If the home was financed at one of the high interest rates that prevailed during the early 1980s, refinancing at a lower interest rate and/or with a longer payment period can greatly reduce monthly payments and bring the payments within reach. Moreover, refinancing a low interest first mortgage and high interest second mortgage into a low interest first mortgage can also reduce payments.

For example, a family with a 25-year, $10,000 first mortgage at eight percent interest and a 15-year, $20,000 second mortgage at 18 percent interest has combined monthly payments of $399.26. Refinancing those two mortgages with a 25-year, $30,000 first mortgage at 10 percent will result in new monthly payments of $272.61. This is $126.65 per month less.

On the other hand, many refinancing schemes are frauds. Even legitimate refinancing options that look like an improvement on closer inspection are far more costly than the existing mortgage. It is imperative to carefully review Chapter Three to decide whether refinancing makes sense.

The major disadvantages in refinancing residential debts are the increased finance charges that result from extending the repayment period, the possibility of having to pay points, the additional closing costs, and prepayment penalties on the old mortgages. The feasibility of refinancing depends on whether the homeowner can obtain a loan at a reasonable rate, usually from a savings bank, a commercial bank, a credit union, or a legitimate mortgage company. Most finance companies and certain mortgage companies do not make residential loans at reasonable rates and terms.

Homeowners in financial distress should *not* assume that legitimate lenders with low interest rates will turn them down. Only by applying can a homeowner determine the availability of a loan from a particular lender.

A study in one state found credit more available from banks than from finance companies. Other studies confirm that most borrowers who receive finance company loans are also usually eligible for bank loans at more favorable terms. Moreover, sometimes special mortgage programs are available, such as federal FHA guaranteed loans, state bonded mortgage funds, or local neighborhood development funds available through community reinvestment programs.

A homeowner applying for a residential loan should present his or her financial problems in the best possible light. The presentation should show how the problems are being solved, and how refinancing will provide substantially lower payments. Homeowners should stress their past financial, residential, and employment stability, and indicate plans for the future. People often refinance high interest rate loans when rates drop; a family in financial distress should not feel that their application will be considered unusual.

Under the federal Equal Credit Opportunity Act, lenders who reject a credit application must explain their reasons. The Act prohibits lenders from denying credit because the applicant receives government benefits.

Rejected homeowners should obtain the reasons for their rejection and determine whether the reasons are legitimate. Consumers should try to cure any problems so that the next application will be successful. For more information on the federal Equal Credit Opportunity Act, see another National Consumer Law Center publication called *Equal Credit Opportunity Act* (2d ed. 1988 and Supplement).

Some lenders solicit financially distressed families. Usually the terms of their loans are not just unfavorable, but disastrous for those who subscribe to them. Anyone who considers accepting a solicited home loan or financing arrangement should first seek the advice of a counselor, lawyer, or accountant.

Appraise or List the House For Sale

When foreclosure is threatened, a homeowner may wish to contact a local realtor to obtain an appraisal of the home or even list the home for sale. Doing so provides the owner with information about the home's marketability and its likely sale price, without necessarily obligating the owner to sell.

Most homeowners do not want to give up their home, and this chapter and the next will discuss strategies to try to save the home. But sometimes no other solution exists or the family wants to move on in any event. Selling the house may be painful, but it is always a better solution than letting a bank sell the house.

If they find a buyer, homeowners may sell their homes privately before a foreclosure sale takes place. The proceeds of a private sale are first applied to the existing debt on the house, then to any realtor fees, and to closing costs. The homeowners keep the surplus. If the sale will only produce a small surplus, before rejecting the offer, the consumer can try to negotiate a smaller commission for the realtor.

The primary advantage of a private sale is that the homeowner will realize more equity than if the house is auctioned at a typical public foreclosure sale. Public foreclosure sales frequently produce a price less than the amount of the mortgage, meaning that in most states the consumer will still owe the balance of the debt. Foreclosure sales almost never produce a sale price greater than the amount owed, meaning the homeowner's equity will be wiped out.

The disadvantages of a private sale are obvious. There can be no private sale unless there is a buyer willing to pay more than the existing debt on the home or unless the lender will approve the sale for the lower amount. (Lenders might do so if they are afraid they will do worse in a foreclosure situation.) Another disadvantage of selling the home is that the family's housing expenses in a new residence may be higher than they were in their old home.

Rent the House to Someone Else

Another strategy is to lease the home temporarily to someone else and rent a less expensive dwelling. This necessitates finding credit worthy tenants, locating a substitute dwelling, and incurring moving expenses. Homeowners assume the role of landlords, with maintenance obligations and new tax implications.

This strategy only makes sense if the rental will stop the foreclosure. The rent payments must be enough to allow the homeowner to pay rent on a new residence, keep up payments on the mortgage, and also to catch up on any delinquent amounts owed the mortgage holder. Moreover, some mortgages contain anti-leasing clauses, prohibiting this strategy. A variation on the theme of renting out the whole house is to rent a room within the home to an individual who has been carefully screened and who is credit-worthy.

Qualifying Under a State Mortgage Assistance Program

Pennsylvania, Maryland, and New Jersey have developed mortgage assistance programs in response to the high number of foreclosures against displaced workers that followed multiple plant closings in their states. The programs provide loans to homeowners from state funds. The loans pay a portion of monthly mortgage payments for several years. Homeowners who are behind in their payments for reasons beyond their control, such as a lay-off, but who are likely to be able to resume full home loan payments within several years, are eligible for the program.

Be Alert for a State Moratorium on Foreclosures

During the economic depression of the 1930s, many states enacted moratorium statutes postponing foreclosure sales of homes and farms. Still in effect, the statutes prevent foreclosures by requiring lenders to accept smaller payments during moratorium periods. For example, the Iowa foreclosure statute provides general relief in cases of natural disasters and both Iowa and Minnesota provide relief when the governor declares an economic emergency.

Occasionally a state will declare a local emergency and allow foreclosure relief in areas where plant closings have created widespread distress and depressed housing markets, giving dislocated workers time to put their affairs in order. For example, during a plant closing crisis in the early 1980s in Pennsylvania, local judges and sheriffs postponed home foreclosures against dislocated workers without resorting to a moratorium law. Massachusetts had a temporary moratorium in 1991 on foreclosures. The legislature was responding to widespread instances of home improvement fraud and other second mortgage scams.

File for Bankruptcy

This immediately stops a threatened foreclosure and may help the family cure delinquent payments and get back on track on future payments. Bankruptcy as a remedy for stopping foreclosure is discussed immediately below under "Defending Against an Actual Foreclosure."

Defending Against an Actual Foreclosure

Curing a Default

Even when a creditor is seeking to foreclose on a home and is demanding the full note in repayment, sometimes the consumer can "cure" the default and reinstate the loan. The consumer does this by just paying past due installments, and in some cases late charges or other fees due, such as an attorney's collection fee.

Many creditors voluntarily reinstate a mortgage when the delinquency is cured if they believe there are reasonable prospects that the homeowner will start making timely payment on future installments. Make sure the consumer receives a promise in *writing* that payment of the cure amount will reinstate the mortgage.

If a creditor refuses to voluntarily reinstate a mortgage if the default is cured, this fact can be presented to the court. Some courts will require that the homeowners be given an opportunity to cure prior to foreclosure, even where a state statute does not explicitly give the homeowner the right to cure.

A number of state and federal statutes also provide homeowners with the legal right to cure certain types of home mortgages and thus reinstate the mortgage. This right to cure may apply to all home mortgages in some states or only to second mortgages or mobile home mortgages. FHA, VA, and FmHA mortgages in all states also are subject to cure rights, as detailed in Chapter Ten.

Sometimes a creditor will demand large attorney fees or other expenses as a prerequisite to a consumer curing a mortgage, and will refuse to accept installment payments to cure this large amount. The consumer should still offer the creditor as much as the consumer can afford. This offer puts the consumer in a good position when the consumer later asks a judge to apply equity in denying a foreclosure.

Negotiate a Work Out Agreement, Refinance the Mortgage, Sell the Home Privately, or Look for Government Assistance

Earlier in this chapter various strategies were set out when a foreclosure is merely threatened. These strategies, such as negotiating with the lender, refinancing the mortgage, selling the home, or various forms of government assistance, apply to an actual foreclosure as well. The only difference is that the homeowner will be under more pressure to reach a solution and to do so quickly.

Usually Do Not Voluntarily Turn Over the Home to the Creditor

Homeowners often will be tempted to turn over their deed to the creditor. This is called "deed in lieu of foreclosure" or "deed in lieu." Instead of fighting the foreclosure, the homeowners just give up and turn the home over to the mortgage holder.

There are several points to warn homeowners about offering the deed in lieu. Deed in lieu is generally a very bad idea if the consumer has significant equity in the home. That is, if the home's value exceeds the amount of the indebtedness, the consumer would ordinarily receive this surplus. By turning over the deed to the mortgage holder, the consumer may forfeit any right to this equity in the home.

Similarly, the consumer may have valid claims or defenses against the creditor, and by turning over the deed, the consumer will be giving up these valuable claims for no consideration.

Often, significant consumer claims and defenses will totally stop a foreclosure, so consumers must carefully consider their options before foregoing these claims.

A major motivation for a homeowner turning over the deed to the creditor is the expectation that the consumer will not owe the creditor a deficiency. That is, there is a fear that the foreclosure sale price will not equal the amount owed on the mortgage plus expenses, and that the consumer will have to pay the creditor the difference. This is not a concern in some states that prevent deficiency actions, but in most states this is a legitimate consumer concern—although the deficiency obligation will just be an unsecured obligation.

If avoiding a deficiency is the consumer's motivation, it is imperative that the creditor put in writing a promise not to seek a deficiency. Simply handing over the deed will not stop a creditor from selling the home and seeking a deficiency.

Similarly, if a consumer does offer the creditor a deed in lieu of foreclosure, make sure that there is a written agreement giving the family sufficient time to vacate the premises. The family will need time to find alternative housing and move in an orderly fashion.

Conversely, a homeowner should not assume that every creditor will accept a deed in lieu agreement. Some creditors will not do so, and consumers can lose valuable time if they pin all their hopes on a deed in lieu agreement.

Procedural Defenses May Delay the Process

In most areas of the country, foreclosures are seldom contested, and lenders' attorneys tend to assume that there is no defense to foreclosure. Consequently, lenders tend to be sloppy in their procedures and frequently do not comply with foreclosure requirements. Lender noncompliance can benefit homeowners contesting foreclosure, forcing the lender to start over, or, at the very least, to comply with the procedural requirements. This will provide the homeowners with additional time to refinance, sell privately, or work out a forbearance.

State foreclosure procedures and defenses to foreclosure vary significantly from state to state. Therefore, a lawyer or some other professional will have to determine whether lenders have fully complied with all the required procedures and whether defenses to foreclosure are available. This will require scrutiny of state statutes establishing foreclosure procedures and judicial decisions interpreting those statutes.

Most state foreclosure procedures are designed to produce a swift sale of real estate, but they usually contain some protection for homeowners. Because foreclosure is harsh, courts generally require strict compliance with statutory procedures.

Examples of possible defenses include the failure to give proper notice to the homeowner, failure to properly advertise the sale, the failure of a lender to introduce the original note in the foreclosure proceeding, or the lender's discouraging bids at the foreclosure sale.

A Creditor's Habitually Accepting Late Payments May Be Grounds to Stop a Foreclosure

Late payment on a mortgage generally triggers the creditor's right to "accelerate" the loan—to call in the full amount of the mortgage due immediately. Failure to pay the full amount then leads to foreclosure.

Nevertheless, many courts refuse to allow foreclosure if the lender surprises the homeowner by suddenly calling a loan in when the lender has been lenient in accepting late payments in the past. If a lender habitually accepts late payments, it must warn the consumer before it calls the whole loan in and attempts a foreclosure. Failure to do so may provide the consumer with grounds to stop a foreclosure and give the consumer a second opportunity to catch up on late payments.

Lender Must Give Consumer Notice of Available Counseling Before Foreclosure

Federal law[1] requires that, for *all* mortgages (except certain Farmers Home Administration mortgages), the creditor must send the homeowner a notice of the availability of financial counseling. This notice must be sent *prior* to any foreclosure action on a consumer's principal dwelling.

This notice must be sent whenever the delinquency is due to an involuntary loss or reduction of employment of either the home-owner or a person contributing to the homeowner's income. The requirement applies to a mortgage on any principal dwelling, including condominiums, cooperatives, and mobile homes where the homeowner owns the land the home is situated on.

The federal government believes that failure to give the notice may prevent the lender from foreclosing on the property. While the law in this area is still unclear, at least one consumer has successfully defended a foreclosure action by pointing to the lack of notice. The court ordered a 45-day suspension of the foreclo-sure to give the consumer the opportunity to obtain financial counseling.

In the case of mortgages insured by the Federal Housing Agency (FHA) or the Veterans' Administration (VA), the notice must state the availability of any counseling services offered by the creditor and the location of either FHA-approved home ownership coun-seling programs or the VA counseling agency in the case of VA loans. FHA approved nonprofit counseling agencies are listed by the federal government.[2] They generally include community action programs, consumer credit counseling organizations, and govern-ment offices. HUD provides grants to counseling agencies to sup-port their counseling programs.

Filing Bankruptcy Can Stop a Foreclosure in Its Tracks

Families in financial distress who are about to lose their homes should carefully consider filing a petition in bankruptcy. This can stop the foreclosure process and allow the family time to regroup and try to work out a plan to keep the home. Bankruptcy may also help the family cure past defaults and make future payments.

However, the bankruptcy option may not be effective unless carefully planned and timed. For example, a premature bankruptcy filing may cancel a homeowner's right to receive special state assistance or may remove a good equitable defense case from a sympathetic state court.

Chapter Fourteen provides a more detailed discussion of a consumer's bankruptcy rights and the factors to weigh in deciding whether a family should file bankruptcy. This section specifically explains how families can stave off foreclosure by exercising their bankruptcy rights. Later in this chapter there is a discussion on the use of bankruptcy even after the foreclosure has taken place.

The Automatic Stay

The first reason why bankruptcy is such a potent method of dealing with an imminent foreclosure is the bankruptcy automatic stay. The filing of a petition in bankruptcy automatically stops most creditor actions against debtors and their property, including foreclosure, foreclosure sales, and the filing of liens against property.

The creditor cannot proceed without first obtaining the bankruptcy judge's permission to do so. The bankruptcy judge will often *not* give the creditor permission to proceed. Consumers can often use the bankruptcy process to permanently avoid a foreclosure. The automatic stay is discussed in more detail in Chapter Fourteen.

Curing Delinquent Payments and Reinstating the Mortgage

The automatic stay gives the family time to take advantage of other aspects of the bankruptcy law. Under a chapter 13 bankruptcy filing, called a debt adjustment case, the family can "cure" the delinquent payments gradually over a period of years so long as the family can also keep up on future mortgage payments as they come due each month. For example, if a family is behind on six $400 monthly mortgage payments, it may be able to keep the mortgage current merely by making future $400 payments as they come due and catching up on the past due $2400 in 60 monthly payments of $40 each.

The consumer can cure delinquent payments in a chapter 13 bankruptcy even if a creditor has already accelerated payments so that the full loan amount is due or even, in many states, if the creditor has obtained a foreclosure judgment. The family just pays the creditor its normal monthly payments and also pays the delinquent amount over time. No additional interest is charged on the delinquent amounts (although consumers in Ohio, Michigan, Kentucky, and Tennessee probably do have to pay interest).

One interesting situation is where the family is delinquent on a balloon payment. A balloon payment is a final payment much larger than the normal monthly payment, for example where a family pays $400 a month for five years with a $10,000 balloon payment due at the end. If the family is in default on a final balloon, courts are divided as to whether the family must pay the balloon amount immediately or whether it can also pay that amount over time, for example over a five year period.

The Bankruptcy Code does not define what period of time is reasonable for repaying a delinquency; the answer depends to some extent on the facts and circumstances of each case. In a chapter 13 bankruptcy, the family creates a plan to pay all or some of its debts over a three to five year period. It is not safe to assume that cure over the entire three to five year length of a plan will be found reasonable, although in appropriate cases the full five year time period has been allowed.

When paying off a mortgage through a chapter 13 plan, it will be important to distinguish between payments made as part of the plan and those made outside the plan. Payments within the plan will be subject to an approximately 10% commission, called a trustee's fee. The family's payments to cure the delinquency will be made within the plan and thus will be subject to that 10% commission. If the bankruptcy plan is correctly drafted, the payments on installments not due until the future can usually be paid directly to the creditor, i.e. outside the plan, thus avoiding the 10% commission.

Another important issue when using the Bankruptcy Code to

cure a mortgage delinquency is the extent to which creditors can collect attorney's fees and costs as part of the amount needed to cure. The creditor is only entitled to attorney's fees and costs if the credit agreement clearly and unambiguously provides for collection of such charges. Even then, many state statutes either place significant limitations on fee arrangements or prohibit them entirely.

When fees are appropriate, they should be assessed only if they are reasonable, necessary, and actually paid. A creditor whose litigation is unsuccessful or unnecessary should not be allowed to collect fees from a debtor.

Sale of the Home in a Chapter 13 Bankruptcy

Homeowners who are no longer able to make their mortgage payments will not benefit from the ability to cure past delinquencies. They can use the bankruptcy to sell their homes themselves in an orderly fashion, thereby keeping their equity and avoiding the problems of a foreclosure sale. This strategy is probably only available to debtors who will realize enough from the sale of the property to pay from the sale proceeds both the secured and unsecured creditors in full.

Homeowners who sell their home usually have to request that the court approve their realtor. When a sale is arranged, the homeowners will also have to file with the bankruptcy court a "Complaint to Sell Property Free of Liens" and obtain an order from the bankruptcy court approving the sale and allowing the property to be sold free of liens. (Many title insurance companies require this order for the sale to go through.)

Steps to Take After the Foreclosure

Although a homeowner is better off avoiding a pending foreclosure, sometimes the homeowner can undo the foreclosure sale and keep the family home. Even if the homeowner cannot keep the home, it is still important for the homeowner to get advice after the foreclosure. The homeowner may still be liable for a large deficiency or, on the other hand, may be owed a significant surplus from the creditor.

The Right of Redemption May Still Allow the Family to Get The Home Back

Most state foreclosure statutes provide homeowners with redemption rights, that is, the right to pay the balance of the debt, including foreclosure expenses, and to extinguish a lender's claim. In some states the right must be exercised prior to a foreclosure sale. In others, the redemption right continues for a certain period of time after a foreclosure sale.

Few financially distressed homeowners are able to redeem their homes, but the redemption right gives them the chance either to sell privately or to refinance the debt. It keeps them from losing the equity in their homes, which is virtually inevitable with a foreclosure sale.

If they can find a buyer, the homeowners can arrange for that buyer to put up all the money to redeem the home, and the buyer also gives directly to the consumer any difference between the negotiated sale price and the redemption amount. If the homeowners can refinance, they use the proceeds from the new mortgage to redeem the home, which thereby terminates the old lender's interest in the home.

It May Not Be Too Late to File Bankruptcy and Undo Everything

If a debtor whose home has been sold at a foreclosure sale can show, among other things, that the home was sold at "less than reasonably equivalent value," the sale can be set aside in bankruptcy court as a "fraudulent conveyance." The family then might be able to use the bankruptcy filing to cure the mortgage default in a chapter 13 proceeding or redeem the house through refinancing or negotiations with the original lender. Undoing the original foreclosure sale also allows the consumer to resell the home for a greater amount and keep some of their share of the proceeds as exempt property.

To undo a foreclosure sale as a fraudulent conveyance, the homeowners must establish three facts. First that the foreclosure sale occurred within one year of the filing of the bankruptcy proceeding. Second, the sale price was for less than a reasonably equivalent value. Third, the family was insolvent on the date of the foreclosure or became insolvent as a result of it.

Because of flaws in foreclosure and execution procedures, foreclosure and execution sales often involve auctions attended only by the lender and speculators. At these sales it is relatively common for property to be sold significantly below market value. Thus it may not be difficult to show a sale was for less than a reasonably equivalent value. One leading case uses a 70% figure as a benchmark, that a foreclosure sale can be undone if the sale price is less than 70% of the home's value. Other courts criticize this simple formula as too rigid, and instead look at all the factors involved in a sale.

Once a foreclosure sale is set aside, the original homeowner must still deal with the purchaser at the foreclosure sale. If the foreclosing creditor was the purchaser, there is no problem. If an innocent third party purchased the home at the foreclosure sale, that party may have a lien on the property equal in amount to what that individual paid.

Deficiencies and Surpluses Following Foreclosure Sales

If a foreclosure sale does not bring enough to pay off the full loan balance plus the lender's foreclosure expenses, the consumer is usually liable for this deficiency. Some states have anti-deficiency statutes that prohibit claims against homeowners for this difference. However, certain federally insured mortgages are not subject to these anti-deficiency statutes.

If a lender pursues a permissible deficiency claim, the former homeowners should determine whether the lender purchased the home at foreclosure and then resold it at a profit. Often a lender will purchase property at foreclosure for the amount owed by the debtor, putting up no cash, and then resell it to a private buyer at a substantial profit. In such a case, the homeowners should consult a lawyer to determine whether the deficiency is barred by the resale and whether the windfall belongs rightfully to them.

If a family is obligated for the deficiency, remember that this debt is not secured by any of the family's remaining property. For example, the family at this point could file for bankruptcy and discharge the deficiency as an unsecured debt. Moreover, even if the creditor obtains a court judgment for the deficiency, it still cannot seize exempt property in attempting to satisfy the deficiency.

10

Special Home Defense Strategies

Chapter Nine outlines home defense strategies applicable to virtually all threatened foreclosures. Special protections also apply to the following seven types of mortgages:

1. FHA and HUD mortgages;
2. VA mortgages;
3. Farmers Home (FmHA) mortgages;
4. Second mortgages and first mortgages not used to purchase the home (Truth in Lending rescission);
5. Liens and mortgages resulting from a home improvement scam;
6. Mortgages based on unconscionable loan transactions; and
7. Where the creditor has no mortgage, but is foreclosing based on a court judgment.

Review the section of this chapter relating to the type of mortgage being foreclosed, or the relevant sections if a threatened home foreclosure involves more than one of these seven situations.

Foreclosure of FHA/HUD-Insured Mortgages

Key Rights for Those with FHA Mortgages

Families with FHA or HUD insured mortgages have many significant rights not available to families with conventional loans. To tell whether a consumer has a FHA mortgage, simply look at the mortgage or loan documents. They will have a FHA form number and indicate that a FHA mortgage is involved.

Consumers should challenge any foreclosure where the homeowner is not afforded certain basic rights available to all FHA mortgagors:

1. Lenders must give notice of default no later than the end of the second month of delinquency;
2. Lenders must make reasonable efforts to arrange face-to-face interviews with homeowners before three full monthly installments are due and unpaid;
3. Lenders must accept partial payments in many circumstances;
4. Lenders cannot foreclose if the only default is an inability to pay in a lump sum an escrow shortage;
5. Lenders cannot foreclose on the mortgage until the consumer is delinquent on three full monthly payments;
6. Before the lender forecloses, the consumer can ask the federal Department of Housing and Urban Development (HUD) to accept "assignment" of the mortgage. If HUD accepts the assignment, it takes over the mortgage and temporarily reduces or excuses mortgage payments.
7. Lenders cannot foreclose while a request for such an assignment is pending.

The HUD Assignment Program Provides Relief From Foreclosure

HUD's assignment program is a central protection for those with FHA mortgages. When HUD receives assignment of a mortgage, HUD reduces or suspends payments for one to three years, and then lets the homeowner catch up on delinquent payments slowly over a period of years. While assignment may not be a permanent solution (the homeowner will eventually have to repay all the mortgage payments temporarily excused), assignment brings immediate relief from foreclosure and allows the consumer to make reduced or no payments for a period of years.

HUD can accept assignment when a consumer is at least three months delinquent and the lender intends to foreclose. The foreclosure must be caused by temporary factors outside the home-owner's control (e.g. temporary loss of employment, delay in the receipt of government benefits, loss of income due to divorce, illness or death, or a sudden increase in expenses). The home-owner must be able to resume payments within three years, and catch up within ten years on payments HUD defers. The key is not the homeowner's present situation, but the *future* ability to make payments.

How to Request that HUD Accept Assignment of a Mortgage

A lender will send notice to the consumer about a pending fore-closure, explaining the HUD assignment program. The consumer should immediately request that HUD accept assignment of the mortgage.

Often the lender will recommend that HUD not accept assignment. Ignore this and press HUD to accept the assignment. HUD is generally not influenced by the lender's opinion, and HUD can insist on an assignment despite the lender's opinion.

HUD almost always initially denies an assignment request as a matter of routine procedure. HUD will give the consumer its reasons for that denial. Homeowners should not be discouraged by this initial denial, but should appeal that denial. Often such appeals will be successful.

Appeals must be made within 15 days (25 days if the appeal is in person). Although the appeal can be by mail or telephone, it is best to meet in person with a HUD representative for a face-to-face interview. Even better is to have an advocate familiar with the HUD process accompany the homeowner.

There can be no foreclosure until HUD makes a final decision. So appealing the original HUD denial has the beneficial effect of delaying the foreclosure.

When contesting the HUD denial, the homeowner should bring proof of income, expenses, and the factors creating the hardship. The homeowner should make a list of points he or she wants to get across.

Follow up an in-person interview with a letter repeating the homeowner's key points, to make sure it all gets into the record. Even after the hearing, send in new information or documents that will help the homeowner's case. Do not be discouraged if the homeowner cannot produce all the information requested by HUD—HUD may still accept the assignment.

HUD has a legal obligation to accept assignment where the conditions of assignment are met. If the consumer has a good case and appeals HUD's initial denial, HUD is legally obligated to accept the mortgage assignment.

If HUD issues a final administrative decision denying an assignment, the lender can then go forward with the foreclosure. But if HUD's final denial was wrong, the consumer can ask a federal court to overturn that decision. At this point, it is advisable for the homeowner to be represented by an attorney. The attorney can ask the court for a delay of any foreclosure action while the lawsuit is pending.

Foreclosure of VA-Guaranteed Mortgages

Homeowners whose mortgages are insured by the Veterans' Administration (VA) have rights not available to homeowners with private conventional mortgages. To tell whether a consumer has a VA mortgage, the simplest thing is to look for the VA logo on the top corner of the mortgage or other loan documents.

Restrictions on Lender's Right to Foreclose

Families with VA mortgages have certain protections against foreclosure. The lender cannot foreclose unless the homeowner fails to make three full monthly payments. The lender must give the VA 30 days warning of its intent to foreclose, and must make all reasonable efforts at forbearance before actually foreclosing on the property.

The lender must consider temporary suspension of payments, extension of the loan, and acceptance of partial payments. If the lender still intends to foreclose, homeowners can stop the foreclosure by paying all delinquent payments, late charges and any of the lender's foreclosure expenses to date.

The VA Assignment Program

Theoretically, the VA can stop a lender's foreclosure by accepting "assignment" of a VA mortgage from the lender. The VA would then hold the mortgage and could excuse or reduce mortgage payments for a period of time. When a family's financial crisis has abated, normal payments would resume. Meanwhile, a foreclosure would be averted.

Unfortunately, this is more of a theoretical option than a practical strategy. The VA has sole discretion whether to accept a mortgage assignment. Government studies show that the VA accepts assignment in less than 1% of mortgages subject to foreclosure.

Stopping a Foreclosure Because the Lender Failed to Properly Service the Mortgage

As described earlier, a lender's statutory obligation in servicing a VA mortgage requires the lender to consider whether to excuse some mortgage payments, accept partial payments, or restructure the loan terms. If the lender fails to do this, the consumer probably cannot sue the lender to force it to change its servicing procedures. But some courts find the lender's conduct to be a sufficient reason to prevent the lender from foreclosing on the mortgage.

The best way to show that a lender is not properly servicing a loan is to show that it is not following the VA lenders' handbook and other servicing guidelines. These guidelines are available from the VA, Office of Administration, Publication Service, Washington, D.C. 20420 or from a regional VA office.[1]

The guidelines require lenders to extend all reasonable forbearance in the event a borrower becomes unable to meet the terms of a loan. The lender should contact the consumer directly in person or over the telephone to discuss the reasons for the default. The lender should also discuss possible ways of handling the loan, such as extensions, recasting the terms of repayment, reapplying prepayments so they go to pay delinquent payments, and accepting partial payments. The lender should not institute foreclosure proceedings until every reasonable effort has been made to find a way to allow the consumer to keep the home.

Foreclosure of Farmers Home Administration Mortgages

Farmers Home Administration (FmHA) guaranteed or insured loans provide rural borrowers (whether they are farmers or not) with significant rights unavailable to homeowners with private conventional loans. To tell whether a mortgage is FmHA insured or guaranteed, simply look at the mortgage papers or loan documents.

Key Resources

The National Housing Law Project's *FmHA Housing Programs: Tenants' and Purchasers' Rights* is an excellent and detailed discussion of all aspects of FmHA mortgages, including strategies to prevent foreclosure of such mortgages. The First Edition came out in 1982 and a Second Edition is due in late 1992.[2] Another excellent reference is an article appearing in the November 1984 *Clearinghouse Review.*[3]

Moratorium Relief from Foreclosure

Families with FmHA mortgages can stave off a foreclosure by successfully asking FmHA for a moratorium on payments for up to two years. The moratorium can also be retroactive for up to three months. This would mean that delinquencies over the last three months would no longer be delinquent until the moratorium period ends.

When the moratorium expires, FmHA has various options to restructure the loan, depending on the borrower's ability to pay at that time. FmHA will give the borrower anywhere from two years to more than the remaining term of the loan to catch up the payments excused during the moratorium period. FmHA can even permanently excuse the interest incurred during the moratorium period.

How to Apply for a Moratorium

Borrowers are eligible for moratorium relief if, because of circumstances beyond their control, they cannot continue making scheduled payments without impairing their ability to pay for essential living expenses. Qualifying homeowners should apply at their local FmHA county office.

The initial decision to grant or deny moratorium relief is made by the county supervisor that administers the county office. Supervisors' decisions vary widely depending on the individual supervisor's predispositions. For example, while some county supervisors do not require formal proof that borrowers will be able to resume payments after the moratorium period, other supervisors only grant relief to homeowners with good payment records.

The county supervisor's decision can be appealed, but that appeal must be filed within 30 days of the supervisor's denial of the moratorium request. While the appeal is pending, there can be *no* foreclosure. Appeals involve an informal hearing where the homeowner will have the burden of proof that the homeowner is entitled to moratorium relief.

Refinancing an FmHA Mortgage into a Low-Interest Mortgage

Federal law provides for another effective approach for families with difficulty paying their FmHA mortgages that would significantly lower their monthly mortgage payments. The FmHA provides low interest (as low as 1%) mortgages to low income homebuyers under its "interest credit" program. There is no reason why a homeowner with a regular FmHA mortgage should not be able to refinance that loan into a low interest loan under the interest credit program. Unfortunately, the FmHA to date appears not to offer this right that federal law provides to all eligible homeowners.

Second Mortgages or First Mortgages Not Used to Purchase the Home (Truth in Lending Rescission)

Overview

Federal law provides many homeowners with an extraordinarily effective means of stopping a foreclosure. Instead of just giving the consumer more time to make reduced payments, this federal remedy allows the consumer to permanently *cancel* the mortgage and significantly reduce the amount of the debt owed to the creditor. Once the mortgage is canceled, there can be no foreclosure.

This remedy, called Truth in Lending rescission, is not available to cancel a first mortgage used to purchase a home. But it may be available to cancel other types of mortgages, such as second mortgages, first mortgages not used to purchase a home, and even liens placed on the home by contractors or other workers. Experience finds Truth in Lending rescission most effective when dealing with onerous credit contracts imposed by home improvement contractors, finance companies, and mortgage companies that prey on families in financial distress.

While Truth in Lending rescission sounds almost too good to be true, there are three catches. First, Truth in Lending rescission does not apply to certain types of loans. Second, the creditor must have made one of a list of basic mistakes when signing the consumer up for the mortgage. Third, the consumer must usually go to court to convince the lender to honor the consumer's Truth in Lending rescission rights.

Obviously, a lawyer or other highly specialized professional will be necessary if a consumer is to successfully utilize Truth in Lending rescission. But a successful result will almost always justify hiring the attorney. The home will be free from the mortgage, the consumer's indebtedness may be reduced by thousands of dollars, and the creditor may have to pay for the consumer's attorney.

This section is not a detailed analysis of Truth in Lending rescission, which can be quite technical. This section does help you identify when Truth in Lending rescission is definitely not available and when it may be, thus telling you whether it is worth contacting an attorney concerning a homeowner's rescission rights. The section also explains how Truth in Lending rescission works and where to get more detailed information.

Key Resources

Truth in Lending rescission is highly, technical and this section only provides an overview. The best practice manual on Truth in Lending rescission is the National Consumer Law Center's *Truth in Lending* (2d ed. 1989 and Supplement). Besides a detailed analysis of all aspects of the law, the volume reprints the key sources of Truth in Lending law—the Truth in Lending Act (TILA),[4] the federal TILA regulations,[5] and the official federal TILA interpretations.[6]

When Does Truth in Lending Rescission Apply and When Does it Not?

Truth in Lending applies to most home mortgages except the ones taken when a consumer buys the home. It even applies to liens that contractors and other workers place on a home, such as artisans' or materialmen's liens. When more than one consumer has the right to rescind a transaction (such as husband and wife), any one consumer can exercise the right and cancel the transaction on behalf of all.

Nevertheless, TILA rescission does *not* apply if:

- The creditor has not taken an interest in the consumer's home and the law does not give the creditor such an interest;
- The mortgage loan was used to purchase the home;
- The mortgage loan was not for consumer purposes, but was for business or agricultural purposes;
- The creditor was only involved in a few loans within the last year.[7]
- The mortgage is on investment property, a vacation house, or other property *not* the consumer's principal residence at the time the loan was extended. (A mobile home, condominium, cooperative, two or three-family home, trailer, even a houseboat *can* be a principal residence);
- The consumer no longer owns the home that the mortgage relates to.
- The mortgage is a refinancing of an existing loan where no new money is borrowed and the same property stays mortgaged;
- *Possibly* if the loan was extended more than three years ago (some courts allow consumers to defend foreclosures through TILA rescission even if a loan is more than three years old).

For most consumers, the most important exceptions will be for mortgages used to purchase the home and the possible exception for loans more than three years old. Otherwise, TILA rescission is usually applicable, and the key question is did the creditor make a mistake which allows the consumer to cancel the mortgage.

When Can a Homeowner Rescind a Mortgage?

There are three different situations where consumers can use TILA rescission to cancel a mortgage. The consumer can rescind for any reason within three days of first taking out a loan that uses the consumer's home as collateral. This obviously will have little relevance in most foreclosure situations, but is very useful when dealing with high pressure lenders and home improvement salesmen.

The consumer can also cancel a mortgage loan if the consumer never received proper notice that the consumer could rescind the loan. Creditors must deliver two copies of the notice of the right to rescind. The notice must be on a separate document that identifies the transaction, discloses that the creditor has a mortgage on specified property of the consumer, and that the consumer and joint owners have a right to rescind. The notice must also give directions on how to rescind, with a form for that purpose, with the appropriate addresses, the effects of rescission, and how long the consumer has to rescind.

Failure to include all this information or the consumer's failure to receive the notice are grounds for the consumer to cancel the loan. As long as the consumer never receives the correct notice, the consumer has a continuing right to cancel the loan (at least for the first three years).

The consumer may also cancel if the creditor otherwise interferes with a consumer's use of the rescission notice. For example, a home improvement contractor might begin work during the three day cancellation period and tell the consumer that, because the work has already started, the consumer cannot cancel.

The third basis for canceling the loan is if the creditor makes a mistake in its disclosure to the consumer of certain important terms of the loan. If the disclosure is improper, the consumer can rescind the loan until the consumer is given the correct disclosure. In practice, since lenders rarely correct mistakes, the consumer can cancel even as late as just before the foreclosure (at least for loans less than three years old).

For many loans, the key issue for the homeowner will be whether the creditor has made a mistake on the disclosure form sufficient to allow the consumer to cancel. For a loan with fixed payments (a closed end loan), an error in any of the following is grounds to cancel: the loan's annual percentage rate (the interest rate),[8] finance charge (the total of interest payments), the amount financed (the amount of the loan),[9] the total of payments, and the payment schedule. For open end lines of credit, the disclosures that have to be correct are the annual percentage rate, the method of determining the finance charge and the balance upon which a finance charge will be imposed, the amount or method for determining any membership or participation fees, and certain payment information.

Hints on Uncovering Truth in Lending Errors

Any decision to pursue Truth in Lending rescission should be approved by an attorney or other professional experienced with financial calculations and Truth in Lending issues. In fact, the analysis necessary to uncover creditor mistakes may be intimidating for many. Nevertheless, there are several steps even the most math phobic counselor can take to explore whether a consumer's home can be saved through Truth in Lending rescission.

Ask someone comfortable with financial calculations to check the numbers. Based on the payment schedule, is the total of payments accurate? Is the annual percentage rate calculation correct? Does the amount financed and finance charge add up to the total of payments? The National Consumer Law Center's *Truth in Lending* manual will explain what mathematical errors to look for and how to show that the creditor made a mistake.

As a general rule, there is more likely to be a creditor error in an extremely high interest rate loan, such as from a home improvement contractor, finance company, or mortgage company, than in a low interest bank loan. Another reason to concentrate on high interest loans is that consumers benefit the most from cancellation of those loans.

Another tip is to look to see what happened to the "amount financed" (that is the money borrowed). The contract itself may tell you where all the money went or you can ask the creditor for an "itemization of the amount financed." Be suspicious if most of the amount financed does not go to the borrower or for the borrower's benefit.

Look for broker's fees, points, insurance, assorted fees, and the like. When a contract is loaded with these charges, it may pay to ask a lawyer familiar with Truth in Lending to scrutinize the contract. NCLC's *Truth in Lending* gives a step by step analysis as to whether the existence of these charges in the amount financed will allow the consumer to rescind.

Especially note any insurance charges, such as "VSI" insurance or credit property insurance. Also suspect is any credit life or credit disability insurance that the consumer did not want.

Another pointer is to see if the consumer actually received the three-day rescission notice. If not, the loan is rescindable. Finally, for home improvement contracts, see if the work was begun before the three day period elapsed or whether the lender took other steps to defeat the consumer's ability to cancel.

The most important point to remember about counseling consumers about Truth in Lending rescission is that Truth in Lending is a technical statute. Only a professional familiar with the statute can make a final judgment whether the creditor's errors are sufficient to rescind the loan.

How to Rescind

If the consumer wants to cancel within the first three days or if the creditor trips up on its notice of rescission or its disclosure of the credit terms, the consumer merely sends a notice of rescission to the creditor. The notice to the creditor must be in writing, but can be a simple letter stating that the consumer wishes to cancel, dated and signed by the consumer.

A consumer can use the mail, a telegram, or other means of written communication. The consumer can use the rescission notice provided by the creditor, (which just says that the consumer rescinds), but need not do so.

If the consumer wants to say more in the notice, a lawyer should supervise the drafting of any rescission notice. If not done correctly, the extra verbiage could undo the effect of the notice.

The consumer does not have to give back to the creditor the money the consumer received from the loan at this stage. The rescission notice merely states that the consumer is canceling. The cancellation will require the creditor to do certain things and eventually the consumer will have some obligations. But the notice merely starts the process.

Sending the Rescission Notice Automatically Voids the Mortgage or Lien!

As long as the rescission was proper, the creditor no longer has the right to foreclose on the consumer's home. Within twenty calendar days after the creditor receives the notice of rescission, the creditor must cancel the mortgage and file that release on the public record. Although the consumer may later have to return to the creditor the amount borrowed (not including the various interest and other charges), the consumer need not do so at this point. The mortgage is still void and the home is out of danger.

Of course, a creditor receiving a rescission notice, but no loan proceeds, will not be happy. Typically, the creditor will ignore the notice and pursue the mortgage foreclosure. What this means is that the consumer will have to retain an attorney to fight for the right to rescind.

If the creditor has to go into court to obtain an order to foreclose on the home, the consumer's lawyer should raise the Truth in Lending rescission as a defense to the foreclosure. If the foreclosure does not involve a court process, the consumer's lawyer will have to go into court to stop the foreclosure on the basis that there is no mortgage.

In either case, as long as the rescission was proper, there should be no problem stopping the foreclosure because if there is no mortgage there can be no foreclosure. Fortunately, if the consumer prevails the creditor will have to pay for the consumer's attorney.

Does the Consumer Have to Return the Loan Proceeds?

There is much misunderstanding, even by lawyers, as to the consumer's financial responsibility after rescinding a loan. It is true that rescinding a loan does not mean that the consumer necessarily gets to keep all the loan proceeds. On the other hand, many people *mistakenly* believe that the consumer, when rescinding, must immediately tender the full amount of the loan. Obviously, this usually would be impossible.

The exact answer as to when and if a consumer must pay the loan back after rescission will depend on many factors. But the bottom line is that the consumer should not have to pay anything back before the mortgage is voided, meaning that the home will be safe from foreclosure.

Moreover, the amount the consumer pays back will often be

significantly less than the amount borrowed. The consumer will have to pay back the principal amount of the loan minus all interest and principal payments already made, and minus most fees, closing costs, points, insurance payments and other charges that the consumer paid when first taking out the loan.

For a home improvement contract, the consumer may just have to return the value of the work done, which is often much less than what the consumer paid for it. Furthermore, the lender's Truth in Lending violation will usually mean that the consumer can knock off at least another $1000 from the amount owed, and perhaps significantly more. The consumer should also raise whatever other legal claims are available, such as breach of warranty, deception, and the like as reasons why the amount owed should be further reduced.

Some courts even hold that if the lender did not cooperate with the rescission process or accept the consumer's offer to repay the loan, then the consumer owes the creditor *nothing* in return. Because the consumer was forced to take the creditor to court, the mortgage and loan are canceled, and the consumer does not have to return the loan proceeds.

If the consumer still has to return a sizeable amount to the creditor, the typical family in financial distress will not be able to do so. But there may not be much the creditor can do about that. The amount might become an unsecured debt to the creditor, depending on the situation. Unlike the canceled debt, the consumer's home would no longer be collateral for the loan. The debt goes into the same pile as credit card bills and hospital bills. The consumer's home is safe unless the creditor obtains a judgment lien on the home. If the consumer does decide to repay this amount, the creditor should be happy to accept installment payments.

Alternatively, the consumer can seek to refinance the amount owed (which should be much less than the original loan amount) with a different lender and at lower interest rates. This may well result in affordable payments for the homeowner.

Another approach a consumer's lawyer may want to consider is to send a rescission letter first and then file a chapter 13 bankruptcy, and let the bankruptcy court deal with the whole matter. The foreclosure will be stopped automatically by the bankruptcy filing and will not be able to go forward without the bankruptcy judge's permission.

Because the mortgage or lien has been canceled, the consumer will take the position with the bankruptcy judge that the creditor no longer has an interest in the consumer's home. As a result, the foreclosure is not just temporarily stopped by the bankruptcy, but permanently stopped by the TIL rescission. Because of the bankruptcy, the creditor will not even have a judgment lien for the amount of the loan that must be tendered back to the creditor.

The consumer's bankruptcy plan will propose that the consumer pay the creditor the same (often small) amount on the dollar as other unsecured creditors, and that this will be spread out over three to five years. Moreover, the consumer will not pay the creditor based on the full loan principal, but the much smaller amount arrived at through the various deductions described above. See Chapter 14 for more details on saving a home through bankruptcy.

Liens and Mortgages Resulting from a Home Improvement Scam

A widespread and vicious scam is to pressure a homeowner into a home improvement contract—aluminum siding, basement waterproofing, replacement windows, roofing, etc.—and then have the homeowner sign up for very onerous financing. The home improvement contractor never completes the work or the work is shoddy or wildly overpriced. A different entity, often a finance company or a mortgage company, will then collect on the loan and foreclose when the homeowner refuses to pay or gets behind.

In almost all such situations, the consumer can fight the foreclosure based on the misconduct of the home improvement contractor. That is, even though the contractor and creditor are not the same company, there is enough connection between the two so that the consumer can raise as a defense on the loan the misconduct of the contractor.

While this is a very effective defense to a foreclosure, it is best for the consumer to obtain legal representation to make sure that the defense is raised correctly. More detailed information (than what is presented below) about raising the contractor's misconduct as a defense to a foreclosure is found in another NCLC manual, *Unfair and Deceptive Acts and Practices,* Section 6.6 (3d ed. 1991 and Supplement).

When Is the Lender Liable for the Contractor's Misconduct?

Consumers can almost always defend a foreclosure based on the home improvement contractor's misconduct. In most cases the loan documents will say right in the documents themselves that any holder of the loan is subject to all claims and defenses that the consumer has against the seller. In other words, the very loan the creditor is trying to enforce will say that the consumer can raise the contractor's misconduct as a defense.

Where this provision is not in the loan documents, the consumer still can usually defend on the loan based on the contractor's misconduct. First, distinguish between loans where the contractor was the original lender and loans where the contractor arranged for a different party to be the original lender.

In the first situation, the contractor's name will be on the loan as the lender, and the contractor will then have sold the loan to another creditor. In that situation, the law allows the consumer to raise against the second lender all defenses that the consumer could have raised against the home improvement contractor.

The situation is not so clear-cut when another lender (not the contractor) was the original lender. About half the states have laws that say that the lender is responsible for what a closely related seller did. So if the home improvement contractor referred the lender to the consumer, the lender is responsible for what the contractor did. In the other half of the states, there are various arguments that a lawyer can make why the consumer can still raise what the contractor did as a defense to the foreclosure.

When the Seller's Misconduct Is Enough to Stop a Foreclosure

A contractor's leaving a scratch on a window is probably not enough to stop a foreclosure. It is important to understand what type of contractor misconduct can act as a defense to a foreclosure.

If the seller never did any work or if the consumer's claims against the seller exceed the amount of the loan, that should be sufficient to stop a foreclosure. Similarly, door-to-door sellers have to give the consumer a three day cancellation right, either under Truth in Lending or under door-to-door sales laws. If this right to cancel was never given, or if work began before the three day period expired, the consumer may be able to cancel the home improvement contract. A canceled sales contract would be a complete defense on the loan.

More troublesome is the situation where the consumer has claims against the seller, but the claims may not offset the whole loan. Then the loan may still be a binding obligation even though the consumer will not have to pay all of it.

If the consumer is in default, the lender may be able to foreclose even though the consumer does not have to pay the full note, only part of it. Nevertheless, some courts will delay the foreclosure until the amount owed is established and then the consumer need only keep current on the new loan payments.

A chapter 13 bankruptcy can also be very helpful in this situation. The bankruptcy filing automatically stops the foreclosure. The bankruptcy court then decides how much the consumer owes the lender, after deducting the consumers defenses against the contractor. The consumer, under the protection of the bankruptcy court, pays any back due amounts over a period of years. The bankruptcy court sets out a new schedule for payment of the remainder of the debt.

Unconscionable Loans

Some lenders engage in outrageous loan conduct, and victimized borrowers should defend the foreclosure based on the lender's misconduct. Especially suspect are high interest loans from home improvement contractors, finance companies, and mortgage companies. There are many types of lender practices that may provide the consumer with a defense on a foreclosure.

Conduct That May Void the Loan

If the consumer can show that the loan is not a binding obligation, then there is no obligation to pay and there can be no foreclosure. Look for the following, which may nullify any obligation to repay the loan:

- The lender misrepresenting the document the consumer was signing—"this is just an application."
- Misrepresentations as to the fundamental terms of the loan.
- An interest rate above the state maximum.
- The lender is not licensed to do business in the state.
- The loan contains illegal terms.
- The lender coerced the consumer into signing the loan.

Other Types of Lender Misconduct

Other lender conduct may not nullify the loan, but may influence a court in a foreclosure proceeding to give the consumer more time and lower the amount the consumer owes. Generally speaking, anything that the lender does that is unfair, unconscionable or deceptive should be actionable.

So should the lender's failure to disclose important information, such as the disadvantageous nature of a consumer loan. If the lender's misrepresentation was intentional and knowing, the lender may even be liable for punitive damages in addition to the consumer's actual injury from the misrepresentation.

Consumers may have defenses where the lender knew the consumer could not afford the loan payments, or arranged a variable rate loan knowing the consumer's income was fixed. Also consider challenging consolidation loans with higher monthly payments than the total of the loans being consolidated.

Lenders also should not refinance low or no interest debts, such as medical or utility bills or pre-1979 first mortgages, into a high interest loan. Continually flipping consumers into new refinanced loans may be unfair if prepayment or rebate penalties apply with each flip.

A loan may also violate one of a number of credit statutes, such as a state usury law or the federal Truth in Lending statute. Usually it takes a professional well versed in these areas to identify such violations.

Foreclosures Based on a Judgment Lien

Most foreclosures are based on the consumer's non-payment of a mortgage, a tax lien, or a workman's lien. Creditors without a mortgage or lien can also try to seize the consumer's home, but special protections apply for the homeowner. First of all, the creditor has to go to court to sue on the debt. (See Chapter Five for tips on defending such lawsuits to collect a debt.)

After a hearing, if the judge rules for the creditor, a lien, called a "judgment lien," is usually placed on the consumer's home. The creditor can later "execute" that judgment by asking a court to sell the home and use the proceeds to satisfy the amount of the judgment lien. Even then, state homestead laws usually prevent such a sale.

Homestead Laws Prevent Many Sales to Execute Judgment Liens

A state homestead law will generally exempt from seizure a certain amount of equity in a consumer's home. Homestead exemptions will not protect a consumer from foreclosure on a mortgage, only from an execution based on a judgment lien.

A few state homestead laws totally exempt from execution the consumer's home, no matter how much equity the debtor has in the home. More typically, the exemption will have a maximum dollar amount of equity it will protect.

It is important to understand that this maximum amount is not the value of the home, but the consumer's equity in the home. If a state has a $10,000 homestead exemption, a consumer can totally exempt from execution a $50,000 house as long as there is at least a $40,000 mortgage on the house. That is, the consumer has $10,000 equity and the homestead exemption protects that full amount from execution.

Asserting the homestead exemption is straightforward. Usually a creditor needs the permission of a judge to execute on a judgment lien, and the consumer will have an opportunity to be heard before the judge. The consumer with a homestead exemption need only go into court and assert that exemption to stop the sale.

The homestead exemption will not eliminate the judicial lien, but only stop an execution if the consumer goes to court and the consumer's equity is less than the homestead exemption. The creditor can come back next month or next year and try again, perhaps when the consumer's equity in the home has increased beyond the exemption. In the meantime, the consumer will not be able to sell the house or obtain another mortgage without first satisfying the judgment lien.

Bankruptcy Filing Can Eliminate a Judgment Lien

Consumers are thus better off if they can permanently eliminate a judgment lien. This will clear title to the home and stop the continual threat of an execution. The only way to do this is through a bankruptcy filing.

A bankruptcy can totally eliminate the judgment lien and discharge the underlying obligation, thus permanently resolving the problem. As long as the homestead exemption is sufficient at that point in time to protect the home from execution, the consumer can "avoid" the judgment lien. Make sure the bankruptcy court orders the creditor to record the avoidance (that is, the dissolution of the judgment lien) in the state or local recording office.

If the homestead exemption only protects a portion of the consumer's equity in the home, the bankruptcy will eliminate only part of the judgment lien. For example, consider a $9,000 judgment lien where a consumer has $17,000 in equity, but where the homestead exemption is only $15,000. Only $7000 of the lien can be avoided. There remains a $2000 lien on the nonexempt part of the house. However, bankruptcy gives the consumer various options to try to deal with this lien, including paying off only $2000 to that creditor, not the full $9000.

Another advantage of a bankruptcy filing in dealing with judgment liens is that a broader homestead exemption may apply. In some states consumers can use the federal bankruptcy exemptions, and these exemptions are broader than some state exemptions.

11

Utility Service

Keeping utility service is a critical issue for consumers in financial distress. While consumers cannot afford to pay their utility bills, they cannot afford to go without the service either.

Consumers find it particularly difficult to cut back on their use of basic utilities. In fact, heating, electrical, and water bills may increase as family members who lose their job spend more time at home. Significant savings in utilities normally require major investments in insulation, home repairs, and energy-efficient appliances—none of which financially distressed households can afford.

On the other hand, if utility billings cannot be reduced, the bills are likely to be unaffordable for a consumer with financial problems. Unpaid utility bills can mean termination of service, which has dire consequences, particularly in the winter months.

Loss of water, electricity, and gas service have obvious consequences. Moreover, if tenants allow their utilities to be disconnected in a rental unit, tenants sometimes risk being evicted from the rental unit as well. The loss of telephone service can impede reentry into the job market, prevent access to government benefits and other sources of assistance, and cause painful isolation.

This chapter offers practical advice concerning how to prevent a utility termination before it is threatened and how to contest a pending utility termination. The chapter also explains the rights of consumers to obtain utility service at a new residence, an important issue for consumers whose financial distress forces them to leave their prior residence.

Understanding Who Regulates a Utility

The first step in handling utility problems is to understand who regulates the various utilities in the community. There are three types of utilities, and consumer rights vary with each type.

Private Utilities Regulated by Public Utility Commissions

Most utilities are private companies, owned by their shareholders. These utilities are regulated by a state agency, usually called the public utility commission or the public service commission. Do not be confused by the term "public" in the commission's title. The term refers to the fact that the utilities which the commission regulates, even though private, must offer service to the general public. Typical privately owned public utilities are the local telephone, gas, and electric companies. Some water companies are also privately owned and publicly regulated.

State public utility or public service commissions closely regulate every aspect of privately owned utilities and offer consumers significant protections. Commissions typically have a legal division (or general counsel's office), a consumer complaint division, and separate divisions to handle problems with particular types of service, such as electric, gas, telephones. Individual customers can often obtain help with utility disputes directly from the staff of the state commission. Look for an "800" toll-free number to call for consumer assistance.

Most commissions issue formal regulations governing utility service to residential customers. Copies of the regulations can be obtained from the local public utility commission. Commissions also have informal rules and policies, particularly concerning termination of service. Counselors who are helping families with utility problems should become familiar with both the formal and the informal rules.

Municipal Utilities

A second type of utility is called a municipal utility. Municipal utilities are usually electric, gas, or water facilities owned by a city or town, and usually run by an elected board of commissioners. In most states, they are not regulated by the state public utility commission. The utility's own board of directors or staff sets out policies concerning utility terminations, deposits, and the like. Consumers will receive little or no assistance contacting the public utility commission concerning such municipal utilities, and must instead deal with their own municipality.

Rural Electric Cooperatives (REC's)

REC's are membership-controlled utilities, established under federal law. REC's are usually not subject to state utility commission regulation, so that consumers again will receive little assistance contacting a state utility commission about a REC. Consumers instead will have to look for protections largely from the REC itself, which will have its own policies specifying members' rights. The National Consumer Law Center has also drafted a detailed manual suggesting several innovative strategies to challenge REC actions, titled *The Regulation of Rural Electric Cooperatives* (1992).

Other Key Sources of Assistance

Families with utility problems should consult someone experienced in utility law or practice. Lawyers and paralegals at local legal services offices have suggestions on how to protect consumers. A local community action program (CAP) can be another good source for advice, especially if the CAP administers an energy assistance or weatherization program.

A variety of useful handbooks are also available, the most helpful of which will be state specific. For example, *The Right to Light (and Heat) Handbook,* published by the Massachusetts Poverty Law Center, is an excellent consumer guide to utility service in Massachusetts. Similar guides are available in several other states.

The National Consumer Law Center publishes a bi-monthly report, *NCLC Energy & Utility Update,* that keeps advocates up-to-date about the latest developments concerning utility terminations, the federal LIHEAP program, payment plans for low-income households, and other utility issues. NCLC has also written a series of papers and articles relating to utility terminations, deposit requirements, and payment plans. Those wanting to develop expertise in this area should contact the National Consumer Law Center for a listing of its publications relating to utility issues.

Ten Strategies for Becoming Current on Utility Bills

1. Level Payment Plans

A level payment plan may help customers who are current on their utility bills, but who may have trouble paying their utility bills at certain times of the year, especially in the winter, when heating bills are high. To avoid running up debts during these months, customers can establish level payment plans with utility companies. Many states require utilities to provide these plans.

In a level payment plan, a customer's projected yearly bill is divided into equal monthly installments; monthly bills reflect this amount rather than each month's actual use. For example, a customer whose total gas bill for a year is $1200, would pay $100 each month instead of $200 to $300 a month in the winter, and $30 to $40 a month in the summer. At some point during the year, the average bill and the actual usage are reconciled.

2. Budget Payment Plans

Households in financial distress can quickly get so far into the hole with their utility bills that a level payment plan is not enough. The household cannot catch up on back due payments and also keep up current utility bills. One solution is for the consumer and utility to negotiate a budget payment plan whereby the consumer makes a fixed monthly payment and the utility promises not to shut off service. State utility commissions often require utilities to offer such a plan.

The plan may be designed so that the customer pays current usage, but only slowly catches up on the amount in arrears. Sometimes the consumer can negotiate a plan whereby the monthly payments do not even completely cover current bills, and do nothing to catch up on arrears.

To make a successful payment plan, the customer, preferably with the help of a counselor, must develop a simple budget that the household can reasonably meet, and must be assertive with the utility company employee who negotiates the agreement. Payment plans need not be level. For example, seasonal workers may want to pay less toward arrears in the winter and more in the summer.

The utility company is likely to want a payment plan that requires larger payments than the customer can afford. Large payments are in the company's short-term interest, because they recover past debts more quickly. Too many customers, believing they have no choice, agree to these payments.

However, unrealistic plans harm both customers and utility companies in the long run. The customer is unable to make the payments, and may lose the service, and the company does not collect its debt. In some states, utilities are not required to enter into a second payment plan with consumers who have defaulted on a first payment plan.

If a company should refuse to agree to a reasonable payment plan, help can be obtained from the consumer division of the local utility commission. Some utilities also are more willing to negotiate with consumer counselors than with consumers themselves.

3. Federal Energy Assistance

The federal Low Income Home Energy Assistance Program (LIHEAP), administered by the states, helps low-income families pay their winter heating bills. Some states also use LIHEAP funds to assist families with summer cooling expenses. LIHEAP benefits can even go to some renters and public and subsidized housing tenants, with the energy assistance payments going directly to the landlord's fuel supplier and the amount being credited against the family's rent.

Guidelines for LIHEAP eligibility vary by state, but most states require that family income over the past three or twelve months be below 150 per cent of the federal poverty guidelines. (In some states, income must be even less.) The size of a family's LIHEAP benefits generally depends on the family's income and the number of household members, and may also depend on housing type, fuel type, fuel prices, weather conditions, or actual energy consumption.

To apply for LIHEAP benefits, a household should contact the local agency in its community administering the program. This is usually a nonprofit agency, such as the local community action program (CAP), or a state welfare office. Benefits are paid directly to the utility company or fuel vendor, and the family's utility or fuel obligation is reduced accordingly.

4. Utility Fuel Funds

Many utility companies participate in special funds, sometimes directly subsidized by other customer contributions, to give loans or grants to those who cannot pay their utility bills. To determine the availability of these funds, contact the utility company or the local agency that administers the LIHEAP program.

5. PIP, EAP and Other Special Payment Plans

A growing number of utilities and state utility commissions are experimenting with plans by which families pay only a certain percentage of their income in lieu of the amount called for by their normal utility bills. Typically, a low income family's consistent adherence to this lower payment schedule is rewarded by gradual forgiveness of amounts in arrears.

These plans are sometimes called Percentage of Income Plans (PIPs) or Energy Assurance Plans (EAP's), but each utility seems to have its own unique name for the program. The best way to determine if a utility has such a program is to contact that particular utility or the public utility commission.

6. Telephone Lifeline and Link Up

In most states, households in financial distress can obtain a significant discount on telephone monthly charges under the "Lifeline" program, and can get steep discounts on new service installation charges under the link-up program run by the local phone company. Contact the public utility commission or telephone company for details.

7. Discounted Rates

Some electric, gas and water utilities have special discounted rates for low-income, elderly and/or handicapped households. Ask the utility company or the state public utilities commission.

8. Energy Conservation Programs

Some states provide homeowners and tenants with funds to weatherize their homes, thereby reducing heating costs. Many utility companies provide low cost loans or outright grants for home weatherization, and some have sizeable programs targeting low-income customers, providing weatherization services directly to customers. More information on weatherization programs is usually available through local energy assistance offices.

Most agencies maintain waiting lists for weatherization assistance, and give priority to households that most need the help. Separate from such programs, families in many states can obtain assistance from utility companies to save on energy bills in other ways, such as replacing light bulbs with energy-efficient bulbs, insulating hot water tanks, and providing "low-flow" efficient faucets.

9. Other Government Programs

Other state agencies, such as welfare departments, also run small energy assistance programs. In particular, federally funded Emergency Assistance provides aid to households that within the past six months have had or currently have a member under age twenty-one. Emergency Assistance can be provided only once in a twelve month period. States may restrict the emergencies for which aid is provided, requiring, for example, that the emergency be unforeseen or out of the household's control. Utility shut-offs should be among the emergencies covered by general relief.

10. Charities and Other Private Sources

Many charities, churches, and other private organizations help people pay their utility bills. These groups provide assistance only when they have funds available, and sometimes only at certain times of the year. In some areas, community action programs or agencies maintain referral lists of such private energy assistance programs.

Fighting a Termination of Service

The threat of immediate termination of service, and the need to restore service that has already been terminated, are the two most urgent problems faced by utility customers. In many states, statutes and public utility commission regulations provide a variety of significant protections against utility terminations. These protections include:

1. Financial Hardship

Public utility commission regulations in some states prohibit or restrict termination of service for households whose income falls below certain levels, or whose income is restricted to certain government benefits, or who can otherwise demonstrate financial hardship.

2. Serious Illness

Similarly, state law or public utility commission regulations often restrict termination of service for households whose members face a serious illness, are threatened with serious illness, or depend upon life support systems. Often, the illness must be certified by a doctor. A family with very young children may also be able to use the health risk to the children as grounds to stop utility termination.

3. Winter Protection Rules

Many states and cities have enacted legislation that prevent termination of utility service during certain times of the year, chiefly termination of heat-related services during the heating months. To qualify for the protections, financial hardship may have to be demonstrated.

4. A Moratorium Linked to a Plant Closing

Sometimes a utility or utility commission will impose a temporary moratorium against termination of utility service for customers or neighborhoods particularly hard hit by a recent plant closing. If such a moratorium is not in effect, it may be possible for a counselor for families affected by a plant closing to negotiate one. A moratorium does not erase financial liability for utility service used before or during the moratorium period. The moratorium only prevents the utility company from terminating service if bills incurred during the moratorium period are not paid. When the moratorium period expires, the utility can then start the termination process for amounts not paid during the moratorium. Most utilities encourage their customers to pay what they can afford during a moratorium.

5. Elderly Households

Some states offer general protections for elderly customers, while others protect them against termination if a winter storm is forecast or if the temperature is expected to drop below a certain level. Similar protections may be offered to households with children.

6. Tenant Protections

It is all too common, particularly in difficult economic times, for a landlord to fail to pay for utility service, putting tenants at risk of losing the utility service. Tenants in this situation sometimes have special protections. In some states, tenants must receive a special shutoff notice if the landlord is delinquent. Then, tenants make utility payments directly to the utility, and deduct those payments from their rent.

7. Telephone Bills Unrelated to Local Service

Some states forbid telephone companies from shutting off local telephone service to force payment of overdue bills for long distance service, "enhanced" services (e.g. call waiting, call-forwarding), or calls to 900 numbers. Check with the state public utility commission for additional telephone service protections.

8. Advance Notice of Utility Termination

All customers are protected against surprise termination of service. Utility companies cannot legally terminate service without first providing customers with requests for payment and notices of termination. Many utilities must also provide customers with an opportunity to dispute or contest the reasons for the shutoff.

9. Contesting the Termination

A utility commission's consumer division responds to phone calls, letters, and visits by residential customers. Many of their complaints are resolved informally, by consultation between the consumer division and the utility. Consumer divisions also hold hearings on complaints that cannot be resolved informally. In large states, several hundred of these hearings are held each year.

Consumers generally have a legal right to a hearing whenever they have grounds to contest a utility termination. Simply request the utility commission to provide a hearing before service is terminated. While municipal utilities are generally not regulated by the utility commission, customers of municipal utilities have a constitutional right to a hearing before termination.

Consumers need not retain the services of a lawyer to represent them at the hearing. However, it may be helpful to have a paralegal or experienced utility counselor assist with the hearing. To support their claim, it is important for consumers to bring all relevant documentary evidence, such as a physician's affidavit or past bills. It may also be helpful to have witnesses such as friends and neighbors present.

10. Bankruptcy Protections

The mere filing of a bankruptcy petition automatically requires the utility to restore service or cease a threatened termination. The bankruptcy filing creates a twenty day period where the consumer is entitled to service from all applicable utilities. The utility can only terminate service after that twenty day period if the consumer fails to pay future bills, even if the consumer never pays another penny on past due arrears. The utility, though, can require that the consumer provide adequate assurance that future bills will be paid, such as the consumer providing a new deposit or a co-signer.

Obtaining Utility Service at a New Address

Often families in financial distress must move residences, and then may encounter difficulties in obtaining utility service at the new address, particularly if a family has had previous utility service terminated, or has changed its residence because of a foreclosure or eviction. All customers have the right to obtain utility service. However, companies may refuse service for certain legitimate reasons.

Failure to Pay Prior Bills as Grounds for Denying Service

Utility companies can usually require customers to pay outstanding bills from a previous address before connecting service at a new address. An unpaid bill is the most common justification for refusing new service.

In some states, however, utilities are required to provide service at a new address if the tenant pays off the old debt in installments, in an agreement called a reasonable payment plan. Under these plans, consumers agree to pay outstanding bills over a set period of time, usually several months.

While a utility can precondition service on a consumer paying the consumer's own outstanding bill to that utility, consumers can argue that they do not have to pay someone else's bill before obtaining service. For example, a consumer should not be obligated to pay the delinquent bills of the prior tenant of the consumer's new residence, or bills that the consumer's old landlord was obligated to pay. Similarly, a consumer may not have to pay an old bill where the old service was in someone else's name (an old roommate or former spouse), or where service is now in the consumer's name, and one of the consumer's current roommates has an old delinquent bill.

Where a consumer is obligated to pay an old bill before service will be connected, one option is to file for bankruptcy. The old obligation will be discharged in the bankruptcy. The utility will have to provide new service as long as the consumer provides a reasonable assurance, such as a deposit, of the ability to make *future* payment. The filing of the bankruptcy will immediately entitle the consumer to service at the new address.

Failure to Provide Information as Grounds for Denying Service

Sometimes companies refuse to hook up service because a customer has not provided requested forms of identification or proof of residence. The company will use this information for various legitimate reasons, including to make sure the new customer does not owe money for service received at a previous address. This is not an unreasonable request unless the company carries it to extremes, demanding such identification as a birth certificate, or information about all previous residences.

Deposits and Cosigners

Before establishing service, some utility companies ask households with poor payment histories to pay a deposit, usually equal to an average monthly bill. Utilities cannot unreasonably discriminate against certain types of customers in setting out deposit requirements. Customers who believe that a deposit is being requested unreasonably, or that a requested deposit is too large, should contact a utility counselor or a utility commission's consumer division.

If the issue is not reasonability, but affordability, some of the sources of assistance listed earlier in this chapter may be available to help pay deposits. When a customer has established a good payment record, or when a customer decides to terminate service, request the utility to return the deposit, with interest.

Instead of a deposit, some utilities accept the signature of a cosigner or guarantor, who agrees to be responsible for payments the customer fails to make. In some states, the cosigner is responsible for all payments the customer fails to make. In other states, the cosigner's responsibility is limited to several months' worth of unpaid bills.

Avoiding Utility Company Restrictions on New Service

Where a consumer cannot pay a former bill with the utility or afford the security deposit, there are still ways to obtain utility service. Look for a house or apartment that includes utilities in the rent. Another option is to establish utility service in the name of someone else with a good payment history. However, since that individual becomes responsible for any unpaid bills, this approach must be considered carefully, with full disclosure of the risks to the individual assuming responsibility for the bills.

12

Dealing with Landlords

Tenants who cannot pay their rent typically face one of three significant problems: 1) the tenants want to stay in the residence and the landlord tries to evict them; 2) the tenants want to move to a less expensive rental unit, but the landlord wants significant damages for the consumer to break the lease; or 3) the tenant experiences problems with the new, less expensive rental unit.

Eviction is clearly the most devastating, disruptive experience. It compounds financial hardships because of the extra costs and pressures it entails. Often the speed of the eviction process forces families into untenable situations, extra expenses, and acceptance of a far from satisfactory alternative living arrangement.

A forced relocation to another house or apartment means extraordinary moving costs on top of utility connection fees and deposits that must be paid in advance. Back rent must still be paid on the former residence. Tenants often have to pay their ex-landlord's legal fees. Frequently, the only other housing available is more expensive than that from which the family was evicted.

Sadly, families who are unable to pay their full rent on a regular, ongoing basis, almost inevitably have to move. Private landlords can nearly always remove tenants eventually for nonpayment of rent.

A counselor's role is to ensure that tenants have enough time to find alternative housing that is both affordable and adequate, with minimal disruption to the tenants' lives. The tenant should move when it is best for the tenant, not when a landlord's eviction action throws the family onto the street. The counselor should also help to minimize payments that must be made to the old landlord upon moving and must assure that conditions in the new apartment are adequate.

Getting Out of a Lease

When a consumer's finances appear stable, they often sign long-term leases at rents that seem affordable. In times of financial distress, those rents become unaffordable. The consumers must then seek less costly housing. It is often preferable for the consumer to move to a new residence when the consumer wants to, as opposed to waiting around for an eventual eviction.

Getting out of a lease is not always easy. Even after the tenant has left the apartment, the landlord may hold the tenant liable for future months rent. When a family decides to change apartments, some care should be given as to how to get out of the lease.

Read the Rental Agreement

The first step in terminating a lease is to read the rental agreement carefully. If the agreement provides that either party can terminate by giving advance notice, the tenants need only give that notice. Many tenants have month-to-month rental agreements with their landlords, and state landlord-tenant law will establish the rules for terminating rental agreements. Often the tenant must give 30 days notice before moving, unless something is seriously wrong with the rental property, making it unsafe to remain there.

Approach the Landlord

Even if the tenant is technically liable for lease payments for the rest of the one year lease term (or even longer), tenants need not be trapped by leases they cannot afford. They should first approach their landlord and suggest a rent reduction. Explain that the rent is no longer affordable. Negotiating may prove more cost-efficient for the landlord than going to the expense of trying to evict the tenant. Landlords who are unwilling to reduce the rent permanently may permit an early termination of the lease, so that they can rent to others who are better able to pay.

Explore Subleasing or Find Someone Else to Assume the Lease

Leases should also be examined for restrictions on subleasing or on lease assumption. Some leases prohibit subleasing entirely. Others allow it with the approval of the landlord. Still others are silent.

Whatever the wording of the lease, landlords are more willing to permit tenants to move out early if they have arranged for responsible tenants to sublet or assume the lease. Even when a lease permits subletting, landlords should be consulted before tenants begin looking for new occupants. Cooperation in the early stages makes it more likely that the transition to a sublease will be approved.

When a lease assumption is possible, it is preferable to subleasing. In an assumption, the new tenant becomes completely responsible to the landlord. In a sublease, if the new tenant fails to pay rent, the old tenant usually remains responsible.

Breaking the Lease

If it is impossible to negotiate a friendly early termination, assumption, or sublease, tenants should evaluate the financial cost of breaking the lease. Any party can break a contract, if they are willing to pay damages to the other party. Although the renter will be liable for breaking a lease, the alternative of eviction, or of continuing to bear an expensive lease, is usually worse.

When a lease is broken, the obligation to pay damages is limited. The other party, in this case the landlord, must mitigate the damages by trying promptly to find a new renter. A landlord who does not make a good faith effort to find a new tenant is not entitled to collect additional rent from the tenant who broke the lease.

Until a new tenant moves in, the departing renter's responsibility for damages should be limited to the rent and to costs associated with finding a new tenant. Landlords who take their cases to court are sometimes awarded court costs or attorney's fees.

The tenant, of course, will only have to pay damages if the landlord decides to actually sue the tenant. Otherwise the tenant's only loss is the security deposit, last month's rent, or similar deposit. The obligation for the difference between this deposit and the landlord's damages is an unsecured obligation (that is, the consumer's car or other property is not collateral for the debt).

Incurring such an obligation is normally preferable to continuing to throw limited resources at an unaffordable apartment. Consumers in financial trouble should instead concentrate their limited resources on purchasing food, clothing and other necessities. The family will also have to save something for the various security deposits that a new landlord and utilities will require.

Various factors also come into the decision whether to break a lease. If only a few months are left on the lease, and the landlord is unlikely to fill the apartment with new tenants quickly, there may be no financial advantage to breaking the lease. On the other hand, if a long time is left on the lease, particularly where the landlord will soon find new renters, breaking the lease may be the best course, particularly if the following steps are taken to minimize possible liability for damages:

- Tenants should give the landlord plenty of notice, preferably thirty to sixty days, so the landlord will have time to advertise for new tenants;
- Tenants should consider advertising the apartment themselves, either by word of mouth or through newspaper classifieds;
- The premises should be cleaned thoroughly, so there is minimal delay before the next tenant moves in. The tenant should request that the landlord go over the property after the cleaning to prevent any dispute over damages. Alternatively, tenants should take pictures of the sparkling clean apartment to use in the event of a dispute;

- Tenants should check newspaper ads to verify that the landlord is making an effort to find new renters; and
- Tenants should observe the rental unit from time to time for signs of new occupants.

The renter who breaks a lease will probably lose the security deposit. However, if a renter plans carefully, making sure that the landlord suffers no lost of rent and has no unplanned expenses, he or she may recover some of the deposit. State landlord-tenant laws provide specific procedures for recovering security deposits.

Responding to a Landlord's Eviction Attempts

The legal steps for an eviction vary from state to state, making it necessary for counselors to become familiar with local rules. Most eviction proceedings take place very quickly. Depending upon state law, the entire process may be completed in as little as two weeks.

The Notice to Quit Is a Last Warning

In most states, the first step in an eviction is a notice telling the tenants that they must move within a short time. This is called a notice to quit or a notice to vacate. If the tenants have not paid their rent, the notice usually instructs them either to pay rent or to get out.

Generally, an initial notice to the tenant gives a specified number of days in which to vacate the premises. In many states, the notice must give the tenant a right to stay in the apartment by paying the back rent within a specified number of days.

This notice is not legally binding on the tenant—the sheriff does *not* show up on the date mentioned in the notice and evict the tenant. Instead, if the landlord wants to put legal teeth behind the notice, it must first go to court. A notice to quit should be seen as a last warning, not an eviction notice.

Negotiating With the Landlord

Some renters cannot pay their rent because it is simply too high. Others find it difficult to pay the full rental amount at the time it is due. For tenants having trouble paying their monthly rent in a lump sum, some landlords agree to accept weekly or biweekly installments. Landlords sometimes also agree to lower the rent, at least temporarily.

Whether a landlord will agree to make any long-term adjustments depends upon the landlord's financial obligations, his or her temperament, and the nature of the relationship with the tenant. It is worth suggesting a rental adjustment to the landlord, coupled with an agreement to move in a designated number of months. This permits the tenant to make an orderly transition, without the threat of an immediate eviction. Landlords who know that their tenants will definitely move usually allow them some extra time. This approach is generally better for the landlord than going to the expense of legally evicting the tenant.

Temporary Rent Assistance

Tenants may also want to apply for various sources of rent assistance that can buy the tenant enough time to make an orderly move or to reverse the tenant's overall financial picture. The federally assisted Emergency Assistance program, operated in many states, is one such source. In most states, evictions and utility terminations are among the emergencies that are covered.

Normally, applications are processed by the same agency that administers Aid to Families with Dependent Children (AFDC). Emergency Assistance is available to households which have a member under the age of 21 and which have not received Emergency Assistance in the previous twelve months. Most states impose additional requirements, such as that the emergency be unforeseen and outside the household's control.

General Relief programs also can benefit tenants. Often operated by individual counties under their own guidelines, most of these programs provide housing payments to needy individuals, at least for short periods. Chapter One lists other possible public assistance programs. In addition, church groups and private charitable organizations are potential sources of financial assistance.

Tenants who do not yet receive any housing subsidy can also apply for various kinds of government housing assistance, including Section Eight rental assistance, state or nonprofit housing programs, and traditional public housing. Waiting lists are quite long. Urgent circumstances, such as homelessness, illness, or small children, sometimes move up applicants on waiting lists.

Priorities for assistance and the length of waiting lists vary from program to program and from community to community. Needy individuals should promptly apply for any assistance for which they may be eligible.

Promptly Responding to the Eviction Notice

If the tenants have not paid the full back rent nor moved out by the time specified in the notice, the landlord can file an eviction action in court. This is sometimes called a forcible entry and detainer action.

Eviction actions are usually scheduled for hearing very soon after filing. State laws require that the tenant be served with the complaint and with a summons to appear in court. State law specifies a minimum number of days, often as few as five, between when the tenant is served and when the hearing takes place. Therefore, the tenant should promptly take steps to respond, or consult a lawyer.

A tenant who disagrees with a landlord's complaint, or has any defenses, should immediately contact the court and file an answer or counterclaim. Many landlord-tenant cases are held in less-formal housing courts or justice courts, where tenants are able to file their own answers or counterclaims without using sophisticated legal terminology. Most courts charge a fee for making an appearance; even a person being sued is charged. Anyone unable to pay the appearance fee, including the tenants being evicted, can request that the fee be waived.

Attending the Eviction Hearing

Tenants who have been served with notice of an eviction proceeding should always be advised to attend the proceeding. Even tenants who believe they have no defenses, or who are able to move shortly, should attend an eviction hearing. They may discover legal defenses that could buy them additional time.

Even tenants with no defense can request that the judge give them additional time before moving. A judge is more likely to grant additional time if the tenant is able to offer at least partial rent, or if other housing has been arranged. For compelling circumstances, such as illness, or for families with many small children, judges are more inclined to grant delays.

Raising Defenses

Tenants with defenses to an eviction must raise those defenses at the eviction hearing. Defenses are lost if the tenant does not appear at the hearing. Most courts require that an evicting landlord must strictly comply with all the technical requirements of an eviction statute, including the content, timing, and service of all required notices and court documents. Any mistake in complying with these requirements may cause a landlord's petition to be dismissed, requiring the landlord to begin the procedure anew.

State laws sometimes allow other defenses or claims that might defeat or delay an eviction. Some states recognize a defense called peaceable possession. This defense states that if a landlord neglects to file an eviction action promptly after the expiration of a notice to quit time period, the landlord has consented to the continued occupancy. Peaceable possession may result in dismissal of the eviction.

In most states, courts will recognize defenses or counterclaims based upon the unit not being habitable or that an eviction action is in retaliation of the tenant exercising his or her legal rights. To determine if a residence is habitable, interview the tenant and see if the property has been cited for housing code violations.

To determine if an eviction is retaliatory, check to see if the tenants have filed complaints with the landlord or with housing authorities, or have participated in tenants' organizations. If substandard conditions are present, or if a retaliatory eviction has occurred, a lawyer should be consulted.

Another possible defense is that the landlord habitually accepted late or partial payments, and then suddenly, without warning, started eviction proceedings. The eviction may be improper where it was started even though the tenant was no later in payments than usual.

Yet another defense is based on the requirement in many states that landlords give tenants a notice to pay the specified amount of rent owed. If the notice misstates the rent owed, for example indicating that three months payments are delinquent when only two and a half months rent is delinquent, the notice is arguably defective.

Also determine whether a landlord is subject to federal housing laws, such as HUD or FmHA regulations. In addition to state laws, these laws provide procedural and substantive protections.

Responding to the Court Eviction Order

If the consumer loses a case and the court orders an eviction, one possibility is to appeal the case to a higher court. This may buy the tenant more time to move in a more orderly fashion. In fact, the threat of an appeal may allow the tenant to negotiate more time with the landlord. An appeal may require the tenant to pay certain filing fees or other charges. In addition, frivolous appeals should not be taken.

Tenants should always respond to an eviction order by taking the initiative themselves and make arrangements for the actual move. Often the arrangements should be made directly with the landlord or with a judge's approval. It is always a mistake to ignore an eviction order.

If a tenant has not vacated by the time specified in a court eviction order, a sheriff may move the tenant's belongings onto the sidewalk, or place them in storage. The tenant will have to pay moving and storage costs. In some states, landlords can place a lien on their tenants' furniture and other possessions to cover moving and storage charges. Until tenants pay those charges, tenants cannot get their property back.

Lockouts and Seizures of Personal Property

Seizures of personal property as part of a court-ordered eviction process may be legal. It is usually not permissible for a landlord to seize a tenant's personal property without court permission. In many states, it is against the law for landlords to hold tenant property, to change locks, or to shut off utilities.

Nevertheless, some states do give landlords the right, if a tenant is behind in paying rent, to seize all or part of a tenant's belongings on the rental premises without first obtaining court permission. The tenant may then be forced to go to court to seek return of the property, and may have to post a bond to obtain its release.

A tenant whose property has been seized should seek legal advice. State law may provide that some property is exempt from seizure. There may even be grounds for a constitutional challenge to the procedure itself.

The Landlord's Suit for Back Rent

Landlords sometimes decide to sue tenants who still owe rent after moving or being evicted. As part of that suit, a landlord may ask the tenant to pay for the landlord's attorney's fees. In addition, where a court finds a tenant's conduct to be intentionally wrongful, the court can order the tenant in some states to pay *three* times the landlord's damages or up to three months rent.

Some of the claims that tenants raise in evictions are also potential defenses or counterclaims in suits for back rent. Common defenses include: substandard housing conditions; illegal attempts by landlords to seize tenant property; a landlord's attempt to lock-out the tenant; or any withdrawal of heat or electricity. For any of these claims, tenants should consult a lawyer. A suit for back rent should never be ignored.

Dealing with Problems in a New Rental Unit

All rental property should meet a certain level of habitability. Yet renters who move into cheaper housing to save money sometimes encounter substandard housing conditions. To protect tenants against substandard conditions, the law in most states requires that a dwelling meet minimum standards of habitability. Rental property must meet local housing, health, fire, and building ordinances. Heat and hot water must be supplied. Appliances must be safe and in working order. When housing is inhabitable, tenants have several steps they should take.

Written Requests that the Landlord Make Repairs

When substandard conditions occur, the first step toward correcting them is to request the landlord to make the desired repairs. Because repair disputes tend to arise frequently, the request should be made in writing. Any oral request should be confirmed in writing, and a copy kept by the tenant.

Reporting Code Violations to a Housing Inspector

If a direct request to the landlord does not bring results, then city or county ordinances, available at a city hall or public library, should be checked for possible code violations. If violations have occurred, the renter can complain to the local housing inspector. Again, this complaint should be in writing and copies retained.

Resist Retaliatory Evictions

Some landlords react badly to tenants' complaints and to inspectors' reports, and attempt to evict complaining tenants. However, many state landlord-tenant laws protect tenants from retaliatory evictions, provided the tenants are current in their rent. It is important to get legal advice from a neighborhood legal services office, pro-bono attorney, or other source when a retaliatory eviction is threatened, so that the tenant can properly mount a legal defense consistent with the state statute.

Forcing the Landlord to Make Repairs

If tenant requests and inspector reports bring no results, the tenant may decide to go to court. Courts can order landlords to make repairs, to refund rent, or to pay tenants for damages. A landlord's refusal to make necessary repairs gives tenants the right to terminate their rental agreement and move elsewhere. Sometimes, if conditions become so bad that tenants are forced to move, a landlord may be required to reimburse tenants for the cost of temporary substitute housing.

Neither this strategy nor rent withholding (discussed below) should be considered without first consulting a lawyer, a tenant counselor, or a clerk at a local housing court. Legal education pamphlets published by bar associations, community legal services programs, and public interest groups explain the rules for withholding rent, for court injunctions, and for terminations. These laws should be carefully followed, or the tenants' rights may be affected.

Rent Withholding

Depending upon the circumstances, some state laws permit tenants to withhold rent to pay for repairs. Because some laws require that tenants follow specific steps before withholding rent, tenants should consult their state's laws before taking any such action.

13

Government Collection of Student Loans and Taxes

Special considerations apply when the government is collecting a debt, such as a student loan or back taxes. The government has enacted laws that give it special powers to collect such debts. At the same time, the government offers consumers special protections when they cannot afford to pay such debts. This chapter details the two most common forms of government collection—student loans and taxes. FHA, VA, and FmHA mortgages are detailed in Chapter Ten.

Student Loans

How Student Loans Work

There are several different types of government backed student loans, and collection practices are different for each type of loan. Some states have state run programs. NDSL or Perkins Loans go from the school directly to the student and are insured by the federal government. Federally insured student loans (FISL's) go from a lender to the student and are directly insured by the federal government.

A Stafford Loan, commonly called a guaranteed student loan or GSL, is the most common type of student loan, and the type of loan discussed in this chapter. Related to GSL's are Supplemental Loans for Students (SLS's) and PLUS loans. Generally, the rules concerning collection of GSL loans also apply to SLS and PLUS loans.

A student takes out a GSL from a lender (usually a bank) to attend a school. The lender often sells the loan to Sallie Mae (The Student Loan Marketing Association) or some other secondary market lender. The lender holding the loan may contract out with an independent company to service the loan.

Six months after the student leaves school, payments should start. If the student defaults, the lender, after some minimum collection efforts, turns the loan over to a state guaranty agency.

Students in default usually deal primarily with the guaranty agency. Sometimes the guaranty agency will turn the loan over to the federal government, and then the United States or a collection agency working for the United States will try to collect the loan.

Federal law gives guaranty agencies and the United States extraordinary remedies in trying to collect defaulted student loans. Federal law also provides students in default with certain important protections.

Grounds for Writing Off
the Student's Loan Obligation

There are seven major reasons why a student would no longer be obligated on a student loan:

1. The student has paid off the loan in full.
2. The student has died.
3. The student becomes permanently disabled.
4. The student has discharged the loan in bankruptcy. Unlike most debts, a bankruptcy can only discharge a student loan if the loan was first due more than seven years ago or repayment would cause the student "substantial hardship." Ask the bankruptcy court to make a substantial hardship determination at the time of the bankruptcy filing, but if a student failed to do so, the bankruptcy court or a state court can later make

that determination when collection attempts on the student loan are renewed.

5. The school closed, preventing the student from finishing the course. (This only applies to loans disbursed after January 1, 1986.)
6. The school falsely certified the student as eligible for the loan (as long as the loan was disbursed after January 1, 1986). What this means in practice is still unclear, but will be the subject of Department of Education regulations issued in 1993.
7. The school is closely related to the lender and the school defrauded the student. Exactly when students can defend a loan based on the school's fraud or similar misconduct is not yet established, but a number of courts have allowed students to raise this as grounds for not paying a loan. Expect guaranty agencies to resist this claim.

When Can a Student Delay Repayment?

There are two ways for a student to delay making student loan payments. One is to be granted a deferral and the other is to be granted forbearance. A deferment is preferable to forbearance because the student will not be liable for any interest that might accrue during the deferment period. But sometimes a student ineligible for a deferral can obtain forbearance.

The grounds for deferral are listed in federal regulations put out by the Department of Education. The most important grounds for deferral are that a student is in school, unemployed, on active duty in the U.S. Armed Forces, disabled or providing services for a disabled spouse, or a mother of pre-school children and the mother works at a low wage job.

Effective for loans taken out after July 1, 1993, many of the deferments dealing with financial hardship will be replaced by a general deferment for "economic hardship." What economic hardship means will be spelled out by forthcoming Department of Education regulations.

One problem with applying for deferments is that the student should do so immediately, and not wait until years of payments are delinquent. At a certain point (generally if delinquencies persist for more than twelve or eighteen months), deferrals are not available. It is much easier to win a deferral if the student first applies within a few months of becoming delinquent.

If a student cannot obtain a deferment, the lender or guaranty agency may forbear payments for a period of time. Although interest will be piling up, collection efforts should be stopped. The lender and guaranty agency have wide discretion in granting forbearance. In addition, federal law requires a one to three year forbearance where the amount owed exceeds twenty percent of gross income and the student requests forbearance. This is the case even if the student has been delinquent for years.

Responding to a Wage Garnishment

A new law passed in late 1991, but not yet implemented, allows guaranty agencies and the United States to garnish 10% of a student's wages without first obtaining a court order. But the law also includes several important protections.

The guaranty agency or the United States cannot garnish any wages without first providing the student with an opportunity for a hearing within the agency. Make sure the student requests a hearing, and raises any of the following as applicable:

1. That the student wants to enter into a new repayment agreement. The statute says that the agency *shall* enter into a new agreement instead of garnishing wages.
2. That the student was involuntarily separated from work within the last year. There can be no garnishment of such an individual until that individual has been *continuously* employed for twelve months.
3. That the student is not in default of a repayment agreement. Although there has been no official interpretation of the statute, it appears that the agency can only garnish wages after the student defaults in payments pursuant to a repayment plan, and is not merely delinquent on the original debt.
4. That the student does not owe the loan, based on one of the

seven grounds listed above under "Grounds for Writing Off the Student's Loan Obligation."

Ineligibility for New Loans and Grants

Students in default on a GSL technically are ineligible for new federal loans and grants. There are three ways that students can avoid this restriction. One is just to apply for the new loan or grant and see what happens. The Department of Education's computer is not yet fool-proof in matching applications for new loans and grants with lists of old defaulters.

Second, the student can work out a repayment schedule satisfactory to the guaranty agency. The student need not start *making* payments, only *arrange* a schedule of payments agreeable to the guaranty agency.

A new law passed in 1992 also allows students to reestablish their eligibility for new loans and grants by just making six consecutive monthly payments in an amount that is reasonable and affordable based on the student's total financial circumstances. This should allow a student in severe financial trouble to make six *very* small payments, and then be eligible for new loans and grants.

Preventing Tax Intercepts

The federal government has the authority to intercept an individual's tax refund check to pay a delinquent student loan. If this is threatened, there are several steps a family can take. Most simply, do not take too much withholding from paychecks, so that no tax refund is due.

The student also has a right to a hearing prior to any tax intercept, where the student could use as a defense for stopping the intercept one of the seven grounds listed above under "Grounds for Writing Off the Student's Loan Obligation." Finally, if husband and spouse file a joint return, the spouse who is not obligated on the student loan can file certain simple tax forms and receive a refund of part of the amount intercepted.

Dealing With Bad Credit Reports

Federal law requires lenders, guaranty agencies, and the Department of Education to report student loan defaults to credit reporting agencies. The default will be on a consumer's file for seven years. If the student does not owe the money because of a school closing or false certification of eligibility (see above), then the credit report should be corrected.

Do Defaulting Students Owe Large Collection Fees?

The United States sometimes seeks to collect large fees on top of the outstanding loan balance, often as high as 40%. Guaranty agencies sometimes try to do the same. Federal law clearly allows the United States to seek "reasonable" collection fees, but the law is unclear as to whether guaranty agencies can seek them as well. Students should also argue that 40% is not "reasonable." If a student decides to pay off a loan, negotiate with the United States about the amount owed and the payment schedule, and hold firm about not paying collection fees on top of the amount owed.

Can the United States Collect on Very Old Loans?

As a general rule, the United States can and does collect on old student loans, even those dating back to the 1970's. Collection of such old loans will be complicated because few people will retain records going back twenty years. There is at least an argument that collection of such stale loans is unfair, particularly where the government's delay in bringing suit prevents the student from raising valid defenses, such as that the school was a fraud.

Taxes

Families are obligated to pay a whole array of local, state and federal taxes. In general, governments have strong remedies to enforce payment of taxes. This section concentrates on back due federal income taxes.

File the Return on Time Even if the Tax Is Unpaid

One of the worst things consumers can do if they cannot afford to pay their taxes is not to file their tax return. Consumers who fail to file their tax returns may be (although usually are not) prosecuted for a misdemeanor crime. More likely, the government will assess a fine of 5.5% per month, up to a maximum of 50% of the amount owed, plus interest.

It is much smarter to file the return and just not pay the taxes due. Then the matter is simply an issue of debt collection and not criminal law. The penalty will only be .5% per month up to a maximum of 25%, plus interest. Obviously this fine is only a fraction of the larger penalty for not filing a return.

Negotiating With the IRS

When a consumer has filed a return, but cannot afford to pay the taxes due, one option is to ask the IRS to put the tax obligation on the consumer's credit card (if the consumer still has a card that works). The IRS has a new program that encourages doing just that.

Credit card interest will generally be less than IRS interest and penalties. More importantly, an unsecured credit card debt is not nearly as serious a debt as an obligation to the IRS that could quickly turn into a tax lien or seizure.

Another option is to ask the IRS to let the consumer pay the amount due in installments over time. The IRS will generally allow this. Sometimes a consumer can even get the IRS to drop penalties and interest altogether.

Be sure the consumer documents the severe financial hardship the family is undergoing, and why this was caused by factors outside the family's control. Also make sure that any installment payment plan or reduction in the amount owed is in writing.

Steps the IRS Can Take to Force Payment

If a consumer does not set up a payment plan, the IRS will force payment. If the consumer has not filed a return admitting a certain amount as due, the IRS will send a series of about four letters asking for payment of a certain amount. The last letter gives the taxpayer 90 days to file a petition with the tax court disputing the amount owed.

If the consumer still does not respond, or if the consumer has already filed a return admitting the amount owed, the IRS will send an assessment notice saying that it is placing a tax lien on all the taxpayer's property. This will give the IRS the authority to seize any of the consumer's property, with the exception of certain exempt types of income and property. In practice the IRS will wait about thirty days and then go after bank accounts, paychecks, homes and cars.

Exempt from IRS seizure is about $100 a week in wages (depending on the taxpayer's personal exemption and standard deduction), unemployment and workers' compensation, public assistance, job training benefits, income needed to pay court-ordered child support, and certain federal retirement and disability benefits. The only exempt property will be certain amounts of clothing, furniture, personal effects and job-related tools. A state homestead exemption will *not* protect the taxpayer's home from an IRS tax lien or seizure.

Unless most of a family's assets and all its income are exempt from seizure, it makes sense to negotiate with the IRS a payment schedule to avoid seizure of personal property and income. Make sure any agreement is in writing.

Bankruptcy

Bankruptcy is not as effective a remedy when dealing with taxes as with other debts. The only taxes (including interest and penalties) that can be discharged in a chapter 7 straight bankruptcy are taxes over three years delinquent where the tax return for the year in question was properly filed. Any tax liens on the taxpayer's property will remain in force even after the bankruptcy. In a chapter 13 reorganization, the taxes owed can be paid out over the life of the plan, that is paid in installments over a three to five year period.

14

Bankruptcy

Overview

The right to file bankruptcy is an important tool which society provides for those with significant debt problems. It is often stated that bankruptcy should be considered as a "last resort" for financially troubled consumers. This advice is a gross oversimplification of the factors which should inform a decision to file bankruptcy. Bankruptcy should be neither the first option nor the last resort; each case must be examined on its own merits.

Although bankruptcy is not a magical cure, it is an important alternative for a range of financial problems. Bankruptcy may provide immediate protection, particularly for individuals facing foreclosure or repossession of property. (It should be noted that delay in those circumstances *may* undermine a consumer's ability to protect property for the long term.) Even those who are not in short term danger of repossession or foreclosure may often decide upon bankruptcy simply for the relief of having debts lifted in order to get a fresh financial start.

Many consumers who file bankruptcy petitions have researched and considered the step carefully. Others lack basic knowledge of what bankruptcy can accomplish, or are hampered by misinformation, fearing that bankruptcy might cause them to lose all of their property, or that it might prohibit them from ever acquiring property or credit again. Because such misinformation is common, and because bankruptcy is a complex and serious undertaking, those counseling families in financial distress must have a thorough knowledge of how bankruptcy works, and what it can and cannot do.

This chapter is not a complete bankruptcy guide. As will be discussed later in the chapter, consumers who are interested in filing bankruptcy should be encouraged to seek the services of an attorney who specializes in bankruptcy. The materials here are designed to explain generally how bankruptcy works so that those counseling families in financial distress can begin to demystify the bankruptcy process, recognize situations where bankruptcy might be the right choice, and help consumers take the necessary first steps when a bankruptcy is called for. The chapter explains:

- how a bankruptcy filing can help a consumer in financial distress and the two types of bankruptcy filings most commonly utilized by consumer debtors;
- the advantages and possible disadvantages of a bankruptcy filing and when bankruptcy may be the wrong solution;
- choosing which type of bankruptcy to file, when to file, and whether both spouses should file;
- how to hire a bankruptcy attorney, how to prepare the consumer to meet with the bankruptcy attorney, and whether to use a for-profit debt counselor or document preparation service; and
- the basic steps of a chapter 7 straight bankruptcy and a chapter 13 reorganization.

Those seeking more detailed and technical information should consult the National Consumer Law Center's *Consumer Bankruptcy Law and Practice* (4th ed. 1992).

That volume is easily the best available manual on assisting an individual to file for bankruptcy. Designed for attorneys, paralegals, and other sophisticated advocates, the manual contains hundreds of model forms and reproducible blank forms for filing a bankruptcy. The manual also reprints the bankruptcy statute and the bankruptcy rules. Another useful book, published by Nolo Press, is *How to File for Bankruptcy* (3rd ed. 1991). That volume is designed to explain bankruptcy to the general public.

What Bankruptcy Can Do

Bankruptcy may make it possible for financially distressed families to:

- Discharge liability for most or all of their debts and get a fresh start. When the debt is discharged, the debtor has no further legal obligation to pay the debt.
- Stop foreclosure on their house or mobile home and allow families an opportunity to catch up on missed payments. In certain limited situations, families can even recover their house or mobile home after it has been sold at foreclosure.
- Prevent repossession of a car or other property, or force the creditor to return property even after it has been repossessed.
- Stop wage garnishment, debt collection harassment, and the like, and give families some breathing room.
- Restore or prevent termination of utility service.
- Lower the monthly payments on debts, including secured debts such as car loans.
- Allow debtors an opportunity to challenge the claims of certain creditors who have committed fraud or who are otherwise seeking to collect more than they are legally entitled to.

Bankruptcy, however, cannot cure every financial problem, nor is it an appropriate step for every individual. In bankruptcy, it is usually not possible to:

- Eliminate certain rights of "secured" creditors. A "secured" creditor has taken the consumer's property as collateral for the loan. Common examples are car loans and home mortgages. Although a debtor can force secured creditors to take payments over time in the bankruptcy process, a debtor generally cannot keep the collateral unless the debtor continues to pay the debt.
- Discharge types of debts singled out by the federal bankruptcy statute for special treatment, such as child support, alimony, some student loans, court restitution orders, criminal fines, and some taxes.
- Protect all cosigners on their debts. When a relative or friend has co-signed a loan, and the consumer discharges the loan in bank-

ruptcy, the cosigner may still have an obligation to repay all or part of the loan.
• Discharge debts that are incurred after bankruptcy has been filed.

A decision to file for bankruptcy should be made only after determining that bankruptcy is, in fact, the best vehicle for dealing with the problems at hand.

The Two Types of Bankruptcy

The bankruptcy law generally provides for two types of cases. These are generically known as liquidation and reorganization.

Liquidation (Under Chapter 7)

A liquidation case usually takes place under chapter 7 of the bankruptcy law. In a liquidation case, the debtor's assets are examined by a court appointed trustee to determine if anything is available to be sold for the benefit of creditors. Certain property cannot, under the law, be sold, and instead is kept by the debtor despite the bankruptcy. This property is called "exempt".

The trustee may sell only property which is either not exempt at all or which has value which exceeds the exemption limits. In most consumer bankruptcies, virtually all, if not all, of a debtor's assets are exempt; therefore, little or none of the consumer's property is taken away and sold.

Exemption laws vary from state to state and may be fairly complicated.[1] It is impossible to assist a consumer in making a final choice about bankruptcy without understanding the exemption laws for your particular state.

The best way to do this is to ask for a listing from a neighborhood legal services office, a private attorney, or pro bono bar organization. Another approach is to see if there is an accurate and up-to-date listing in a legal publication for your state. See Chapter Five for more detail on state exemption laws.

It is also important to understand that in deciding what can be sold, the trustee will only look to the debtor's *equity* in property. If a debtor owes money on a mortgage or other lien on a home, that mortgage or lien reduces the debtor's equity in the home. The trustee will not sell property if the debtor's equity in the property is fully exempt.

For example, if the applicable state exemption for the consumer's home is $50,000, the home's value is $150,000, and the consumer has a $100,000 mortgage, all of the consumer's $50,000 equity in the home is exempt. The trustee will *not* sell the home in a chapter 7 liquidation.

At the end of a liquidation case, a debtor can obtain a discharge of most unsecured debts. This means that the debtor no longer has a legal obligation to pay those debts. Generally the discharge will include credit card debts, medical bills, utility arrearages, and the like. Other unsecured debts, such as student loans, tax debts and public benefits overpayments, may also be dischargeable, depending on the circumstances.

It should be understood at the outset, however, that liquidation cases rarely can help with secured debts, because the liens of secured creditors generally pass through a liquidation case unaffected. That is, bankruptcy discharges most personal debts, but does not eliminate the right of a secured creditor to recover its collateral if a debt is not repaid.

This means that a liquidation case will not affect, for example, the rights of a mortgage holder or car loan creditor to foreclose or repossess collateral. Although some delay in the foreclosure or repossession may result from the liquidation case, the bankruptcy will not provide long term relief.

Reorganization (Under Chapter 13)

Reorganization cases work very differently from liquidations. In a reorganization case, the debtor puts forward a plan, according to the rules set out in the bankruptcy law, to repay creditors over time, usually from future income. Most consumer reorganizations take place under chapter 13 of the bankruptcy law. However, some debtors with large amounts of debt may be required to (or prefer) to proceed under chapter 11. Family farmers can also proceed under chapter 12.

In certain circumstances, there is an advantage to the debtor of filing a reorganization case rather than a liquidation. Most importantly, in a reorganization case, the debtor is allowed to get caught up on mortgages or car loans over a period of time.

For example, most credit agreements allow a creditor to call the whole loan in where the consumer misses a payment of two. Although a creditor may let the consumer work out an agreement to catch up over time on back payments, the creditor usually is not legally required to do so.

Where a creditor is uncooperative, a bankruptcy reorganization may be the only way to use the law to force the creditor to accept such back payments over time. Reorganization cases allow debtors to put forward plans to pay off or cure the default rather than surrender property.

Additionally, reorganizations allow a debtor to keep both exempt property (which would be protected in a liquidation) and non-exempt property (which would be sold in a liquidation). The debtor can keep the non-exempt property by paying its value to creditors under a court approved plan, usually over a period from three to five years.

The heart of any reorganization is the debtor's bankruptcy plan. This is a simple document outlining to the bankruptcy court how the consumer proposes to make payments to various creditors while the plan is in effect. The law places certain limits on what a debtor may do under a plan.

Nevertheless, there are substantial opportunities for reorganizing the consumer's debt payments and protecting the consumer's property from creditors, including mortgage and other lien holders, as long as appropriate payments are made. The reorganization option is thus particularly useful for someone who has fallen behind on a mortgage or car loan due to temporary financial hardship and is now able to begin making payments again.

A chapter 13 bankruptcy plan generally requires monthly payments to the bankruptcy trustee over a period of three years. However, plans can go for as long as five years with court approval. In most jurisdictions, bankruptcy courts will routinely approve requests by the debtor to have the monthly payments to the trustee paid automatically by wage deduction.

Once the debtor's payments are completed under the plan, the debtor is entitled to a discharge just as in a chapter 7 bankruptcy. The discharge available is slightly broader than a discharge under chapter 7 and may cover more debts. If the debtor has caught up on any mortgage or other secured loan, the loan will be reinstated and the debtor must be treated as if the debtor never fell behind.

It is important for consumers to be aware that reorganization cases can often be quite complicated. Working out the most advantageous possible bankruptcy plan is frequently difficult. Where bankruptcy appears to be an option, encourage consumers facing foreclosure on a home or repossession of a car, to consult with an attorney specializing in bankruptcy as quickly as possible. Delay may result in the foreclosure or repossession proceeding to the point where bankruptcy can no longer help.

The Purposes of Bankruptcy

Bankruptcy achieves two purposes: it establishes equity among creditors and it provides debtors with a fresh start. Equity among creditors is achieved by fair distribution of the consumer's nonexempt property according to established rules guaranteeing identical treatment to similarly situated creditors.

Bankruptcy's fresh start allows individuals who have become mired in debt to free themselves and engage in newly productive lives, unimpaired by past financial problems. Bankruptcy avoids the kind of permanent discouragement that can prevent people from ever reestablishing themselves as hard-working members of society. In the wording of the United States Supreme Court, bankruptcy is meant to provide "a new opportunity in life, unhampered by the pressure and discouragement of pre-existing debt."

Advantages of Bankruptcy

The Automatic Stay of Foreclosures, Evictions, Repossession, Utility Shutoffs, and Other Adverse Actions

One of the most advantageous and straightforward aspects of a bankruptcy filing is that the submission to the bankruptcy court of the consumer's bankruptcy petition automatically, without any further legal proceedings, stops most creditor actions against the consumer and the consumer's property.

The consumer's mere request for bankruptcy protection automatically forces an abrupt halt to repossessions, garnishments, attachments, utility shut-offs, foreclosures, evictions and debt collection harassment. Beyond all this, the automatic stay offers debtors a breathing spell, providing them with time to sort things out and to solve problems.

Creditors cannot take any further action against the consumer or the consumer's property until the creditors obtain permission from the bankruptcy court. Sometimes creditors will seek such permission immediately, and sometimes they will never seek permission.

Note that even when they do, such permission is rarely, if ever, granted to unsecured creditors. While it is common for secured creditors to get relief from the stay in a chapter 7 case to continue foreclosure or repossession (because the lien will pass through the case unaffected), secured creditors rarely get relief in a chapter 13 case as long as plan payments are being made.

While the stay is automatic, creditors may not hear about the bankruptcy filing for some time. If it is important to the consumer to stop a creditor's actions, the consumer should inform the creditor of the bankruptcy filing as soon as it is filed. If the creditor acts against the consumer despite the automatic stay, the creditor can be held in contempt of court and may have to pay the consumer money damages and attorney's fees. The action taken in violation of the stay is then also reversible.

Discharge of Most Debts

The principal goal of most bankruptcies is quite simple. It is to achieve a total discharge, absolving the debtor from most unsecured debts. This discharge is the traditional goal of most individuals who file bankruptcy. Bankruptcy is a relatively easy way, though not the only way, to permanently end creditor harassment, and the hardship, anxiety and stress associated with debt overload. (See Chapter Four for other strategies to stop debt harassment).

As discussed above, the liens of secured debts are not terminated by bankruptcy unless those debts are paid off. However, if the debtor gets a discharge, all that survives the bankruptcy is the creditor's right to foreclose or seize the property. A secured creditor has no right following bankruptcy to seek a deficiency judgment or to harass the debtor to pay.

Protection Against Wage Garnishment and Enforcement of Judgment Liens

Bankruptcy prevents any garnishment of wages or other income after a petition is filed. Thus bankruptcy can restore a debtor to full use of income and may also be a useful strategy for consumers whose employers' frown on wage garnishments. Even recoupment by federal and state agencies of Social Security or of other public benefit overpayments can be prevented by a timely bankruptcy petition, so long as the receipt of the overpayment was not deliberate.

Bankruptcy is also an effective tool to deal with money judgments against the debtor. If the judgment does not create a lien against any property under state law, that creditor is unsecured and the debt may be discharged as if no judgment ever existed. Even if the judgment does create a lien, the debtor may request the bankruptcy court that the lien be lifted if it affects otherwise exempt property. As described in Chapter Five, state exemption laws specify how much of a consumer's property is exempt from seizure by unsecured creditors even after they obtain a court judgment. Consumers can utilize these state exemption laws to also protect the same property in a bankruptcy proceeding.

Added Flexibility in Dealing with Secured Creditors

Bankruptcy can also be advantageous in dealing with secured creditors, that is lenders who have collateral for their loans. Consumers in bankruptcy will generally have to make payments on their mortgages, car loan, and other secured debts if they want to keep the home, car, or other collateral. But bankruptcy does provide added flexibility in dealing with these secured creditors.

First of all, bankruptcy can totally eliminate certain secured creditors' right to seize collateral by "avoiding" the creditor's lien. One narrow but still important situation where liens can be avoided involves liens on household goods taken where the loan is not used to purchase those goods. To the extent that household goods are exempt—and most families' household goods will be completely exempt—such a creditor's ability to seize that collateral is forever eliminated by a bankruptcy filing.

Bankruptcy also allows consumers to keep collateral by redeeming it, that is essentially paying the creditor not the amount of the loan, but the value of the collateral. For example, if a car is only worth $1000, even though the car loan is $3000, the consumer could keep the car by marshalling together various exempt assets and paying the creditor only the $1000.

The greatest flexibility in dealing with secured creditors is available when a chapter 13 bankruptcy is filed. For example, if the consumer is 6 months delinquent on a mortgage, filing the bankruptcy will stop the threatened foreclosure and allow the consumer to gradually catch up on the back payments, perhaps over as long a period as several years. A chapter 13 filing may also allow the consumer to restructure a loan schedule to stretch out or lower monthly payments.

Utility Terminations

A bankruptcy filing will not only stop a threatened utility termination, but will automatically and immediately restore terminated utility service, at least for twenty days. To keep utility service beyond twenty days after the bankruptcy filing, the consumer need only provide a security deposit or other security for future payments and keep current on the new utility charges. To keep service, the consumer need not pay bills incurred *before* the bankruptcy was filed.

Driver Licenses

A driver's license can be critical to a consumer in keeping a job or in finding a new job. In some states a driver's license is subject to revocation because the consumer has not paid off a court judgment stemming from an automobile accident. In that situation, bankruptcy is sometimes the only possible way for a debtor to keep or regain the license. Normally, bankruptcy can be used to discharge the obligation to pay the court judgment, and the consumer then has a right to regain or retain the driver's license.

Possible Disadvantages of Bankruptcy

Loss of Property

Consumers often believe that a bankruptcy filing will result in the loss of all or most of their possessions. This is not true. All consumers will get to keep some of their possessions and whether they get to keep *all* their possessions will depend for any particular family on a number of factors. These factors include whether the consumer files a chapter 7 or 13 bankruptcy, whether certain debts are secured or unsecured, and how much of a family's property is exempt.

For most consumer debtors, the practical answer is that the family will keep all or virtually all their property in a bankruptcy, except property which is subject to a lien which the consumer cannot afford to pay. In fact, bankruptcy should be seen for most consumers as a method of preventing loss of property rather than causing it.

As discussed above, in a chapter 7 bankruptcy, all of a consumer's equity in his or her property is divided into two groups—exempt and nonexempt. State law or in some cases the federal bankruptcy statute will specify which property is exempt. Usually at least a certain amount of equity in the consumer's home, car, household goods and tools will be exempt. In some cases, even if some property is not fully exempt, the trustee will not choose to sell it because the amount received from the sale would not justify the costs of sale.

In valuing property for the purposes of bankruptcy, the trustee will not consider the property's original cost, but rather what the property could be sold for at the time of filing. It is often useful to imagine a hypothetical yard sale to try to estimate what particular items would bring. Remember also that state exemptions vary widely from state to state. It is important to check what exemptions are available in the jurisdiction in which the debtor lives.

If a consumer has significant *non*exempt assets, a chapter 13 bankruptcy often presents a viable alternative through which debtors can retain all of their possessions. In a chapter 13 bankruptcy, consumers keep all their possessions and instead make payments over time on their debts from future income pursuant to a plan approved by the bankruptcy court.

The Effect of Bankruptcy on a Debtor's Credit Record

By federal law a bankruptcy can remain part of a debtor's credit history for ten years. The effect of a bankruptcy on the consumer's credit record is unpredictable, but of understandable concern.

For many debtors, this concern can be easily alleviated. If long term credit problems already appear on an individual's credit record, a bankruptcy is unlikely to make that individual's credit worse. In fact there is some evidence that the bankruptcy will make it *easier* to obtain future credit, because new creditors will see that old obligations have been discharged and that they will therefore be first in line. Moreover once a discharge is received, many new creditors recognize that the debtor cannot then receive a new chapter 7 discharge for the next six years.

For other debtors who do not yet have problem credit, the question is more difficult. Research on the effects of bankruptcy on credit and reputation is inconclusive. It seems fair to say that most credit decisions depend upon the bias of individual creditors and that most creditors look more to a potential customer's income and income stability than to anything else. Some creditors demand collateral as security, ask for a cosigner, or want to know why bankruptcy was filed. Other creditors, such as local retailers, do not check credit reports or inquire about bankruptcy on credit applications.

Debtors should remember that they always have the option after the bankruptcy of voluntarily paying certain creditors, such a preferred doctors or hospitals, with whom they wish to maintain lines of credit. The consumer can just make voluntary payments without formally reaffirming the obligation.

The Effect of Bankruptcy on a Debtor's Reputation in the Community

Creditors might continue to extend credit despite a prior bankruptcy, but what about friends, neighbors, and coworkers? What happens to an individual's reputation? Most people find their reputations suffer no perceptible harm. However, in a small town, where debts are owed to local people, the stigma of bankruptcy cannot be entirely discounted. Embarrassment and damage to reputation must be personally evaluated and weighed against bankruptcy's potential advantages. Consumers may want to pay selected debts, just as they may want to pay favored creditors. Voluntary payment of discharged debts is specifically authorized by the Bankruptcy Code.

Feelings of Moral Obligation

Occasionally, a debtor's feelings of moral obligation mitigate against bankruptcy. It is not easy for conscientious individuals suddenly to discard values that have guided them since childhood. For them, the stigma against bankruptcy remains strong. They may think of bankruptcy as a sort of public declaration that they do not intend to pay their debts; this kind of declaration is difficult to accept, especially if they have insisted to creditors that they sincerely intend to make good on their obligations.

Consumers who object to bankruptcy on moral grounds should be reminded to consider certain factors. Bankruptcy is their right under the United States Constitution, intended to provide a fresh start for individuals in precisely their situation. Big corporations like W. T. Grant, TWA, Pan Am, A.H. Robbins, and Penn Central, and famous people like Jerry Lewis, John Connelly, Mickey Rooney, Craig Morton, and Les Crane have not hesitated to utilize this right.

Creditors know that a small portion of the people to whom they extend credit will be forced to go bankrupt; therefore they protect themselves by charging enough interest and overhead to cover these losses. The so-called stigma of bankruptcy is largely the creation of creditors who have every reason to make it appear unattractive. Bankruptcies are not generally announced in newspapers, although they are a matter of public record.

Some debtors find comfort in the fact that the Bible mentions the need for periodic release from debts. The book of Deuteronomy states:

> At the end of every seven years thou shalt make a release. And this is the manner of the release: every creditor shall release that which he has lent unto his neighbor and his brother; because the Lord's release hath been proclaimed. (Deut. 15:1-2.)

Most importantly, whatever its negative connotations, bankruptcy should be considered in relation to the hardships it can avoid. Debtors who remain reluctant to file for bankruptcy must picture for themselves the results of doing nothing. During hard times, bankruptcy may be the only way to provide a family with food, clothing, and shelter. Debtors often decide that their moral obligation to provide for their children and loved ones outweighs any obligation to pay creditors.

Debtors who continue to object to bankruptcy on moral grounds will want to explore alternatives. Are there other ways to defend against the largest and most troublesome of their debts? What would be the consequences of waiting before filing a bankruptcy petition?

If bankruptcy is indeed the last resort, they should be reminded that filing for bankruptcy does not prevent them from voluntarily paying their debts at a later time if they wish. This fact should reassure those who cannot come to terms with the idea of turning their backs on their creditors forever.

Potential Discrimination After Bankruptcy

The federal bankruptcy law offers consumers filing bankruptcy some protection against later discrimination by creditors and others. Government agencies, such as housing authorities, cannot deny benefits because of previously discharged debts.

Similarly, utilities cannot deny service because of a bankruptcy, although a utility company can require a deposit to cover charges incurred after the bankruptcy is filed. No private employer can discriminate against employees or terminate employment on the basis of bankruptcy.

Consumers are fully protected by law from any such discrimination and can enforce their rights in court, if necessary. However, the bankruptcy law does not prevent discrimination by others, including private creditors deciding whether to grant new loans, and does not prevent discrimination based upon future financial responsibility or capability.

Cost of Filing a Bankruptcy Petition

There may be costs associated with hiring an attorney to handle the bankruptcy. Hiring an attorney and the advisability of alternatives are discussed later in this chapter. In addition to an attorney's fee, a bankruptcy petition requires a $120 filing fee. This filing fee cannot be waived, but can be paid in installments. In a chapter 13 reorganization case, the trustee is usually entitled to a commission of about ten percent of the payments made through the plan. These payments must be included in with the amount that the debtor pays the trustee under a plan.

In addition, utility companies may be entitled to collect a security deposit following a bankruptcy (usually equal to approximately twice the average monthly bill) just as if the debtor were a new customer. Some, but not all utility companies take advantage of this right. In most localities, the debtor can request up to 60 days to make this payment.

When Bankruptcy May Be the Wrong Solution

For some individuals bankruptcy is simply the wrong solution. These individuals usually find themselves in one of these four situations:

1. They have only a few debts and strong defenses for each. Instead of filing for bankruptcy, the consumer can simply raise these defenses vigorously. Usually the disputes can be settled out of court in a way acceptable to the consumer. (Consumers can also raise all their claims and defenses in the bankruptcy court.)
2. The debts at issue are secured by the consumer's property— such as home mortgages or car loans—and the consumer does not have sufficient income to keep up payments and also catch up on past due amounts, even with all of the help bankruptcy

provides. That is, bankruptcy may not be able to help those who solely want to keep their property, but where the long term expense of doing so exceeds their long term incomes.

3. The consumer has significant assets that cannot be exempted, and does not want to lose these assets. (Note that a chapter 13 filing may still be appropriate.)

4. Because of a prior bankruptcy, the consumer cannot receive a discharge in a chapter 7 bankruptcy. However, in most cases a chapter 13 petition can still be filed.

Occasionally, the protection bankruptcy offers is already available through other laws. Where state exemption laws are generous, many consumers will be totally judgment-proof already at the time they seek bankruptcy advice. Legally, creditors can do virtually nothing to harm them. Because there may not be a compelling urgency for these individuals to file for bankruptcy, it often makes sense not to file immediately. If those debtors wait, additional debts may arise which can also be included and discharged in the bankruptcy case. For a more detailed analysis of the advantages and disadvantages of a bankruptcy filing, see the National Consumer Law Center's *Consumer Bankruptcy Law and Practice* ch. 6 (4th ed. 1992).

Choosing the Type of Bankruptcy

Related to the question of whether to file a bankruptcy petition is the question of which type of bankruptcy to choose, a chapter 7 liquidation case or a chapter 13 debt adjustment (reorganization). Another issue is whether both spouses or only one should file. The final decision on these questions must await consultation with the attorney handling the bankruptcy, but it is helpful to understand the options in explaining what bankruptcy is likely to mean to a particular family.

Considerations Favoring Chapter 7

A straight chapter 7 bankruptcy is the simpler bankruptcy choice, particularly for low-income debtors. It is certainly appropriate when the bankruptcy filing will discharge most debts and not result in the loss of any property.

Generally, chapter 7 is the best option when three factors are present:

- All or nearly all of the debtor's property is exempt;
- The debts which are causing problems for the debtor are unsecured; and
- The debts which are causing problems for the debtor are dischargeable under chapter 7.

In some cases, even if consumers would lose certain property in a chapter 7 because the property is not exempt, consumers may be able, before filing for bankruptcy, to convert this property to other property that is exempt from seizure. This is called exemption planning and is legitimate in most cases, just as tax planning is an appropriate course for wealthier families.

Some view chapter 7 as appropriate only where a consumer's debts are all unsecured, with chapter 13 being the appropriate choice if there are secured debts. But even where there are secured debts, a chapter 13 filing may not be necessary. This is particularly the case if the consumer is current on the mortgage, car loan or other secured debt payments. (A chapter 13 filing is generally preferable where the consumer is delinquent on a secured debt and wants to cure this default over time.) If the consumer can keep current on secured debt payments, the consumer can keep the home or other collateral, if it is exempt, even while going through a chapter 7 bankruptcy.

Where chapter 7 is the best choice, the big advantage is that the process is simple and quick. Basically, once the papers are filed, unless unusual issues are raised, the debtor will receive a discharge within six months. (A more complete time-line for both chapter 7 and chapter 13 cases is included below.)

Considerations Favoring Chapter 13

Probably the most common reason for filing a chapter 13 petition is that one or more secured creditors cannot be dealt with satisfactorily in any other way. Few legal steps create opportunities to deal with foreclosures and repossessions as quickly and effectively as a chapter 13 petition and plan. The plan can lower monthly payments and even reduce the balance due on car loans and mortgages.

Another reason to file a chapter 13 bankruptcy is to protect non-exempt assets, which would be liquidated in a chapter 7 case. However, the current value of the non-exempt property usually has to be paid to unsecured creditors over the course of the plan.

Other important reasons favoring a chapter 13 filing include:

- Debts that are not dischargeable in chapter 7 can be discharged in chapter 13, including some taxes, debts incurred through false financial statements, false pretenses or fraud, willful and malicious torts, and breach of fiduciary duties, as well as debts for which a previous bankruptcy discharge was denied or waived. Even for nondischargeable, priority debts such as taxes, a chapter 13 plan allows debtors to stretch out payments over a longer period than would otherwise be possible, and to avoid severe interest and penalties.
- In a chapter 13 case, it is less likely that objections such as fraudulent transfer, concealment of property, or inability to explain loss of assets, will be raised. However, a court may consider such behavior to be violative of the Bankruptcy Code's "good faith" requirement.
- A chapter 13 case helps consumers who want to pay their debts, but who need the protection of the bankruptcy court and who can profit from the discipline of a chapter 13 plan.
- Chapter 13 usually eliminates any further finance charges and late charges for debts that have no collateral.
- Some experts consider a chapter 13 filing, compared to a chapter 7 filing, to be less harmful to the consumer's credit rating and reputation.
- For debtors who have obtained a chapter 7 discharge within the

previous six years, a chapter 7 filing is not available, leaving only the option of a chapter 13 filing.

It should also be noted that the choice of one form of bankruptcy over another is not irrevocable. It is easy for a debtor to convert at least once from chapter 7 to chapter 13 or vice versa.

Should Both Spouses File?

In cases where both a husband and wife are living together, it is usually preferable for both to file bankruptcy jointly. The filing fee is the same whether one or both file, and filing provides both with the advantages of a bankruptcy discharge.

Most couples are jointly responsible for their debts; therefore a spouse who does not file remains liable as a codebtor, and can continue to be pursued by creditors. (However if one spouse files under chapter 13, the other spouse obtains some protection at least to the extent that the plan provides for joint debts).

There is, of course, no requirement that married people file together. Therefore, if one spouse wants to file and the other does not, or if the spouses are estranged, there is nothing to prevent a married individual from filing alone. However, the consequences of not filing jointly should be considered carefully.

Timing of Bankruptcy Filing

Immediate Filing

Some debtors have no choice but to file immediately to forestall a foreclosure, repossession, eviction, execution sale, or utility shutoff. Filing immediately for bankruptcy is sometimes the only way to stop a state court proceeding and to avoid much unnecessary work. Bankruptcies in an emergency can be filed with as little as ten minutes preparation. A good discussion of how to do this is set out in the National Consumer Law Center's *Consumer Bank-*

ruptcy Law and Practice ch. 7 (4th ed. 1992), "The Emergency Bankruptcy Case, or How to Prepare a Bankruptcy Case in Under Ten Minutes."

Anticipation of Further Debt

If a debtor is not facing immediate loss of property to creditor action and anticipates further unavoidable liabilities, such as new medical, utility or unpaid rent bills, a bankruptcy filing should be delayed until after these debts occur. That way the consumer gains maximum benefit from the discharge.

Debts incurred after the bankruptcy filing are *not* discharged in that bankruptcy case—the consumer will still be obligated to repay them. As a general rule, bankruptcy should not be filed until a debt load has peaked.

Once a chapter 7 bankruptcy has been filed, the consumer will have to wait another six years before filing another chapter 7 bankruptcy and obtaining another chapter 7 discharge for debts incurred after the first bankruptcy was filed. The consumer can file a chapter 13 case with no waiting period after the chapter 7 discharge, as long as bad faith is not involved.

While consumers may wish to delay a chapter 7 filing until additional debts are incurred, this must be distinguished from another type of behavior, that of obtaining goods or services while having no intention of paying for them. In a chapter 7 bankruptcy, debts incurred in this way can be declared nondischargeable.

Fortunately, the line between these two kinds of debt is not as difficult to draw as it might seem at first. Most courts have found nondischargeable only the most obvious examples of debts incurred without intent to pay, such as prebankruptcy vacation trips and credit card shopping-spree debts. Expenses for medical bills and other essentials are rarely challenged.

Exemption Planning

Most debtors can take a number of steps to improve their legal position prior to filing; these steps come under the general rubric of exemption planning. Basically, exemption planning means arranging one's affairs so that a maximum amount of property can be claimed under exemption provisions, and a minimum amount is lost to creditors. It is similar to making arrangements to take maximum advantage of tax laws, and, if done reasonably, is perfectly legal.

Of course, debtors cannot simply give away nonexempt property or sell it at nominal cost. Any transfer of property within a year of filing must be disclosed. Fraudulent transfers of property can be recovered and may be grounds for denying a discharge.

Anticipation of Future Property

Sometimes an individual expects a significant upturn in his or her financial picture in the future through inheritance, a divorce settlement, or a life insurance payment. It makes sense to obtain a fresh start in bankruptcy *before,* rather than after the family receives this future property.

Filing bankruptcy after receipt of this property may just result in payment of this property to creditors. Discharging debts through bankruptcy and *then* receiving the property means the family can keep the property.

If a family anticipates receiving significant assets in the future, several rules should be kept in mind. Certain types of property received within 180 days of filing bankruptcy are treated as if the property was received before the bankruptcy. These types of property include inheritances, bequests, divorce decrees, spousal property settlements, and life insurance proceeds.

Moreover, any property or earnings received while the consumer is paying out a chapter 13 bankruptcy plan (which usually takes 3 to 5 years) is considered included in the bankruptcy process. Finally, property not actually received until after the filing may still be part of the bankruptcy if the property was earned, awarded or vested before the bankruptcy filing. This might include settlements on insurance or accident claims, tax refunds, or benefit payments.

Hiring a Bankruptcy Attorney

Hiring an attorney to handle any legal case is a difficult process. Nowhere is this more evident than in hiring a bankruptcy attorney because many of the profession's least reputable attorneys have latched onto bankruptcy as a way to make easy money by handling hundreds of cases at a time without considering individualized needs.

As with any area of the law, it is important to carefully select an attorney who will be responsive to a debtor's personal situation. The attorney should not be too busy to meet clients individually and to answer questions as necessary. Every client should take care before hiring an attorney to meet the attorney personally and to be comfortable with the attorney's style.

At all points in the case, the attorney should take time to answer questions either directly or through an office paralegal. If an attorney does not respond to telephone calls, a client should keep trying and demand an answer. If a chapter 13 bankruptcy is filed, make sure the attorney will continue to represent the consumer during the several year life of the bankruptcy.

The best way to find a trustworthy bankruptcy attorney is to seek recommendations from family, friends or other members of the community. Retainers and other documents should be read carefully. In some cases the retainer will not cover important aspects of the case.

In bankruptcy, as in all areas of life, you get what you pay for. Remember that the lawyer advertising the cheapest rate is not necessarily the best.

For-Profit Debt Counseling and Document Preparation Services

Two bankruptcy related services have recently generated a large number of consumer complaints. These are for-profit debt counseling and document preparation services. For-profit debt counseling is almost never a good idea. There is almost nothing that a for-profit debt counselor can offer other than a recommendation about whether bankruptcy is appropriate and a list of highly priced debt consolidation lenders. When bankruptcy is the right choice, they will simply recommend a lawyer.

There is no good reason to pay someone for this service. A reputable attorney will offer counsel on whether bankruptcy is appropriate and prepare the case only if relief is available. This avoids the double charge of having to pay a counselor and then an attorney. If bankruptcy is not appropriate, a good attorney will offer a range of other strategies which the debtor can pursue independently.

Document preparation services involve non-lawyers who offer to prepare bankruptcy forms for a fee. Problems with these services often arise because non-lawyers cannot offer advice on difficult bankruptcy cases and they offer no services once a bankruptcy case is commenced. This means that their clients are effectively abandoned with completed forms at the steps of the bankruptcy court. Often, the actual case will involve complications or even simple problems which the consumer is unprepared to meet.

Preparing the Consumer to Meet With the Bankruptcy Attorney

The consumer should be prepared when first meeting a bankruptcy attorney to answer the following:

- What types of debt are causing the most trouble?
- What are the debtor's significant assets?
- How were the debts incurred and are they secured?
- Is any creditor action imminent to collect any debt, or to foreclose or repossess property? The debtor should be prepared to report on the status of any pending lawsuits or foreclosures.

The answers to these general questions will reveal not only whether bankruptcy is likely to provide relief, but also the dimensions of the problem—its cause, its scope, and its likelihood of recurring.

Many bankruptcy specialists, finding introductory interviews both time-consuming and repetitive, give their clients a written questionnaire, and then supplement that information in interviews. Because the information required is extensive, specific, and critical to a successful bankruptcy, counselors should consider volunteering to help the consumer fill out this written questionnaire. Even the simplest parts of a questionnaire can be misunderstood, while other parts may be confusing. Some clients fail to list debts they wish to pay, or property they do not consider legally theirs.

Stress that complete information is a prerequisite to an effective bankruptcy. If information is not complete, then unexpected rights such as tax refunds might be denied, major debts might turn out to be nondischargeable or unaffected because of security interests, and undervalued property might be considered nonexempt and be lost.

Furthermore, without complete information, lawyers cannot make use of the maximum benefits that bankruptcy offers. For example, a debtor's right to avoid or modify a lien may be lost if the existence of the lien is not discovered in the fact-gathering stage. Debts not listed in bankruptcy papers sometimes survive a discharge. Even if they are discovered during the pendency of the case and are included later, they can mean additional fees for the debtor and more work for the debtor's attorney.

The consumer's answers to oral and written questions should be supplemented and checked against available financial documentation. Most financial documents provide the addresses of creditors and give precise amounts due. In addition, loan documents may reveal that security interests have been taken in property or may elucidate available defenses and counterclaims.

Consumers tend to overlook (to their detriment) certain of their property and liabilities:

• *Property.* Long-dormant accounts with banks and credit unions are among the types of property that consumers sometimes forget about in reporting their assets. Consumers also may fail to recognize their entitlement to tax refunds or credits, security deposits given to landlords or utilities, accrued vacation pay, future commissions from sales positions, salary or pension rights, causes of action, and valuable leased holdings. They may overlook their share in a housing, shopping, or agricultural cooperative, entitlements to government grants, such as energy assistance grants, or to accrued insurance interest.

- *Liabilities.* Obviously, every conceivable liability should be unearthed so that the opportunity to discharge debts can be used to its fullest. Debts not listed in the bankruptcy often will not be discharged. Consumers do not always realize the full extent or nature of their debts, especially if payments have not been demanded for those debts. Just as a cause of action can be a form of property, so too it can become a liability if the client is the defendant.

More on what information a debtor should provide an attorney in preparation of a bankruptcy filing is set out in the National Consumer Law Center's *Consumer Bankruptcy Law and Practice* ch. 5 (4th ed. 1992).

Chapter 7 Bankruptcy: The Basic Steps

This section describes the routine steps in a typical chapter 7 case, from start to finish, with emphasis on the procedures in no-asset cases. A no-asset case is one in which the debtor has no assets available to unsecured creditors because all of his or her assets are exempt or where secured loans equal the value of the collateral. For more detail on the basic steps of filing a chapter 7 case, see the National Consumer Law Center's *Consumer Bankruptcy Law and Practice* ch. 3 (4th ed. 1992).

In a chapter 7 case, all of the debtor's nonexempt assets are distributed to creditors, and the debtor receives a bankruptcy discharge at the end of the proceedings. From the beginning of the case until its conclusion, each step in the process is directed toward one or both of these ends.

1. Who Can File?

Any individual who lives in the United States or has property or a business in the United States can file a chapter 7 bankruptcy. There are no preconditions to a bankruptcy filing, such as insolvency, although a judge can dismiss a chapter 7 case if the debtor is engaged in a substantial abuse of the bankruptcy system. Moreover, any debtor who received a bankruptcy discharge within the past six years (with some exceptions for chapter 13 cases), or who is guilty of hindering, delaying or defrauding a creditor, is likely to be disqualified.

2. Initial Forms

The first step in a chapter 7 bankruptcy is the filling out of certain basic forms. The most important is a one page initial petition to file the bankruptcy case. The fee for filing a petition is currently $120. The fee for a husband and wife filing jointly is the same as for an individual filing alone.

If the debtor has not paid an attorney, bankruptcy courts will accept a petition without a fee if the petition is accompanied by an application to pay the fee in installments over the next few months. Unfortunately, the statute specifically states that the filing fee cannot be waived. If the fee is not ultimately paid, or if the required forms are not filed, the case will be dismissed.

A number of other forms must also be filed either at the same time as the petition or shortly thereafter. These include the debtor's statement of affairs and schedules, and a list of creditors, if not already filed with the petition.

3. First Steps After Filing

Filing the petition itself triggers the automatic stay. With few exceptions, this stay stops any actions or claims that arose before the petition was filed. It has the general purpose of freezing the debtor's property so that it can be examined and administered in the bankruptcy proceedings. The consumer's attorney or the court clerk will notify any creditors poised to take action against the consumer or consumer's property that a bankruptcy has been filed.

A consumer should also be aware of the automatic stay so that the consumer can respond to any attempts by a creditor to collect a debt. While there is no legal requirement that the consumer do so, this will prevent creditors from inadvertently seizing property before they receive notice from the attorney or bankruptcy court.

Within a few weeks after filing, the bankruptcy court mails a notice of the stay and of the date and place for a "section 341(a) meeting," known also as the first meeting of creditors, to all creditors, to the consumer, and to the consumer's attorney. The notice also contains deadlines for creditors who wish to file claims or complaints raising objections to the discharge or to the dischargeability of a particular debt. If it appears that all the consumer's property is exempt, the court may notify creditors that claims need not be filed unless they are later notified that the debtor possesses assets.

4. The Chapter 7 Trustee

For both chapter 7 and chapter 13 bankruptcies, a trustee is appointed to represent the interests of unsecured creditors (i.e., creditors who do not have any collateral). In a chapter 7 bankruptcy, the trustee collects the debtor's property that will be sold, if any, handles the sale, distributes the property to creditors with valid claims, and makes a final accounting to the court.

5. The First Meeting of Creditors

The first court appearance for the consumer usually occurs at a meeting of creditors, known as the "first meeting of creditors" or a "section 341(a)" meeting. This proceeding gives the various parties a chance to examine the debtor's affairs. It is usually the way the chapter 7 trustee learns whatever is necessary for the performance of the trustee's duties.

Despite the name, creditors rarely appear at the first meeting in a consumer bankruptcy. The meeting consists of a series of routine questions addressed to the consumer by the court-appointed trustee covering most of the information in the statement of affairs and schedules, and lasts from five minutes to half an hour.

6. After the First Meeting

Unless there is an objection, property claimed as exempt is always kept by the consumer. Property that has little nonexempt value is abandoned by the trustee, which means that the consumer gets to keep it. At this point the consumer can surrender collateral to the secured creditor if this is the consumer's intention, or the consumer can keep the collateral outright by paying the creditor the value of the collateral.

If larger assets remain, they are turned over to the trustee at or after the first meeting. The consumer is usually offered the option of paying the non-exempt value of the assets to the trustee in cash instead of turning over those assets. The trustee then collects any other property of the estate that is neither exempt nor abandoned, and liquidates the estate, converting it to cash.

In most states the trustee must give twenty days notice of intent to sell the property. Any party, including the debtor, can object (within specified time limits) to the proposed sale, which is either private or by public auction.

The consumer's attorney will review creditors' proofs of claims and file appropriate objections. If the trustee collects any property, the proceeds are distributed to creditors in order of their priority pursuant to the Bankruptcy Code.

7. The Discharge

The final step in most chapter 7 bankruptcy cases is the discharge, at which the debtor sees the judge for what is usually the first and only time. In some jurisdictions the discharge hearing is waived. At the hearing the court formally grants the discharge, except for rare cases when an objection to discharge is sustained. The discharge is effective for all debts with the exception of:

- Certain taxes;
- Debts not listed in the schedules;
- Some debts for alimony and child support;
- Most fines and penalties owed to government agencies;
- Some student loans;
- Debts listed in a prior bankruptcy where discharge was denied or waived; and
- Debts incurred through driving while intoxicated.

In addition some other debts may be determined to be nondischargeable, but only if the particular creditor seeks such a determination of nondischargeability within certain strictly enforced time limits. These include:

- debts incurred by certain types of fraud;
- debts incurred while acting as a trustee over someone else's property; and
- debts for causing willful or malicious injuries.

Chapter 13 Bankruptcy: The Basic Steps

A chapter 13 bankruptcy allows debtors to adjust their financial affairs without having to give up their assets. It allows them to choose between making payments on debts out of future income or out of current assets. Debtors can keep and use all property, whether exempt or not, and use it to pay some or all of their debts according to a court-approved plan.

Chapter 13 also gives debtors an opportunity to cure defaults. That is, the chapter 13 filing can allow consumers to catch up—often gradually over time—past due delinquencies. At the completion of this plan, or before, the debtor is given a discharge which is basically similar to the discharge received in a chapter 7 case. More on the basic steps of a chapter 13 bankruptcy can be found at the National Consumer Law Center's *Consumer Bankruptcy Law and Practice* ch. 4 (4th ed. 1992).

1. Who Can File?

Chapter 13 is available to "individuals with regular income" who live in the United States, or have a place of business or property in the United States. An "individual with regular income" includes not only wage earners, but also recipients of government benefits, alimony or support payments, or any other regular type of income.

As with chapter 7, the debtor need not be insolvent. A chapter 13 discharge can be obtained even by a debtor who has received a chapter 7 discharge within six years before filing, or who would not be granted a discharge because of some other provision in chapter 7.

2. The Initial Forms

As with chapter 7, a chapter 13 bankruptcy begins by filing a one-page petition. As with chapter 7, the petition must be accompanied by a $120 filing fee, charged both to single individuals and to husbands and wives filing jointly, or by an application to pay that fee in installments. No waiver of the fee is permitted.

Several other required forms are usually filed at the same time as the petition, including the schedules, the statement of financial affairs, the statement of compensation, and the chapter 13 plan, which is the consumer's description of when creditors will be paid, how they will be paid, and how much they will be paid.

For consumers unable to file a chapter 13 statement and plan with the petition, the case can begin simply by filing the petition, along with the fee (or the application to pay the fee in installments), and the list of creditors. The other papers must be filed within fifteen days, unless that time is extended by the court. Local practice may require that certain other papers be filed, either with the petition or shortly thereafter.

As with chapter 7, filing a petition sets the bankruptcy process in motion. A trustee is appointed, and, if applicable, an order for paying the filing fee in installments is entered.

The filing immediately establishes the automatic stay, which prevents any further creditor acts against the consumer or the consumer's property. Filing a chapter 13 petition also puts into effect a prohibition that prevents creditors from taking any action against any codebtors (for example, co-signers and sureties) who have not filed bankruptcy who would otherwise be obligated to pay claims against the consumer.

The consumer's attorney will usually give notice of the stay to creditors poised to take action against the consumer. This prevents seizures before the bankruptcy court formally notifies the creditor. Permission of the bankruptcy court is necessary before creditors can proceed with any of the acts prohibited by either stay.

The debtor must begin making plan payments within thirty days of filing the plan, unless the court orders otherwise. These payments are held by the chapter 13 trustee until the chapter 13 plan is approved by the court. If the court does not approve the chapter 13 plan, the payments are returned to the debtor after deduction of administrative costs.

Within a relatively short time, the court issues a notice of the "first meeting of creditors", also known as the "section 341(a) meeting." This form also notifies creditors of the automatic stay and of the deadlines for filing their claims with the court.

3. The Chapter 13 Trustee

The chapter 13 trustee has considerably more to do than the chapter 7 trustee. In addition to the duties of a chapter 7 trustee, the chapter 13 trustee must attend all hearings dealing with how to handle secured loans, and on approval or change of the consumer's plan for payment of debts.

Once the consumer starts making payments according to this plan, the payments are made to the trustee, who then sends them to the appropriate creditor. The trustee can also advise the debtor on matters related to the bankruptcy and assist the debtor in performance of the plan.

Depending upon the type of case or the matter involved, and in some cases the trustee's personality, a trustee is either a debtor's friend or a debtor's foe. In either case, the trustee's opinion is not necessarily the last word on any matter. The consumer has the right to raise the issue with the bankruptcy judge. Trustees are not judges and have no power to rule on disputes between creditors and debtors.

4. The First Meeting of Creditors

As with chapter 7 bankruptcy, the primary purpose of the first meeting of creditors is to give the trustee an opportunity to ask the debtor questions and discover any grounds for objecting to the plan. The trustee will inquire generally into the information presented in the statement and plan, including the debtor's ability to make the proposed payments.

Despite the popular name for the proceedings, creditors rarely appear, and the bankruptcy judge is not permitted to be present. The meeting is likely to last between five minutes and a half hour, and follows the same pattern of routine questioning as chapter 7 cases.

5. The Confirmation Hearing

The confirmation hearing occurs either on the same day as the first meeting of creditors, or some time within the next several months, depending upon local practice. The purpose of the hearing is to provide a basis for ruling on whether the plan will be confirmed, to inquire into whether the requirements of chapter 13 have been met, and to hear any objections to approval of the debtor's chapter 13 plan.

Prior to the hearing, the consumer's attorney will review the creditors' proofs of claims (i.e. the creditor's statement of how much the consumer owes that creditor), and can object to these proofs. The effect of confirmation is to bind the consumer and all of the consumer's creditors to the terms of the plan.

For various reasons, consumers sometimes want to modify their original plan. Before confirmation, a plan can be modified as a matter of course, so long as the modified plan meets the chapter 13 requirements. After confirmation, plans can still be modified, but only upon notice and hearing subject to creditor objections.

6. Consumer Failure to Complete the Plan

Some consumers are unable to complete chapter 13 plans as proposed, usually because of loss of income. When this occurs, four options are available, each having somewhat different consequences:

• *Hardship Discharge.* The federal bankruptcy law provides for a hardship discharge if problems are caused by circumstances for which the debtor is not justly accountable, such as the debtor's death and serious deterioration of the debtor's financial circumstances.
• *Modification.* It is possible to modify a plan to accommodate new problems, but creditors have a right to object to the modification, and, if so, the court will decide whether to allow the modification. Plan payments can be reduced or even terminated if the modified plan still complies with the requirements of chapter 13.
• *Conversion.* Consumers have the right to convert to a chapter 7 bankruptcy as of right; in most cases such a conversion provides the same relief as a hardship discharge. After the conversion, nonexempt property is liquidated and the debtor receives a chapter 7 discharge. If the debtor has no nonexempt property, the debtor simply receives a discharge. Debts arising after the chapter 13 case was commenced, but before conversion, can be included in the chapter 7 discharge.
• *Dismissal.* Occasionally, dismissal is preferable to any of the other options. Consumers have the right to dismiss their chapter 13 case unless the case was previously converted from chapter 7. This route is particularly attractive if it appears that the case may be converted to chapter 7 against the consumer's will, and if the consumer has nonexempt property that he or she does not wish to see liquidated.

7. Discharge

The final step in a successfully completed chapter 13 case, or in a case ended under hardship provisions, is the discharge. In the wording of the law, a discharge must be granted by the court "as soon as practicable" after completion of all payments under a confirmed plan.

The discharge received in a chapter 13 bankruptcy is usually broader than in a chapter 7. It includes all debts provided for by the plan, except for most support and alimony payments and for long term debts with final payments due after the completion of the plan. Thus, a chapter 13 discharge can eliminate liability on debts not dischargeable in a chapter 7 case, including debts incurred through fraud or false pretenses, fines or penalties for willful and malicious injuries, and fines for driving while intoxicated.

Promptly after the discharge, a notice of discharge is mailed to all creditors and to the trustee. The consumer and the consumer's attorney also receive a copy of this notice. Shortly thereafter, the trustee files his or her final report and the case is officially closed.

Notes

2 • Debt Counseling

1. The $127.50 is the weekly minimum wage. Federal wage garnishment protections are pegged to the minimum wage, and the amount protected will increase when the minimum wage increases.

4 • Dealing With Debt Collectors

1. Volume 15 of the United States Code Section 1692. The best analysis of consumer rights under this statute and other debt collection harassment law is found at National Consumer Law Center, *Fair Debt Collection* (2d ed. 1991).
2. Delete reference to the Fair Debt Collection Practices Act where the letter is to a creditor instead of to a collection agency.
3. However, creditors collecting their own debts are covered if they use a different name suggesting that they are a third party collector.

5 • Lawsuits to Collect on a Debt

1. Volume 15 of the United States Code Sec. 1673. The law provides the debtor may retain thirty times the federal minimum wage, per week. Currently the federal minimum wage is $4.25 per hour.

7 • Protecting the Family Car from the Repo Man

1. If the consumer has paid 30% of the loan.

9 • General Home Defense Strategies

1. Volume 15 of the United States Code Section 1701x(c).
2. The agencies were listed at Volume 54 of the Federal Register at 20967–21037 (May 15, 1989). Contact the Housing and Urban Development agency in your region for a more up-to-date list.

10 • Special Home Defense Strategies

1. The most important guidelines are found in the lenders' handbook Section F, Manual (M) 26-3, Pamphlet 26-7, and Circulars 26-75-8, 26-78-21, and 26-80-3.
2. Information on this manual is available from the National Housing Law Project, 2201 Broadway Street, Suite 815, Oakland, CA 94612, (510) 251-9400.
3. Massey, *Farmers in Crisis,* Volume 18 of the Clearinghouse Review, page 702 (Nov. 1984). To order this article, contact the National Clearinghouse for Legal Services, 407 South Dearborn, Suite 400, Chicago, IL, 60605, (312) 939-3830.
4. Also found at Volume 15 of the United States Code, Section 1601 and after.
5. Known as Regulation Z and found at Volume 12 of the Code of Federal Regulations Section 226.
6. Known as the Federal Reserve Board Staff's Official Commentary on Regulation Z, found at Volume 12 of the Code of Federal Regulations Section 226, Supplement 1.
7. If the creditor made six or more mortgage loans or twenty-six or more loans of any kind in the last year, the rescission rules should apply.
8. The "annual percentage rate" is not always the same as the stated interest rate on the note. The rules for calculating the two are somewhat different. So do not assume that there is an error because the two figures differ. See NCLC's Truth in Lending manual for more details on calculating annual percentage rates.
9. Just as the annual percentage rate is not the same as the interest rate,

so to the "amount financed" is often smaller than the loan amount stated in the promissory note. The issue is not whether the two numbers are the same, but whether the creditor followed Truth in Lending rules in calculating the amount financed.

14 • Bankruptcy

1. Exemptions are determined either by state or federal law. In 14 states, a debtor may choose either state or federal exemptions. In the other states, a debtor must utilize state exemption options.

Bibliography

All National Consumer Law Center publications can be ordered from Publications, National Consumer Law Center, 11 Beacon Street, Boston, MA 02108, (617) 523-8010.

Books

Center on Budget and Policy Priorities, *EITC Community Outreach Kit* is a particularly helpful resource for counselors on how to inform low-income families about their potential eligibility for tax refunds. The kit contains a fact sheet, eligibility guidelines, campaign posters, flyers printed in English and Spanish, and a summary of effective outreach strategies. To receive the kit, write to the EITC Campaign, Center on Budget and Policy Priorities, 777 N. Capitol St., Suite 705, Washington D.C. 20002, (202) 408-1080.

Elias, Leonard, & Renauer, *How to File for Bankruptcy* is an excellent guide for those attempting to file bankruptcy on their own. Available from the Nolo Press, 950 Parker Street, Berkeley, CA 94710, (800) 992-6656.

Federal Home Mortgage Association, *Sellers' and Servicers' Guide* contains the guidelines all Freddie Mac lenders must utilize in foreclosing on a home and negotiating repayment schedules. The cost is $275, which includes a one-year update service. Available from Freddie Mac, Attn: Subscription Services, 8200 Jones Branch Drive, McLean, VA 22102.

Federal National Mortgage Association, *Servicing Guide* contains the guidelines all Fannie Mae lenders must utilize in foreclosing on a home and negotiating repayment schedules. The cost is $300, which includes a continual upkeep service. Available from Fannie Mae, 510 Walnut St., 16th Floor, Philadelphia, PA 19106 and from other Fannie Mae regional offices.

Food Research Action Center, *Guide to the Food Stamp Program* (1988 and Supplement) is an excellent resource on the federal food stamp program and is available from the Food Research Action Center, 1875 Connecticut Ave. NW, Suite 540, Washington, D.C. 20009-5728, (202) 986-2200. In 1992 the guide cost $12.

Leonard, Robin, *Money Troubles: Legal Strategies to Cope With Your Debts* (1991) is a good consumer self-help manual for certain types of less serious consumer debt problems, such as straightening out a credit report of dealing with billing errors. Available from the Nolo Press, 950 Parker Street, Berkeley, CA 94710, (800) 992-6656.

National Consumer Law Center, *Consumer Bankruptcy Law and Practice* (4th ed. 1992). The best resource available on all aspects of consumer bankruptcy filings, including hundreds of model forms.

———, *Fair Debt Collection* (2d ed. 1991 and Supplement), the definitive treatise on consumer remedies to fight debt collection harassment, including extensive treatment of the federal Fair Debt Collection Practices Act.

———, *Repossessions* (2d ed. 1988 and Supplement) covers all aspects of consumer repossession law, including seizure of automobiles, mobile homes, and household goods.

———, *Unfair and Deceptive Acts and Practices* (3d ed. 1991 and Supplement) is a unique resource covering all types of unfair and deceptive conduct in the marketplace, including special sections on student loans, the federal racketeering statute, other consumer remedies, and insurance issues.

———, *Truth in Lending* (2d ed. 1989 and Supplement) is the essential guide for anyone handling a Truth in Lending case, either to obtain statutory damages or to cancel a loan. Also included is a detailed analysis of the federal Consumer Leasing Act.

———, *The Regulation of Rural Electric Cooperatives* (1992) provides a number of innovative strategies that REC customers can utilize to combat utility termination and bill collection.

———, *Fair Credit Reporting Act* (2d ed. 1988 and Supplement) explains a consumer's rights in dealing with credit reporting agencies, including extensive treatment of the federal Fair Credit Reporting Act.

————, *Sales of Goods and Services* (2d ed. 1989 and Supplement) is a detailed manual on all aspects of consumer warranty law and the rights of consumer purchasers of goods and services.

————, *Equal Credit Opportunity Act* (2d ed. 1988 and Supplement) covers consumers' rights when they are denied credit, including a thorough analysis of the federal Equal Credit Opportunity Act.

————, *Usury and Consumer Credit Regulation* (1987 and Supplement) is a unique legal resource, covering federal and state law regulating interest rates and other credit terms for consumer loans and credit sales.

————, *Odometer Law* (3d ed. 1992) explains consumers' special remedies where they purchase a used car with a tampered odometer. The best treatment available of the federal Odometer Act and state laws.

————, *Consumer Class Actions: A Practical Litigation Guide* (2d ed. 1990) explains how even a small law firm can mount a consumer class action, thus obtaining widespread relief for victims of a consumer scam.

National Health Law Program, *Advocates' Guide to the Medicaid Program* (1991) is the best source for information on Medicaid benefits. It is available from NHELP, 2639 S. La Cienega Blvd., Los Angeles, CA 90034, (213) 204-6010.

National Housing Law Project, *FmHA Housing Programs: Tenants' and Purchasers' Rights* is an excellent resource for any FmHA housing issue. The first edition was published in 1982. Contact the National Housing Law Project, 2201 Broadway Street, Suite 815, Oakland, CA 94612, (510) 251-9400 for the current edition.

Periodicals

Clearinghouse Review (National Clearinghouse for Legal Services) is an invaluable monthly magazine covering recent developments in all areas of poverty law, including government assistance, rights of consumer debtors, housing issues, health law, and special issues relating to the elderly, migrant workers, immigrants, and veterans. Annual subscription is $75 and is available from the National Clearinghouse for Legal Services, 407 South Dearborn, Suite 400, Chicago, IL 60605, (312) 939-3830.

The Health Advocate (National Health Law Program) is a quarterly publication concentrating on Medicaid benefits and other low-income health law issues. It is available from NHELP, 2639 S. La Cienega Blvd., Los Angeles, CA 90034, (213) 204-6010.

Memorandum to Welfare Specialists (Center on Social Welfare Policy and Law) is a free series of memoranda that are produced periodically on current topics of welfare law. To subscribe, contact the Center on Social Welfare Policy and Law at 275 Seventh Ave., 6th Floor, New York, NY 10001-6708, (212) 633-6967.

NCLC Energy & Utility Update (National Consumer Law Center) keeps readers current on low income utility issues, such as utility terminations, low-income payment plans, the federal fuel assistance program, low-income weatherization, and telephone and water issues.

NCLC Reports (National Consumer Law Center) covers the latest developments in all major areas of low-income consumer law. Twenty-four issues a year are divided into four different editions, each published bi-monthly: Bankruptcy & Foreclosures Edition; Debt Collection & Repossessions Edition; Consumer Credit & Usury Edition; and Deceptive Practices & Warranties Edition.

Index

About the National Consumer Law Center

The National Consumer Law Center (NCLC) is the nation's expert on the rights of consumer borrowers. Since 1969, NCLC has been at the forefront in representing low income consumers before the courts, government agencies, Congress, and state legislatures.

NCLC has appeared before the United States Supreme Court and numerous federal and state courts and has successfully presented many of the most important cases affecting consumer borrowers. It provides consultation and assistance to legal services, private, and government attorneys in all fifty states. It authored an influential model statute in 1974 to protect the rights of consumer debtors.

NCLC publishes a nationally acclaimed series of eleven manuals on all major aspects of consumer credit and sales. It also conducts state and national training sessions on the rights of consumer borrowers for attorneys, paralegals, and other counselors.